THE OPERATIONS OF THE ALLIED ARMY,

UNDER THE COMMAND OF HIS SERENE HIGHNESS

PRINCE FERDINAND, DUKE OF BRUNSWICK AND LÜNEBURG,

DURING THE GREATEST PART OF SIX CAMPAIGNS, BEGINNING IN THE YEAR 1757, AND ENDING IN THE YEAR 1762.

BY

SIR CHARLES HOTHAM-THOMPSON

Cover Design by Dr. G.F.Nafziger

Originally Published: London, T. Jeffreys, 1764

This edition: Edited by Dr. G.F.Nafziger Copyright (C) 2016

Winged Hussar Publishing LLC edtion © 2018

ISBN 978-1-945430-41-1
LOC 2018939883

Bibliographical References and Index
1. History. 2. Seven Year's War. 3. Germany

Winged Hussar Publishing LLC
1525 Hulse Road, Unit 1, Point Pleasant, NJ 08742

Cover: Ferdinand, Duke of Brunswick.

For more information on Winged Hussar Publishing, LLC, visit us at:
www.wingedhussarpublishing.com

ADVERTISEMENT

By the **PUBLISHER.**

THE author[1] of the following work has been concerned in many of the transactions related therein; prudence, therefore, would not suffer him to prefix his name to them. Had the publisher been permitted to do it, he flatters himself, that that alone would have been a sufficient recommendation of them to the public; however, he makes no doubt but the performance will recommend itself by the strict regard that is everywhere paid to truth; and as the facts here related are at this time recent in our memory, everyone will be a competent judge of the merit of this work.

NOTES ON THIS EDITION

To the degree that it was possible, the names of the villages, towns, and cities have been corrected to the modern spellings. I owe a great debt of gratitude to Dr. Dirk Rottgardt, who reviewed the "interesting" spellings of German town names by the author and provided me with the current names. Because the population of Germany has expanded since 1757 many of the smaller villages have been absorbed into larger cities and now are districts. This is indicated in footnotes.

Some grammatical structures have been changed, i.e., "the river of Alle," has been changed to read the "Aller River." Similar changes were made to other phrasings.

The original maps in this work were not satisfactory and I turned to Roesh, J.F., *Collection de quarante deux plans de batailles, sieges, et affaires les plus mémorables de la guerre de sept ans* (Frankfurt am Main: Jaeger, 1790). The maps were taken from this work and subjected to the minimum of changes, i.e. specificially, no town names were altered to match those used in the rest of the text and the "Key to Map" retains those spellings.

ON THE AUTHOR OF THIS WORK.

According to Medinger[2], Hotham is the author of this work on Duke Ferdinand's of Brunswick campaigns in the Seven Years War that has been anonymously published in English at London, in 1764. Medinger used it as a source when writing his own book on Ferdinand's campaigns as well as many primary sources from different German archives. He also used Mackesy's book on Lord George Sackville's court martial mentioning the friendship between the Sackvilles and the Hothams, and especially the friendship between Lord George and the Hotham brothers. He does not include, though, biographical data on Hotham.

Mackesy analyses Sackville's court martial after the Battle of Minden. His book contains some biographical data on Hotham.

---

1. Editor: The author of this work was originally anonymous, but I have determined the author's identity to be Sir Charles Hotham-Thompson.
2. Walther Medinger: *Herzog Ferdinand von Braunschweig-Lüneburg und die alliierte Armee im siebenjährigen Krieg* (1757 – 1762) (Hannover: Thomas Klingebiel, 2011)

Sir Charles Hotham-Thompson

Charles Hotham (* 1729; + 25 January, 1794) belonged to a family of squires that owned land in Yorkshire from the Middle Ages. In 1622, they were created Baronets of Scorborough in the County of York in the Baronetage of England, and, in 1797, the Barons Hotham appeared in the Peerage of Ireland (the 1st Baron was Admiral William Hotham from a different branch than Charles Hotham). The family still owns their manor, Dalton Hall, Beverley, East Riding of Yorkshire. The family had a longstanding friendship with the Sackvilles. Charles and his predecessors were Members of Parliament and often soldiers.

Charles Hotham was the son of the 7th Baronet, Sir Beaumont Hotham (+ 1771), and a nephew of the 5th, Sir Charles Hotham (1693 to 1738). He was educated at Westminster School and at the Middle Temple. In 1746, he was commissioned as an ensign in the 1st Foot Guards and took part with his regiment in the campaigns in Flanders. In 1747, he fought in the Battle of Lauffeld. Subsequently, he became aide-de-camp to the Earl of Albemarle, the British commander-in-chief in the Low Countries. He proved most efficient and remained in that position until the end of the War of the Austrian Succession. Thereafter, for much of his military career he served in staff positions. At the beginning of the Seven Years War, he became aide-de-camp to Lord Ligonier, then commander-in-chief of the British Army. In 1758, as a lieutenant-colonel, he was appointed adjutant of the British forces attacking St. Malo, and thereafter adjutant of the British forces in Germany until the end of the war.

Hotham was a personal friend of Lord George Sackville, who, after the Battle of Minden, was succeeded as commander of the British forces by Lord Marlborough. He also testified as a witness for Sackville in his court martial. However, he also had friendly connections with Lord Ligonier and Ligonier's nephew, Edward Ligonier, then a captain and one of Duke Ferdinand's British aides-de-camp, who testified against Sackville. In addition, he made friends with the Hanoverian adjutant-general, Johann Wilhelm von Reden, with whom he closely cooperated on official business. Reden issued Duke Ferdinand's orders in German to the Hanoverian, Hessian and Brunswick troops and in French to Hotham who translated them for the British troops into English. By his position as an adjutant, Hotham knew the whereabouts of the British troops, and by this friendship, he might have gathered information on the movements of non-British troops or detached corps of the Allied Army, which he used in preparing his book.

In 1761, Hotham was elected as a Member of Parliament for St. Ives, Cornwall. In this, his brother-in-law, John Hobart, 2nd Earl of Buckinghamshire, supported him by exerting great influence and paying the obligatory bribes to voters. As Hobart was married twice and it appears one of his wives was one of Hobart's sisters. Apparently, the Hobarts were not only landowners in Norfolk, but also in Cornwall.

In 1763, Hotham tried in vain to become adjutant-general of the British Army. He remained in the army for 12 more years but lacked the experience for an own high command. However, like Sackville, he was a favourite of King George III, who made him a groom of the bedchamber. In 1763, he became a colonel, and was re-elected for St. Ives.

In 1765, he became colonel of the 63rd Regiment of Foot, and served until 1768 with his regiment in Ireland – at least when Parliament was not in session. In 1768, he took possession of the family estates in Yorkshire. In 1768, he left Parliament and became colonel of the 17th Regiment of Foot. In 1771, he succeeded his father as the 8th Baronet, and started re-building Dalton Hall, from 1771 to 1775. On 15 January 1772, the king created him a Knight of the Bath, so that he became Sir Charles Hotham. In 1772, he chose the surname Hotham-Thompson as part of the inheritance of his mother.

By 1775, he was a major general. However, he was apparently too old for command in America. So, Hotham retired from the army to his manor, and among other things expanded his library. Apparently, he was promoted to general, on 18 October 1793.

After his death, he was succeeded as the 9th Baronet by his younger brother John (1734 to 1795). John had served during the Seven Years War as a chaplain with the British forces in Germany. He served in the Anglican Church of Ireland as the Bishop of Ossory from 1779 to 1782 and as the Bishop of Clogher from 1782 to 1795.

CONTENTS

The OPERATIONS of THE ALLIED ARMY Under the COMMAND of HIS SERENE HIGHNESS PRINCE FERDINAND, DUKE OF BRUNSWICK and LÜNEBURG. THE CAMPAIGN OF 1757

THE following narrative commencing only from the time His Serene Highness Prince Ferdinand, Duke of Brunswick and Lüneburg assumed command of the Allied Army, renders it absolutely necessary to premise and mention, though in a concise manner, some previous transactions relative to the contending powers; as they may serve to inform the reader of the situation of the two armies at that juncture, and cast a light on the separate views of each party, whereon only the future operations, but also the motives of those operations, so immediately depend.

After the remarkable Convention of Kloster Zeven, signed on 8 September 1757, the Army of Observation remained in the neighborhood of Stade, and the French army was distributed into five camps at Bergen, Verden, Rethem, Bottmor, and Celle, in order to wait the breaking up of the Army of observation, according to the articles agreed on; and 'till their own winter quarters were regulated. They had also separate corps at Hanover, Brunswick, and Wolfenbüttel; some whence Mr. de Voyer was advanced into the country of Halberstadt, as far as Osterwieck, with a detachment consisting of three battalions, four squadrons, and Fisher's corps, M. de Soubise, with a body of 30,000 French, having joined the Army of Execution under the command of Prince of Hildburghausen, they were both advancing about this time into Saxony; but on advice of the King of Prussia was in full march towards them with a body of 35,000 men, they halted at Erfurt, which they abandoned on his approach, and retired with the greatest precipitation to Eisenach, where they strongly entrenched themselves in a post already fortified by nature. Hither His Majesty followed them, using all possible means to bring them to an action, which they as cautiously declined, as they expected reinforcements, though already greatly superior in number he, therefore, judging it imprudent to attempt to force so advantageous a post defended by an army of near double his strength, determined to return to Naumburg. He had several motives for taking this step: forage was scarce, M. de Richelieu had sent detachments to join M. Soubise; and, above all, he wanted to be nearer at hand either to protect his own dominions or support his other corps as necessity should require. While His Majesty was marching against the Combined Army, Prince Ferdinand was detached with seven battalions, ten squadrons, and some artillery, into the country of Magdeburg, in order to cover that province and alarm the French in those quarters. He accordingly advanced to Halberstadt, and detached Colonel Horn with about 600 men, who surprised a party of French at Egeln, and made the greatest part of them prisoners. The French everywhere retreated and, abandoning all their posts in that principality, retreated behind Hornburg in such condition, that they left behind them a large magazine, which they had at Osterwieck.

THE Russian Army, which had entered the Prussian territories under the command of Marshal Apraxin, suddenly evacuated the same; and about the middle of September retired by forced marches, to the great surprise of the French and Austrians, and indeed of the whole world, as the real cause thereof never transpired.

M. de Richelieu, having received information of those marches of the Russians, and having no other enemy at that time to deal with, resolved to turn his whole force against the King of Prussia. He for that purpose collected, on the 26th of September, all his troops at Renen near Wolfenbüttel; and having sent M. de Broglio with 20 battalions and 18 squadrons to reinforce M. de Soubise, Richelieu with the rest of his army marched to dislodge Prince Ferdinand from his advanced posts of Zillingen and Adersheim. Ferdinand, unable to withstand so superior a force, retired first to Halberstadt, and afterwards to Winfleben[3] near Magdeburg; and the enemy encamped in the neighborhood of Halberstadt, where they committed unheard of excesses and devastations, utterly ruining that small principality, according to their general maxim.

THE Combined Army, being thus greatly reinforced, again advanced towards Saxony by the way of Erfurt; and, passing the Saale River about the end of October, summoned the town of Leipzig to surrender. Marshal Keith, who commanded in that city with a garrison of 8,000 men, returned for answer, that his master had ordered him to defend it to the last extremity, and he was for preparing everything necessary for that purpose. But His Prussian Majesty, always rapid in his motions, prevented their intentions; for having foreseen that they would again advance, he had on his return so distributed and disposed of his army that they might speedily be collected, giving at the same time orders to each detachment to be ready to march at a moment's warning. He quickly reassembled his troops, and advanced to Leipzig. The enemy, on his approach immediately re-passed the Saale at Weissenfels, Merseburg, and Halle, destroying the bridges behind them. These were soon repaired by the Prussians, who passed that river on the 3d of November and encamped opposite the enemy, between the villages of Rossbach and Rederow, intending to begin the attack the next morning. It was, however, deferred for that day; and, on the 5th, the combined army was seen to be everywhere in motion, making the necessary dispositions both on the right and left to surround His Majesty, as they were near treble his number. He immediately took his resolution and marched up to attack them. The engagement was obstinate, but the enemy at length gave way and at five in the afternoon the rout became general. They were totally defeated, abandoned most of their artillery and baggage, and, under cover of the night, retired to Freyburg. In a word, they were entirely dispersed, flying in small parties, destitute for many days even of bread, and every other necessary proper for their support.

THE Combined Army before the battle looked with so much contempt on the small handful of Prussians, that they declared they should get no honor by beating them; and so certain were they of success, that they boasted their design was to enclose them in a

3. This may be Wanzleben.

triangle, and, by that means intercepting their retreat, reduce them to the necessity of subscribing to such conditions as they should please to dictate; but the event manifested the vanity of those boastings.

M. de Richelieu on the first notice of that action, sent a considerable detachment to support M. de Soubise, and secure his retreat. This body had advanced as far as Duderstadt, in the neighborhood of which place it found the shattered remains of the French army reuniting, about the middle of the month. Their loss in the whole was computed at about 12,000 men, and the remainder were rendered incapable of keeping the field by the loss of their baggage.

M. de Richelieu received the news of this defeat the day after the battle. The consternation it occasioned among the French was inconceivable. Their whole army immediately evacuated the country of Halberstadt, and retired towards Brunswick, only leaving garrisons at Regenstein, Sterwick, and Hornburg on the frontiers.

AT the latter end of September, the Army of Observation still remained in the neighborhood of Stade. Some corps had advanced as far as Bardowick, on their way to take up their winter quarters in the country of Lauenburg; the troops of Hesse and Brunswick had also began their march, in order to repair to their respective countries, as had been stipulated by the convention; but they all received orders to halt. His Royal Highness embarked for England in the beginning of October and the command of the army then devolved on General Zastrow. In this position the Allied Army remained 'till the month of November, as some difficulties had arisen between the Courts of London and Versailles, with respect to the Convention; but about that time the French were everywhere in motion, and their different corps posted along the Aller, were assembling by order of M. de Richelieu, who, on the 23d of November, advanced to Lüneburg with 32 battalions and 38 squadrons, having before issued orders for all his army to assemble in the neighborhood of Celle with the greatest expedition. He also ordered the 6,000 Palatines, who were quartered about Hamm and Lippstadt, and some cavalry from the Duchy of Cleves, to join him. His intentions were, as he declared, to bring General Zastrow to an eclaircissement; but they in reality were to enforce whatsoever farther unreasonable demands his master might think proper to exact: for the French, ever haughty on the least seeming advantage, had set no bounds to their ambitious views.

THE Army of Observation, in consequence hereof, began also to move forward. They had corps near Harburg, Buxtehude, Bremervörde, etc. and likewise some small advanced parties, which were obliged to fall back on the approach of M. de Richelieu.

As it is only our intent to relate bare matters of fact, without entering into political reflections, we shall not attempt to point out the particular flagrant infractions of the articles of the Convention which the French were guilty of, but refer the reader to the following manifesto:

A preparatory Manifesto of the Motives which oblige His Majesty the King of Great-Britain, in Quality of Elector of Brunswick Lüneburg, to oppose with Arms the Army of France in its new March against his Forces.

"IT is notorious, that on the 8th and 10th of September of this present year (1757), at Bremervörde and at Kloster Zeven, a convention was respectively agreed upon between His Royal Highness the Duke of Cumberland and the Marshal Duke de Richelieu, the copy whereof is in possession of either party.

"THE Court of France was no sooner informed of this, then it plainly manifested that she neither could nor would acknowledge the validity of the said convention, but on this single condition; namely, that the Hanoverian troops should formally engage not to serve any more, during the present war, against France and her allies. And, not content even with this pretension, she positively insisted upon disarming the auxiliary troops upon returning to their own country.

"His Royal Highness the Duke of Cumberland, who had on his part fulfilled all the conditions of the convention, and caused part of the troops, desired on their return for the country of Lauenburg, to begin their march, could not consider this new demand otherwise than as a manifest contravention; as the M. Duke de Richelieu had engaged not only to let the auxiliary troops depart freely, but the convention also setting forth in express terms that they should not be regarded as prisoners of war, under which quality alone the condition of laying down their arms could subsist: upon this his Royal Highness sent orders to the said troops to halt.

"ENDEAVORS were used to reconcile the difference by all imaginable means. Expedients were proposed, which left no shadow of pretext to the opposite party. But all in vain. The French would never be brought to give up so mortifying a demand, and 'tis but lately they have learned to soften their language a little. In the meantime, the troops, pent up in a narrow district assigned them, were exposed to the rigor of the season, and cut off from their business and emoluments of every kind.

"THE French at this time presume to treat the convention as a bare military scheme: and indeed (in consequence of the above declaration of the Court of France, in express opposition to its validity, and on account of the negotiation for the disarming, which the French general would never answer categorically without waiting for the resolution of the Court of Versailles) the nature of that act is totally changed between general and general, and is now become a court affair.

"HARD as were the conditions of the Convention for the troops of His Britannic Majesty, Elector of Hanover, the King would have acquiesced in them, if the French had not glaringly discovered their design of totally ruining his army and his dominions. It is themselves, who, by the most evident contraventions and outrageous conduct, have set the King free from everything which the Convention could render obligating to him.

"THE great end of the convention was an end in itself of the very nature and essence of every provisional armistice was to enter directly on negotiations of peace, in order to prevent the total ruin of the countries which compose the Electorate of Brunswick-Lüneburg and procure an accommodation for His Majesty's allies. The Court of France, turning a deaf ear to the propositions offered has for that end not only declared, time after time, that it would not lend a hand towards a definitive pacification with His Majesty in his quality of Elector; but has shown too plainly, by its continual violences, excesses, and insupportable exactions, since the signing of the convention, that its resolution is the absolute destruction of the King's electoral estates, as well as those of his allies. In the midst of a truce the most open hostilities have been committed. The Schartzfels Castle has been forcibly seized, and the garrison made prisoners of war. The prisoners made by the French before the Convention have not been restored, though this was a point expressly stipulated between the delegated generals and was exactly satisfied on our part by the immediate release of the French prisoners. The bailiffs of the reserved districts, into which the French troops were on no pretense to enter, have been summoned, under pain of military execution, to appear before the French commissary, with the design of compelling them to deliver the domainal receipts, of which they are the administrators. They have appropriated to themselves part of those magazines which, by express agreement, were to remain with the electoral troops; and they still go on with seizing the houses, revenues, and corn, belonging to His Majesty, in the city of Bremen, in spite of all the reciprocal engagements, whereby they are held to regard that city as a place absolutely free and neutral; and lastly, have proceeded to menaces, unheard of among a civilized people, of burning, sacking, and destroying all before them without remorse.

"ALL these violent and unjust proceedings are so many incontestable proofs that the French will not admit the convention as obligatory, any farther than as it may prove ruinous to His Britannic Majesty. They deny that they are tied down to anything and alert a power of acting at will. To so insupportable a degree of indolence have they carried matters, as to have born too heavily upon the King's patience; who holds himself before God, and all the impartial, not only at liberty, but even necessitated, without farther regard to the Convention, so often and so openly violated by the French, to have recourse to arms, as the means which the Almighty has put into his hands for delivering his faithful subjects and allies from the oppressions and vexations, which they now grow under.

"As His Majesty (conformable to his solemn declaration-made and repeated to all nations, and to the Germanic body in particular, from the beginning of the present unhappy war). Has never thought of arming offensively against any power whatever, but solely with a view of defending himself and his allies, he reposes his confidence in God, and hopes for his benediction on the justice of his enterprises."

I shall also subjoin the following copy of a letter, written by M. de Richelieu to His Serene Highness Prince Ferdinand at that critical juncture, as it may serve to give the reader some idea of French moderation and humanity

SIR,

ALTHOUGH for some days past I have perceived the Hanoverian troops in motion, in order to form themselves into a body, I could not imagine the object of these movements was to break the Convention of neutrality, signed on the 8th and 10th of September, between his Royal Highness the Duke of Cumberland and me. The good faith which I naturally supposed on the part of the King of England and Elector of Hanover, and of his Son who signed the said convention, blinded me so far as to make me believe that the assembling of these troops had no other design than to go into the winter-quarters that had been assigned them. The repeated advices, which came to me from every quarter, of the bad intentions of the Hanoverians, at length opened my eyes, and at present one may see very clearly, that there is a plan formed to break the articles of a convention, which ought to be sacred and inviolable.

"THE King my master, having been informed of these dangerous movements, and of the infidelity of the Hanoverians, is still willing to give fresh proofs of his moderation, and of his desire to spare the effusion of human blood. It is with this view that I have the honor to declare to your Serene Highness, that if, contrary to all expectations, it should take any equivocal step, and still more, if it should commit any act of hostility, I shall then push matters to the last extremity, looking on myself as authorized so to do by the laws of war. I shall set fire to all the palaces, royal houses, and gardens; I shall sack all the towns and villages, without sparing the smallest cabin; in short, this country shall feel all the horrors of war. I advise your Serene Highness to reflect on all this, and not to lay me under the necessity of taking steps so contrary to the natural humanity of the French nation, and also to my personal character.

Signed: RICHELIEU.

"P. S. MONS le Comte de Lynar, Ambassador of the King of Denmark, who was mediator for the Convention, has been so kind as to take upon him to say everything in his power to Your Serene Highness, in order to prevent the fatal consequences with which this country is threatened."

His Serene Highness Prince Ferdinand returned this laconic reply, "that he would come at the head of his army and answer him in person."

SUCH was the posture of affairs when His Serene Highness Prince Ferdinand, Duke of Brunswick and Lüneburg, arrived at Stade, where he assumed the command of the Combined Army. He directly caused it to be published, at the head of every regiment, that it was with regret he saw himself reduced to the necessity of keeping the troops in the field during so severe a season, but the good of their country rendered it absolutely unavoidable; he therefore hoped their solidity and courage would enable them to persevere with patience; that it should be his particular care, not only to recompense their faithful services, but also to provide them with all the necessaries the circumstances would allow him, in order to enable them to support the fatigue. Orders were immediately issued to increase their allowance of bread, and to furnish every man daily with one pound of meat and a glass of brandy. The troops on this occasion expressed the greatest ardor and alacrity.

As M. de Richelieu in his march to Lüneburg had already commenced hostilities, His Serene Highness drew nearer to the town of Harburg. On his approach M. de Pereuse retired into the castle, with his garrison consisting of about 1,500 men. His behavior on this occasion was ungenerous and cruel, for he carried along with him some of the wives and children of the principal inhabitants of the town, among whom was General Schulenburg's lady, at the same time threatening to set fire to the town. This incendiary method of proceeding is not surprising, when we consider their excessive ravages and devastations in Saxony before the battle of Rossbach; a country they pretended they came to relieve from the imaginary depredations of the Prussians. The jägers entered the town on the 3d, and General Hardenberg the same day invested the castle with three battalions and two squadrons. The reduction of the garrison was committed to his care. The army then advanced, and in consequence of some motions which it made in order to intercept the French troops in Lüneburg, they evacuated that city, and Major Freytag with some light troops took possession of it on the 3d of December. A considerable quantity of forage and provisions, besides 3,000 pair of shoes, were found there, which the enemy could not carry off in their hurry. The garrison of Harburg made a vigorous sally, but were repulsed, and suffered considerably. The enemy fell back everywhere towards Celle, and M. de Richelieu sent reiterated orders to press the march of the different corps to join him there. The heavy artillery from Hanover, the 6,000 Palatines quartered at Hamm and Lippstadt, and a body of cavalry quartered in the Duchy of Cleves, received also the same repeated orders.

THE reigning Duke of Brunswick, having signed a private convention with the French, sent orders in pursuance thereof to his troops to withdraw from the Army of Observation, and march home to winter quarters; but his brother Prince Ferdinand detained them, and the Crown Prince remained with them of his own accord.

His Serene Highness continued to advance, and on the 4th encamped at Amelinghausen, where he halted the next day. By this step our communication with the Elbe was thoroughly secured. On his march to that place, Gen. Schulenburg, who commanded an advanced party, overtook near Ebsdorf a detachment of Fischer's Corps, supported by the Caramans Cavalry Regiment and as his foot was not come up, attacked them with the single regiment of Breidenbach's Dragoons, some jägers and hussars. The action was very sharp for some time, as each party was spirited up with a kind of animosity; but at last the French were entirely routed with the loss of 11 officers and 400 private men, killed and wounded. General Schulenburg was slightly wounded in the affair. A reinforcement was immediately after sent to join him.

ON the 6th, the army crossed the Lopau River in four columns, and encamped with the right to Wittenwater village, and the left in the rear of Melzingen. The headquarters were fixed at Ebsdorf. Count Schulenburg joined the army with his advanced corps, and Major Luckner was detached towards Hermannsburg, where he seized 24 laden wagons. Major Esdorff, who took possession of Medingen, found there 100,000 rations of hay, 60,000 rations of oats, with a considerable quantity of wheat, rye, and straw. There were also small magazines at Bienenbüttel, Bad Bevensen, and Ulzen, all which the enemy had abandoned, so precipitant was their retreat.

ON the night between the 6th and 7th, one of the magazines in Harburg Castle was set on fire by a bomb, and entirely consumed. On the 8th, the garrison made a sally on the side of Lauenburg and brought off some live cattle. An armed vessel was immediately posted upon the Riegerstieg, a branch of the Elbe, to curb them on that side, and to cut off any support they might receive by the said river. The army halted on the 7th and 8th but on the 9th it passed the Gerdau River, encamping between the small Hardau and Schweinebach Rivers, the former being on its right, and the latter on its left, with its center in the front of the village Suderburg, where the headquarters were established. Major Luckner dislodged a party of the enemy posted at Hermannsburg. The 10th was a day of halt; then General Spörcken was ordered to advance towards Gifhorn with eight battalions and eight squadrons.

On the 11th, the army advanced to Weyhausen, where the headquarters were fixed. Here intelligence was received, that a large body of the enemy were posted at Ribbesbüttel and had afterwards been considerably reinforced; whereupon General Oberg, on the 12th at daybreak, moved forward with an advanced corps of six battalions and nine squadrons supported by the whole army in four columns; but the enemy had retired in the night. The army encamped with its center in the rear, and the advanced corps in the front of that village, where His Serene Highness had his quarters. Major Luckner advanced towards Gamsen with three companies of grenadiers, four squadrons, and some irregulars, where he skirmished the whole day with the volunteers of Hainault and Dansret. General Spörcken joined the army at nine this night with his detachment. On the 13th, the army marched in the same order as on the preceding day. As we advanced the enemy retreated; and, when we arrived within a league of Celle, it evidently appeared that they had no intention to stand their ground; whereupon General Oberg moved briskly forward with the advanced corps, and they all retired on the other side of the Aller through the city, burnt their magazines which they had in the suburbs of Lüneburg, and kept up a continual fire from a battery that defended the head of the bridge. In the night they also set fire to the suburbs and the bridge. Their cruelty and inhumanity on this occasion was enough to excite horror in any but a savage. The children were burned In the Orphan House, and several of the inhabitants also perished in the flames, not being apprised thereof. The army encamped on the heights opposite the suburbs, its headquarters being at Altenhagen. The French army at this time consisted of 44 battalions and 42 squadrons. The enemy passed that night and all the next day under arms, and then encamped with the city of Celle in the front of their right, and their left extending towards Schaffery. The whole country, through which these marches were made, is open, but intersected by small rivers, whose sides are mostly marshy ground, and difficult of access, so that they are only passable through the villages: it is, therefore, amazing that the French so easily gave way everywhere on our approach, without ever attempting to dispute one foot of ground to retard our progress in a country which afforded by nature so many strong posts. Numberless were the fatigues and difficulties the soldiery had to encounter in a march made in the severe season of the year through a country so full of defiles; but they bore them with the greatest cheerfulness, fired with emulation and animated by the hopes of relieving their distressed country from the rapine and avarice of a licentious army; an army of freebooters! An army maintained by depredations at the express commands of their monarch an army that paid no regard to the laws of war or humanity, whose very officers were guilty of the meanest actions! Out of the many instances that might be enumerated, I shall only mention one: when the Hanoverians represented to the French generals, that their officers had taken the sheets from off their beds to make them shirts, the only redress they had was an order immediately issued out for them to furnish the army with shirts, shoes, stockings, etc. by way of a contribution.

ON the 14th, the army made no movement. His Serene Highness having determined to pass the Aller, the following dispositions were made for that purpose.

ON the 15th, General Spörcken was ordered to march towards the right to Boye with eight battalions and eight squadrons, and some irregulars. The pontoons were that night also ordered to be conducted to the same place. On their arrival the grenadiers, irregulars and pioneers belonging to that corps, were to pass the river, and, with all expedition, throw up a bridgehead. Two bridges were at the same time to be constructed, over which the whole detachment was to pass. On the 16th, the army was under arms at five in the morning in order to march and pass the river at that place as soon as Gen. Spörcken should send notice that the bridges were perfected; His Serene Highness's intentions being to attack the enemy's left. General Oberg was also detached towards the right to Hehlen with two battalions and eight squadrons; at the same time, General Isenburg marched towards the left to Lachtehausen, with three battalions and two squadrons. Both these detachments were to make a feint of passing the river, and to act in such manner as might be conducive to deceive the enemy, on that occasion: and cause them to imagine the affair serious. Count Kielmansegg had two battalions under his command, with orders to endeavor to force into the city the instant the enemy should abandon it. The pontoons through some mistake, took a wrong route, and did not arrive at the place of destination; by which disappointment the whole of the intended scheme was frustrated. General Spörcken, with his detachment returned to the camp; but Generals Isenburg and Oberg each encamped near his respective post.

ON the 16th and 17th, M. de Richelieu was reinforced by a body of the troops from Brunswick; and his army consisted of 74 battalions and 70 squadrons, and more were still on the march from different quarters to join him. Meanwhile, on the 19th, Gen. Spörcken's corps fell into the line, also two battalions and two squadrons of General Isenburg's detachment returned and did the same. The other battalion remained at Lachtehausen. General Oberg's corps also marched back to its first camp, being a part of the advanced guard of the army.

M. de Richelieu, his army being now greatly superior in numbers to the Army of Observation, decided to cross the Aller; and, in consequence thereof, made the following maneuver:

M. de Broglio was ordered to go and assume the command of a body of troops which had been assembled in the Duchy of Bremen, consisting or 12 battalions and 8 squadrons. His orders were to advance by the Wümme, to turn our right, and cut off our convoys. He was to proceed even beyond Wolthausen, if it could be done with safety. On the 21st, 22d, and 23d, they made several different movements, with a design to alarm us on our left and rear; and frequent skirmishes passed between the light troops. On the 24th, the Marquis de Willimer, with 10 battalions, 14 squadrons, and a body of light troops, passed the Aller at Münden, to cover the construction of two bridges that were to be thrown over the river at Offensen and Schwachhausen. He was likewise to lend an advanced guard of 1,500 men to dislodge any of our parties that might be in the villages of Ahnsbeck, Jarnsen, and Lachendorf; and if possible take post on the heights beyond them, in order to favor the construction of some bridges designed to be thrown over the Aller and the Lachte Rivulet. A detachment of the same corps, consisting of 400 horse, was to advance towards Ulzen the same night, to burn our magazines, and intercept our convoys. M. de Caraman, with two regiments of infantry, two companies of grenadiers, two picquets, and Fischer's Corps, were to pass the Aller at Schaffery, and make a false attack on our right at Klein Hehlen and Gross Hehlen. M. d'Auvet, with seven battalions, four squadrons, and a party of hussars, was by the way of the suburbs of Lüneburg also to make a false attack and might be reinforced according as the different events should render it necessary. The Duke d'Ayen, with three brigades of infantry, one of cavalry, and four squadrons of Gendarmerie, was to pass at Altencelle. The rest of the army was to assemble at Offensen and Schwachhausen in two lines; the second to have the care of constructing the two bridges, while the first remained in order of battle on the banks between the two villages

ON the 23d in the evening, General Spörcken was detached with five battalions and five squadrons to the right, to observe M. de Broglio; and, on the 24th in the morning, the Prince of Brunswick was sent to Hermannsburg, to join General Spörcken, with four battalions and four squadrons. M. de Broglio had advanced as far as Fallingbostel.

His Serene Highness, being thoroughly informed of all the motions and designs of the enemy, determined to decamp on the 25th and retire to Ulzen, whereby all M. de Richelieu's schemes were rendered abortive. Several reasons concurred to induce him to take this step: 1st, he was nearer at hand to cover the siege of Harburg, which the enemy had an intention to relieve: secondly, he thereby secured his communication with the Elbe: thirdly, by that advantageous situation he covered the march of a body of Prussian cavalry which was advancing to reinforce him, and could then join him without the least obstruction: fourthly, the French were greatly superior to him in numbers: the fifth and principal motive was the inclemency of the weather, which was so excessively severe as to render it next to impossible for the soldiery to remain any longer in the field. They had moreover undergone great fatigues and wanted refreshments. The troops were therefore sent into quarters of cantonment about Ulzen and Lüneburg, at both which places the headquarters were occasionally established. This march was made without any loss, as the enemy never once attempted to molest them. A party of about 400 men had indeed made their appearance, but immediately retired on the approach of a party sent against them. The French likewise cantoned their troops, distributing them about Verden, Celle, Brunswick, and Hanover. M. de Richelieu fixed his headquarters in the latter; M. d'Armentières commanded a large body in the city of Celle and M. de Broglio remained between Bremen and Verden with another.

ON the 29th, the castle of Harburg capitulated after a brave defense. The garrison consisting of 1,700 men, was allowed the honors of war, on condition of not serving against His Majesty or his allies during the war. The artillery, ammunition, etc. were to be faithfully delivered up; in pursuance, whereof they marched out on the 31st, and a party of our troops took possession thereof. Major Luckner, with his hussars, had a smart engagement with a detachment of the enemy, consisting of 200 hussars and 60 dismounted troopers, wherein the latter were entirely dispersed. Their commanding officer M. de Grandemaison, two captains, three subalterns, and 60 men, were made prisoners, besides a number killed and wounded.

THE CAMPAIGN OF THE YEAR 1758

JANUARY 1, General Oberg, who was posted at Soltau with a detachment of the Allied Army, having received intelligence that a large body of the French were advanced as far as Visselhövede, immediately ordered out Colonel Dreves with 400 infantry, 100 cavalry, and some light horse, to dislodge them. The Colonel surprised and entirely defeated the enemy, making five officers and 114 private men prisoners; took three drums, killed and wounded about 30: the rest saved themselves by flight.

AFTER the reduction of the castle of Harburg, the troops that were employed in the siege were ordered to Bremervörde and Buxtehude, towards the Lower Aller on the right of the river Wümme, in order to descend the passage of that river, and cover the country of Bremen, as also to alarm the French, and keep them in awe in that quarter, as they had a considerable corps posted along the river in the neighborhood of Rotenburg an der Fulda and Ottersberg. On their march they surprised a party of 400 of the enemy at Tesse Hoeusde[4], whom they entirely defeated, taking 108 prisoners, and cutting a considerable number of them to pieces. Detached parties were advanced, who took possession of Vegesack, Ritterhude, etc. in the former of which places they found a considerable magazine. M. de Richelieu, having intelligence hereof, immediately sent orders to M. de Broglio to advance by the Lower Wümme, in order to dislodge us from beyond that river, and, by opening a passage for themselves into the Duchy of Bremen, preserve their communication with their troops at Rotenburg an der Fulda and Ottersberg. Moreover, they were jealous of our intentions to possess ourselves of the city of Bremen, which they had before planned to seize. About the 3d of January he entered the suburbs of that city, and proceeded to Burgh, where he crossed the Wümme and advanced by the way of Vegesack, etc. which our advanced parties were obliged to abandon, not being able to withstand a force so superior. General Oberg, as soon as he was informed of the enemy's motions, gave orders for same troops from Bremervörde and Buxtehude to join him, and by forced marches advanced to attack the enemy; but the Duke de Broglio, though he had been reinforced by 11 battalions, retreated with the utmost expedition. Our advanced guard, however, came up with their rear, on the 12th, near the village of Ritterhude. A smart engagement ensued in which the enemy suffered considerably and were obliged to fly with the greatest precapitation. Repassing the Wümme at Burgh, they broke down the bridge as soon as they had got on the other side. On the 14th the bridge was repaired. General Oberg passed that river and took possession of Borgfeld Fort; but the French had retired towards Bremen, where they arrived on the 15th. M. de Broglio directly drew up his forces on the edge of the ditch; and, having ordered some cannon to be advanced to the gates, demanded

4. Editor: This may be Tiste or Tostedt

immediate admittance, threatening to have recourse to extremities in case of refusal. The magistrates prayed he would wait 'till the next day; but he allowed them only two hours, insisting that, if the gates were not then thrown open, he would beat them down, and order the walls to be scaled. Admittance was then granted on his consenting to sign a kind of articles, whereby he promised that their rights and privileges should not be infringed, nor their city any way damaged or molested in its trade. A party of his troops ac-cordingly took possession of one of the gates at midnight, and the whole detachment entered that city the next day. Both the Hanoverians and French were reinforced from time to time in those parts. Frequent skirmishes happened, which I pass by in silence, as nothing material or decisive was the consequence; for we still continued masters of the passage of the Wümme, and the Duchy of Bremen, at the time the forces took the field.

THE following account is not immediately a part of Prince Ferdinand's operations, yet the affairs in those quarters had a strong connection, and were in a great measure interwoven with them, as they greatly contributed to their success; for the Prussians were to act on that side against M. de Richelieu's army, at the same time that His Serene Highness should advance in front on their left and center; I therefore thought it necessary to keep up the chain of events that occurred on that side, so far as they were relative to the matter in hand

WHEN M. de Richelieu, as was observed before, had been obliged, in consequence of the battle of Rossbach, to evacuate the country of Halberstadt, the governor of Magdeburg detached General Jungkenn, with a part of his garrison, consisting of two battalions of infantry and 1,100 cavalry, to cover that country from the incursions of the French. He accordingly proceeded to Aschersleben, where he was joined by another battalion. He thence went to Halberstadt, where he took post with two battalions, sending the other to Quedlinburg. With this small body of troops, he kept the French in continual alarm, even as far as the gates of Brunswick.

M. de Voyer, who had for some time commanded at Wolfenbüttel, was ordered to re-enter that country, with a detachment consisting of 11 battalions, 36 piquets, two regiments of cavalry, one of hussars, and 400 cavalry. He flattered himself with the hopes of surprising General Jungkenn and purposed to cut off his retreat by surrounding him. For this purpose, he divided his force into three columns, which were all to begin their march on the night between the 10th and 11th. The right column set out from Schladen, and, marching to the right of the Holtemme Rivulet, was to take post on the road near the gate which leads from Halberstadt to Quedlinburg; the center set out from Hornburg, and, directing its march by Osterwieck and Zilly, was to take post at the gate to which that road led; the left was to march from Achim; and, passing the rivulet of Holtemme below Halberstadt, take post at the gate leading to Ascherleben.

A small party of the Prussians, who had been patrolling, met their right at 3 o'clock in the morning, and brought intelligence of their march to General Jungkenn, who, being unable to make head against so superior a force, retired at daybreak to an eminence at some distance from the town, where he halted for some time to cover the junction of the regiment from Quedlinburg; and as soon as that was effected he retreated without any molestation to Ascherleben. Some skirmishes passed between the cavalry on this occasion. Excessive were their demands both in money and corn. In vain did the magistracy represent the ruined state of the country, which they had already entirely exhausted. M. de Voyer's answer was money and corn, or flames, threatening to burn every house wherein there should be found more than four crowns in money, or three bushels of rye. These threats were partly put in execution; for, under the pretense of searching for corn, the soldiers plundered the houses of what they thought proper. In this manner they collected 121,000 crowns in money, and 79,000 in bills, and taking with them all the cattle and grain they could find, they, on the 16th, again evacuated that unfortunate country; the view of this expedition plainly appears to be entirely lucrative, and their behavior everywhere similar, makes good what has been before asserted.

THE 31st, a detachment of Prussians re-entered the city of Halberstadt, and, on February the 1st, pushed forward a party to Hornburg, who made there, and in the neighboring village about 500 prisoners and on the 2d, a party of cavalry and hussers advanced to the gates of Steinfeld before the garrison had received the least notice of their march; killed the sentinel, and immediately entered the city, where they made 600 of Turpin's Regiment of hussars prisoners of war, and seized all their horses and baggage; the rest of the garrison fled in the greatest confusion towards Schlade, but being reinforced they returned in pursuit, and came up with the Prussians on their return to Halberstadt. Several smart skirmishes ensued between them and the Prussian cavalry: in the meantime, the hussars conveyed their prisoners and booty safely off. This corps was the vanguard of a body of about 18,000 men commanded by Prince Henry, who afterwards invested the fortress of Regenstein, which surrendered on the 12th, where was found a considerable quantity of artillery, ammunition, etc. This unexpected appearance of the Prussians, especially at this juncture when the Combined Army was on the point of taking the field, threw the French into the greatest consternation. The commandant at Wolfenbüttel recalled all the neighboring posts and out-parties, and kept the gates shut for fear of a surprise and a reinforcement was also sent to him from Brunswick. Prince George of Holstein-Gottorp joined the Combined Army with a body of 7,000 cavalry from Pomerania and as everything had been previously prepared that was necessary for taking the field, the Combined Army marched out of their cantonments, resumed operations, and advanced towards M. de Clermont, who had just succeeded M. de Richelieu in the command of the French army. His Serene Highness, with the main body directed his march towards Bremen and Verden. The French seemed determined to maintain the former of these fortresses, as they had not only been greatly reinforced in that quarter, but also had for some time worked day and night on the repair of its fortifications. General Zastrow advanced at the head of the remainder towards Celle and Gifhorn.

FEB. 18, Prince Ferdinand's quarters were this day at Schneverdingen, and Prince George advanced on Soltau. On the 19th, the headquarters advanced to Neukirchen, on the confines of the Duchy of Verden; and on the 20th. at Visselhövede, on which day the castle of Rotenburg an der Fulda surrendered to General Wangenheim, after a cannonade of about six hours. M. de la Mothe, with the garrison, consisting of about 150 men, were made prisoners at the same time the enemy retired from their post at Ottersberg, abandoning all their artillery and ammunition: on the same day, they likewise evacuated the town of Verden, and M. de St. Chamans, who commanded therein, retired to Bremen, with the garrison, as did also those from Ottersberg.

FEB. 23, the Crown Prince of Brunswick was detached at 7 o'clock this morning, with two battalions of Hanoverians, two battalions of the Brunswick Guards, one squadron of dragoons, and a body of light horse, to Hoya, a place of great importance, with orders to dislodge General Count de Chabot, who had been posted there with a considerable body of French, consisting of the two battalions of the Gardes Lorraines, two companies of grenadiers, some piquets of the Bretagne Regiment, and a detachment from the Mestre de camp Dragoon Regiment, being some of the best troops in France. He accordingly proceeded to Döverden, near which place he expedted to have got some floats of timber to transport a part of his troops over the Weser, but he only found one float and two or three boats capable of carrying about eight men each. The battalions of Oberg, and the squadrons of dragoons were to make a false attack on the left of the river, while the other three battalions entered the town by the bridge on the right; but by the time the Hauss Regiment and one half of the 2nd Battalion of Brunswick Guards had passed over, the wind blew so strong as to render the passage of the rest impracticable: whereupon they moved forward as they were, and advanced to the bridge without any molestation: there the fire became exceeding hot; our attack was vigorous, and the resistance as obstinate, no ground being either gained or lost. The Prince immediately formed the design of turning the enemy, and for that purpose marched with the half battalion around the town, and, with bayonets fixed, forced his passage through a house and garden. Here the affair was very bloody; but the French being driven from the bridge, our two parties were again joined each other, and the enemy retired into the old castle. As we had no cannon, and the Bretagne Regiment, with some squadrons of dragoons, were on their march to relieve them, they were granted the capitulation to march out with the honors of war to the next French post, delivering up all the artillery, ammunition, and stores. Our loss on this occasion was negligible, not amounting to 100 men killed and wounded. Those of the enemy were also very great, for exclusive of the number killed and wounded we made 670 prisoners, who had in the time of action been intercepted from entering the castle. A great quantity of baggage, belonging to several of the principal officers of the French army, was found in this place.

ON the same day there happened a severe action, between a party of the Prussian Black Hussars and Poleretzky's Hussar Regiment, near Norddrebber; wherein the latter were entirely defeated and dispersed, having three officers and 50 men killed; their colonel, four officers, and 100 and 30 private men, made prisoners, ten standards, one pair of kettledrums, and 300 horses taken: the remaining troops fled to Hanover.

M. de St. Germaine, who had relieved M. de Broglio in the command of the French troops in the neighborhood of Bremen, having received information of the reduction of Hoya, and that His Serene Highness was at that time in full march towards that city with his advanced guard, immediately determined to evacuate it, as the communication with M. de Clermont was intercepted, and their retreat would have incurred the same danger by a longer stay. Accordingly, on the 24th in the morning, being the time, the account came, he issued orders for all the troops, as well cavalry as infantry, to assemble that same evening at Bassum. So great was their diligence, that their artillery and baggage marched out before 2 o'clock in the afternoon, abandoning their hospital and magazines. They lay that night on their arms, as not being far from Hoya. On the 25th they quitted Bassum and passing the Hunte River proceeded to Wildhusen. On the 26th they got to

Vechta, where they halted the next day; but hearing that a party of the Hanoverians had passed the Hunte they marched on the 28th to Vorde, and on the 1st of March arrived at Osnabrück in the greatest disorder and confusion, quite worn out with the fatigue of forced marches through bad roads. This body consisted of 22 battalions and 21 squadrons.

ABOUT an hour after the French had quitted Bremen a party of about 50 Hanoverian jägers appeared at the Doven Gate; and about 9 o'clock Major General Diepenbrock, with a detachment of the Allied Army, demanded admittance: but after some messages, between him and the magistrates, he desisted from his demand for that night. However, a body of 150 of his light troops were per-mitted to march through the town at two in the morning, and about noon the next day five Hanoverian battalions, two squadrons, and two companies of the jägers on foot, entered the city on a convention of preserving the liberties and immunities of the burghers. His Serene Highness detached a body of light troops in pursuit of the enemy, who greatly harassed them, daily sending in numbers of prisoners, such as had either straggled for the sake of marauding, or being unable to bear the fatigues, could not keep up with the main body. The enemy would have suffered a great deal more in their retreat, or more properly flight, had not our hussars been otherwise diverted and amused by the immense quantity of baggage wagons which, being deserted by the French, were left sticking in the mire; the roads being everywhere covered with them. The effects of M. de St. Germainee, La Valette, and St. Chamant, fell into their hands at Wildhufen, and, in general, the regiments lost almost all their tents and baggage. What remained of their heavy baggage was, immediately on their arrival at Osnabrück, sent forward by the way of Münster to Wesel and the Duchy of Cleves.

AFTER His Serene Highness had taken possession of Bremen, he passed the Aller River, and directed his march towards Hanover, while Prince Henry of Prussia, at the same time, advanced on their right from the country of Halberstadt towards Wolfenbüttel and Goslar, The enemy, on the 26th and 27th, abandoned Celle, Brunswick, Wolfenbüttel, and all the neighboring posts, retiring with great expedition by Hanover. On the 27th, the town of Nienburg was invested by the allies, and surrendered the 28th on capitulation. The garrison were granted the liberty to march out with the honors of war, which they accordingly did on the 1st of March.

AT 5 o'clock in the morning of the 28th, the city of Hanover was evacuated by the enemy, and M. de Clermont retreated towards Hameln, having already ordered on February 6, his heavy artillery to be conducted, part to that place, to both Hameln and Einbeck. Before his departure he ordered the arsenal to be destroyed and took with him the Baron de Münchausen and M. de Hardenberg as hostages for the payment of the arrears of the contributions, as they had also done from Bremen, and all the places they had abandoned. The next day following, a party of our Prussian hussars passed through the city in pursuit of them. The great humanity and benevolence which the French governor, the Duke of Randan, showed, not only on this occasion, but also during his whole government, will forever render his name and memory grateful to the inhabitants, who were under the greatest consternation at that juncture, expecting to be pillaged, but he caused the strictest discipline to be kept up, and ordered a considerable quantity of all sorts of provisions, which they could not carry away, to be distributed among the poor burghers. Neither did he suffer the least damage or injury to be committed upon their retiring from that city.

ON the 2d of March, His Serene Highness made his entrance into the city of Hanover amidst the acclamations of the inhabitants. He immediately gave orders for taking proper care of the sick, who were left by the French in the hospital, amounting to 1,500 men.

THE Combined Army immediately moved forward in pursuit of the French in two bodies. His Serene Highness marched at the head of one on the left of the Weser, the Prince of Holstein with the vanguard being advanced one day's march before, while General Oberg with the Crown Prince, who commanded his van, at the same time kept at an equal distance on the right of that river, by which means the junction of the two bodies might on any occasion be speedily effected. On the 3d the Prince's headquarters were at Sachsenhagen. The retreat of M. de Clermont was made with the same precipitation and confusion as that of M. de St. Germaine, having lost the most part of their tents and baggage, which they were obliged to abandon on the roads, as they were closely pressed by our hussars and advanced parties, who made an immense booty on that occasion. On their arrival at Hameln, the French with the greatest diligence sent forward their heavy baggage by the way of Paderborn towards the Rhine, over which river they had constructed bridges at several different places.

PRINCE Henry advanced from Halberstadt to the country of Hildesheim, having his headquarters at Hessen, where some of our chasseurs who had been left on the Aller joined him. He threw garrisons into Wolfenbüttel and Goslar. On the 2d a party of his hussars passed through the town of Hildesheim, where he arrived on the 3d; and on the 5th, established his headquarters at Liebenburg.

ON the 3d of March, a detachment of 600 Prussian dragoons and hussars overtook a party of French, composed of 600 cavalry and 300 infantry. A severe action ensued, during which the French lost 300 killed, and 176 made prisoners: the rest were entirely dispersed.

MARCH 5. The Crown Prince of Brunswick appeared before the town of Minden and summoned it. The French commandant, the Marquis de Morangiers, returned his answer, that, as the place was well supplied with everything requisite, he would endeavor by his defense to merit the esteem of a prince equally distinguished by birth and bravery. Whereupon General Oberg with his corps invested the town on the right, while General Spörcken did the same on the left; and a bridge of communication was thrown over the Weser. His Serene Highness's headquarters were on the 6th at Stadhagen, and on the 7th at Frille near Minden.

M. de Clermont was then encamped in a very advantageous situation near Hameln, with his left covered by that town, and his right by a morass: his front could only be approached by defiles well defended by artillery and redoubts. He had also thrown five bridges over the river.

MARCH 8. Prince Ferdinand's headquarters were at Hartum, within a mile and a half of Minden. His Serene Highness, having received intelligence that M. de St. Germaine had on the 7th marched out from Osnabrück towards Melle and Herford, in order to join M. de Clermont, who had also sent forward a detachment towards those places to favor his junction, immediately passed the Weser to prevent their design. M. d'Armentières stopped short, and halted at the villages of Diflen, Enger, etc. where they committed excessive ravages and horrid outrages, conformable to their usual behavior. On the night between the 7th and 8th, the garrison of Minden made a sally, but were quickly repulsed. On the 9th, the heavy artillery being arrived, a brisk fire began from the batteries of the besiegers,

MARCH 14. His Serene Highness's headquarters were at Hille and this day the town of Minden surrendered. The garrison consisted of eight battalions and eight squadrons besides a detachment of the Hainaut Infantry Regiment, amounting in the whole to 3,516 men, officers included, who were made prisoners of war. General Kielmansegg took possession of it with one battalion, and found there 67 pieces of cannon, besides a considerable magazine. On the 18th, the French evacuated the town of Hameln, and also their strong camp in that neighborhood, retiring towards Paderborn. They had first sent off all the heavy artillery and baggage, blown up the bridges, and destroyed the arsenal with all the military stores. As soon as they had marched out, four companies of Colonel Scheither's regiment were ordered to take possession of that place.

On the 19th, His Serene Highness removed his headquarters to Melle, near Osnabrück, and Prince George of Holstein, with a strong detachment, took post at Herford, Bielefeld, and Rinteln; the two former of which places the French, who had come from Bremen under M. de St. Germaine, had abandoned, and retired towards Münster. A party of the Prussian Deathhead Hussars overtook a body of French at Bielefeld, made several prisoners, and took a great many wagons laden with baggage. Major Estorf, with a body of cavalry, was also sent to take possession of Osnabrück, where the French had left a considerable magazine.

ON the 17th, Commodore Holmes[5], with His Majesty's ships the Seahorse and Strombolo, came to an anchor between Delfzijl and Knock; and, on the 18th, came to their station between Knock and Emden. On the 19th, at six in the morning, the French, to the number of 2,520, marched out of the town; and, on the 20th, the Austrian troops, amounting to 1,220, did the same; at noon, the commodore received intelligence, that they had, the night before, been transporting their baggage and cannon up the river in small vessels. He, thereupon, dispatched an armed cutter with two boats in pursuit of them, who took two of them notwithstanding the fire of the enemy, who had lined both sides of the river. On board one of those vessels there were some French officers, and three of the chief inhabitants, whom the French were carrying away as hostages for the payment of the contributions exacted. M. de Clermont had sent orders to General Pisa to evacuate East Friesland lest his communication should be cut off, as he had received information that the troops in the neighborhood of Bremen were to be joined by a detachment from the Allied Army, in order to march into that principality. General Pisa also gave into a report which had been artfully spread, that the English men-of-war which had intercepted his communication down the river were part of a convoy to a fleet of transports who were landing a body of 10,000 British troops about ten

5. Commodore Charles Holmes

miles from thence, which was the cause of his evacuating that city so suddenly. He directed his march on the right of the Ems towards the country of Bentheim, not only destroying the bridges at Rheine, Meppen, and Lingen, but also sinking all the boats they found on that river, the better to secure his retreat. However, a party of about 500 Hanoverian hussars, not long after they had quitted Lingen, arrived there, made two French commissaries prisoners, and seized on a large magazine which was in that place. They also obliged the peasants to weigh up the vessels and repair the bridge, which was accomplished the following night. They immediately set forward in pursuit of the enemy, a body of whom, consisting of about 1,500 men, were overtaken between Githuysen[6] and Bentheim: these they entirely defeated, killed and wounded a great number, and made many prisoners. They afterwards pursued their march to north, where they made an Austrian major prisoner, and took 14 baggage wagons richly laden.

THE Prussian troops under the command of Prince Henry about this time advanced towards Duderstadt. A party of 70 Austrians who were in that town retired on the night between the 19th and 20th with great precipitation, on intelligence that a detachment of the Prussians were on their march thither. A party of 100 hussars belonging to Wunsch's corps were sent in pursuit of them and made one subaltern and 50 men prisoners. The main body of the Prussians arrived soon after in that neighborhood in their rout towards Hesse.

ON the 20th the French abandoned the town of Münden without committing the least disorder and, on the 21st, they likewise evacuated the city of Kassel and the greatest part of Hesse, having first removed their hospitals, artillery, and heavy baggage, to Hanau and Mainz. M. de Broglio, who came there from Bremen to take the command of the French troops in that country, directed his march, with a body of 27 battalions and 22 squadrons, to join M. de Clermont. Before his departure he ordered the arms and trophies, which were in the arsenal, to be sent to Marburg; but at the same time would not suffer any damage to be done to the inhabitants when he quitted that city. A party of Prussians took possession of it the next day, just as the Count de Lorges who commanded the French troops at Hanau was preparing to evacuate that place he received orders not to quit it, but on the contrary to maintain and defend that post to the last extremity. In consequence thereof, he used the greatest diligence to have the fortifications repaired: he also ordered new works and entrenchments to be thrown up. A battalion of the Royal Regiment of Artillery, which had crossed the Rhine at Mainz, on the 26th received orders to return to that city, with several pieces of cannon and mortars; and several engineers also returned to oversee the works that were to be added to the fortifications. They likewise ordered the post at Aschaffenburg to be entrenched, and the old works repaired; and a body of 14 battalions and 18 squadrons were left between the Rhine and Maine Rivers.

THE Allied Army halted on the 20th and 21st, and nothing material passed during that time, except that numbers of prisoners were brought into the camp, but, on the 22d, it resumed its march, and the headquarters were established at Borgholzhausen, at a small distance from Ravensburg. On the 23d, the army decamped and marched to Versmold, and, on the 24th, it continued its march, and encamped near Sassenberg, where His Serene Highness fixed his headquarters.

6. Editor: This may be Gildehaus, which is today a suburb of Bad Bentheim.

THE main body of the French army removed at the same time from Paderborn to Neuhaus, and from thence filed off along the Lippe by Lippstadt, Soest, etc. towards the town of Wesel; and the corps under the command of M. de St. Germaine, having sent all their heavy baggage to Haltern-am-See, directed its march also to the same place, so that the enemy moved in three columns. M. de St. Germaine with the troops from Bremen being on the right, M. de Clermont with the main body kept in the center, while M. de Broglio with the troops from Hesse composed the left column, proceeding along the Rhine; but he was not so far advanced as either of the other two.

THE enemy left a hospital of more than 800 men at Paderborn: they likewise left considerable ones at Lippstadt and Münster; at the same time abandoning great quantities of provisions and forage, as well as artillery and ammunition, at all those places.

A party of hussars belonging to the Allies came up with the rear guard of the main body of the French near Soest in the country of Marc; and having attacked them made a considerable number prisoners, took ten pieces of cannon 24-pounders, and five 6-pounders, together with a large magazine.

His Serene Highness decamped from Sassenberg, and encamped near Freckenhorst on the 27th, having detached Prince George of Holstein with a considerable body of foot and horse in pursuit of the enemy, with orders to use his utmost efforts to break in upon them.

ON the 28th, the division of the French which came from East Friesland arrived at Emmerich, where it passed the Rhine, and went into quarters of cantonment in Cleves and its neighborhood.

APRIL 2. His Serene Highness removed his headquarters to Haltern-am-See.

THE two columns of the French army which came from Münster and Paderborn encamped, on the 1st, 2d, and 3d of April, near Wesel; after which they separated, and went into cantonments on the other side of the Rhine: at the same time M. de Broglio, with the corps from the country of Hesse, also crossed the Rhine at Cologne, and took up their quarters between Cologne and Neuss. The whole of the French army was distributed into quarters in three lines, extending with its right to Cologne and its left to Cleves. The first line was posted along the Rhine the second lay farther up in the country, between the Meuse and the Rhine and the third along the Meuse and Ruhr Rivers. They were distributed, as if in the field, into brigades: the general officers were stationed with their divisions according to the order of battle and took up their quarters as near the center of their brigades as possible. M. de Clermont, thoroughly sensible of the dissoluteness and want of order in his army, did his utmost endeavors to reform the abuses and confusion which naturally flowed therefrom: in order to effect this, he firmly determined to bring every offender to exemplary punishment, and laid the strongest injunctions on his generals to see that discipline was strictly observed, requesting them to omit nothing that might enforce it; but all was ineffectual, a general discontent and contempt of their general's conduct having spread itself even through the officers discipline. He, at the same time, issued orders for all the officers either to sell off their baggage wagons, or send them back to France, as they were for the future only to be allowed bat-horses for carrying their baggage. His headquarters were established at Wesel, where he placed a garrison of nine battalions and four squadrons. The Duke de Chevreuse had at Ruhrmond a garrison of six battalions and four squadrons: there were at Düsseldorf ten battalions of the Palatine troops, at Cleves four battalions and one squadron, at Cologne six battalions, at Kaiserswerth[7] one battalion. The whole of the French army, at that time, amounted to 105 battalions and 104 squadrons.

ON the separation of the French army, the troops of the Allies also marched into cantonments which extended from Münster to Dülmen and Dorsten, with detachments along the Lippe and Ruhr. The headquarters were established at Münster. The hussars and light troops were not idle however, but advanced up to the Rhine, making excursions even to the walls of Wesel, and from thence as far up as Cologne, and down to Emmerich. Several smart skirmishes passed between them and the enemy's light troops during the time the troops were in quarters; but as nothing interesting happened on these occasions, they are omitted.

THE inhabitants of the Bishopric of Münster were greatly alarmed on the approach of the Hanoverians, after it had been abandoned by the French; but His Serene Highness Prince Ferdinand, on his entrance with the Allied Army into that country, soon dissipated their terrors by the immediate publication of the following declaration:

"WE, Ferdinand Duke of Brunswick and Lüneburg, make known by these presents, That, finding ourselves obliged, not only to pursue the French army in their retreat, who had invaded the territories of His Britannic Majesty, and those of his confederates, but also to enter for that purpose into the Bishopric of Münster, with the army of which we have the command; we enjoin all the forces under our orders not to molest the inhabitants, in any manner, in the exercise of their religion; we most expressly forbid them to do any damage to the public edifices, or to the churches, schools, convents, or other religious houses for as much as it is our intention, that all who shall presume to make any exactions in the country, shall be punished with death according to the rigor of the law. Accordingly, in order to remove all apprehension, we have caused public notice to be given of these presents to all the subjects ecclesiastics, or lay, both of the territory in which we are with our army at present, and of those territories into which circumstances may determine us to follow our enemy, that they may lay aside their fears, and, instead of quitting their country, remain quietly at home, and enjoy the security and protection we grant. We moreover permit them by these presents to give information of all excesses or contraventions which may, contrary to our expectation, be committed, and, to secure those who may disobey our orders, and to cause them to be conducted to the headquarters to undergo the punishment they merit. We promise ourselves, on the other hand, that no person will abuse the protection we give, by succoring the French troops either by intelligence or otherwise: in which case, we shall be obliged to treat the offenders according to the rules of war."

ABOUT the beginning of this month orders were dispatched to General Hardenberg to march with the garrisons of Bremen, Harburg, and the detachments that were left behind, in order to join the army. He accordingly proceeded by the way of Vechta,

7. Editor: Today Kaiserswerth is part of Düsseldorf.

which castle surrendered by capitulation. The garrison consisting of seven companies were made prisoners, and a large quantity of artillery was found there, consisting of 100 pieces of cannon and mortars.

PRINCE George of Holstein-Gottorp sent a detachment from his corps to take possession of East Friesland in the name of the King of Prussia, and they were also ordered to pass by Bentheim to dislodge the Münsterian garrison quartered there.

ABOUT this time His Serene Highness received a very fine sword, which had been sent to him by His Britannic Majesty, as a mark of his royal regard and esteem.

ABOUT the middle of May, Baron Dombast, Lieutenant-Field-Marshal of the Imperial armies, who had last year joined the French, began his march to Bohemia with the Austrian corps under his command, consisting of the Prince Charles of Lorraine, Los Rios, Platz, Ligne, Saxe-Gotha, and Arberg Regiments, besides six squadrons of Széchény's Hussars and 4,000 recruits. He was to pass the Moselle at Alken, and the Rhine at Mainz.

THE French army, during the time the troops were in quarters, was very diligent in fortifying the towns of Wesel, Düsseldorf, Gueldres, and Kaiserswerth. Reinforcements daily arrived from Flanders, consisting of several thousand regular troops, besides a large body of militia, which was to be incorporated into the old corps in order to recruit them. In short, M. de Belleisle in the cabinet, and M. de Clermont in the field, used their utmost endeavors to set their army on a respectable footing, and introduce order and regularity. The French about Hanau remained all this time inactive in their quarters; but as they were under a continual alarm and apprehensions from a body of the Prussians, who were in Thuringia and Franconia, they incessantly worked on the repairs of the fortifications, not even Sundays excepted. They also received reinforcements from time to time. On the other hand, the Hessians assembled all their militia, who together with some Hanoverian jägers kept a strict guard over all the roads in that country. They had a garrison in Marburg of three battalions, besides a regiment of dragoons, some militia, and hussars. The Landgrave of Hesse returned to Kassel on the 6th day of May.

THOUGH Prince Ferdinand, ever attentive, as far as the nature of affairs permitted, to whatsoever was either requisite or conducive to the welfare and ease of his troops, thought proper at this juncture to canton the army as it necessarily wanted refreshment after so long and fatiguing a march, yet several other stronger motives obliged him to postpone his operations for a time. Many things were wanted, which it was absolutely and immediately necessary to provide for the ensuing service. The greatest diligence was pursued on this occasion by that general: he collected from different quarters considerable quantities of provisions and forage to form sufficient magazines; large convoys from Lüneburg, Emden, etc. came in daily; pontoons and other necessary implements arrived from Hamburg and Holland: numerous artillery, with ammunition, etc. were got ready at Hameln, and embarked on the Weser for Minden, in order to be transported to the army; the fortifications of Lippstadt were repaired; six bridges were re-established on the Lippe, which the French had destroyed in their retreat towards the Rhine; a road was cut through the wood of Duisburg; a considerable detachment was sent into the country of Burgues[8], and several dispositions were made in order to favor his intended schemes. In a word, His Serene Highness was indefatigable, and labored incessantly to get everything ready for taking the field; as he was anxious to resume his operations in order to prevent the designs of the French general, who intended to form five different camps along the Rhine by the middle of June. The first was to be at Neuss, the second near Moers, the third at Büderich opposite to Wesel, the fourth between Cleves and Xanten, and the fifth facing Emmerich, with a view to descend the passage of the Rhine. On the contrary, the Prince had determined to pass that river, and if possible to push the French beyond the Meuse.

ABOUT the 20th of May, everything was ready, the Allied troops were on all sides in motion, and, on the 25th, the chief part of the troops encamped at Nottuln. Here they were not to remain long, this camp being only intended as a rendezvous for assembling them from the most distant quarters, in order to put them in a condition to march forwards. A part of these troops went in the night between the 26th and 27th from Nottuln to Coesfeld, to join those which were already there, as well as the different regiments which were come there from Dülmen. The rest of the army marched some hours sooner from Nottuln for Dülmen, where the headquarters were fixed, in the morning of the 27th. The army marched before sunrise of the 29th from Dülmen towards Dorsten, and encamped at Lembeck from whence the next day, Lieutenant General Wutgenau was detached towards Wesel with a body of infantry and cavalry. The 30th, he encamped at Raesfeld, and the 31st, at Ringenberg. The Duke left the army during its march from Dülmen to Lembeck, and went to Bocholt, where he found the advanced guard of the body assembled at Coesfeld. That advanced guard marched, on the 30th, to Emmerich, and was followed by the rest of the corps which were encamped at Vrasselt. About 5 o'clock in the afternoon of the 31st, the whole was in motion to cross the Rhine, and the advanced guard went on as far as Lobith. The Duke's design was to pass the river there that night; but an unforeseen accident broke all the measures which had been taken for that purpose, and His Serene Highness was obliged to march the troops back again in the night to Niederelten. The 1st of June was employed in removing the obstacles which had occurred; and, in the following night, the passage was again attempted, and attended with all possible success, near Herwen.

Two hussars with a detachment of grenadiers passed, on the 2d of June at 2 o'clock in the morning, in flat-bottomed boats, which went and returned with so much diligence, that, besides the hussars, a regiment of dragoons, and 10 or 12 battalions, were, before noon on the other side of the river. During all this time, workmen were employed about the bridge; which, however, was not completed 'till four that morning. The remainder of the cavalry and infantry passed immediately and marched towards Cleves.

The hussars, supported by the volunteers, surprised these patrols, which were made prisoners of war; and, continued to advance, defeated the cavalry which showed themselves, and took a pair of kettledrums, and a standard from the Bellefonds Regiment. This country is entirely divided by dykes, so that it is as easy to dispute the ground, as it is difficult to advance. The enemy, sensible of this advantage, advanced with 7 or 800 foot to stop the head of our vanguard, and fired some pieces of cannon upon them,

8. Editor: This may be the Herzogtum Berg, which was near Düsseldorf.

which, however, hurt nobody; but a detachment of 20 men having found means to slip along a dyke, and get possession of a house, which the French had in part passed, fired upon them. This had such an effect, that they retired immediately. Everything else which happened, even to the gates of Cleves, only related to the hussars, and they had only five men and two officers wounded.

ON the 26th, a detachment consisting of several battalions and squadrons, together with Scheither's light troops and Luckner's Hussars, assembled at Dorsten, and in its neighborhood, under the command of Major General Wangenheim, who had orders to pass the Ruhr, and advance up to the gates of Düsseldorf, and likewise to cause M. de Scheither's corps to pass the Rhine at Duisburg.

ON the night between the 29th and 30th, M. de Scheither accordingly passed over, and with bayonets fixed attacked the battalion of the Cambresis Regiment, who were at Homberg and Eschenburg; the greater part of whom were cut to pieces. The rest saved themselves by flight. They also repulsed two battalions of the Navarre Regiment, who came to support them. They took two officers and 30 men prisoners, together with five cannon, six-pounders, and all the new clothing of the Navarre Regiment and repassed the river with such success, that he had only two men wounded in the passage over, and not one either killed or wounded in the action.

ON the night between the 30th and 31st, General Wangenheim attacked Kaiserwerth, and carried it, having killed or taken prisoners the greatest part of the garrison; the remainder saving themselves by crossing the river. He placed in that town a garrison of light troops, some foot, and Bock's dragoons; the whole commanded by Lieutenant Colonel Walthausen. He then advanced up to Düsseldorf.

JUNE the 3d, Prince George of Holstein-Gottorp, with a large body of horse and dragoons, at 8 o'clock in the morning, marched to Goch, in order to take possession of that place, and cut off the communication of the enemy between the Rhine and the Meuse; and at the same time to seize on some magazines which were in that neighborhood. The French, on the approach of the allies, had not only abandoned Cleves, but also Kranenburg, Gennep, Kalkar, and Xanten, retiring with the utmost precipitation towards Wesel; their army were assembling near Rheinberg, at the same time sending off their baggage to Ruhrmond.

THE headquarters of the Allied Army were removed to Goch, and on the 8th they were transferred to Uedem. The jägers and hussars daily sent a great number of French prisoners, and took a large amount of booty. Among the rest the baggage of the Duke of Randan, and that of the Duke of Fronsac, son to the Marshal de Richelieu, were taken. The former was immediately sent back, in testimony of a grateful remembrance of his generous and disinterested behavior in Hanover. The bridge over which the Allies had crossed the Rhine near Herwen was removed to Rees, in order to facilitate the communication between the different corps of the army.

AT this time M. de Clermont was encamped near Rheinberg in a most advantageous camp fortified by nature: the country which separated the two armies, being broken and full of banks, hedges, hollow ways, and other impediments, rendered it almost inaccessible. Here he thought himself so secure, that he bid defiance to the Allies. His Serene Highness could not possibly come up with him too soon as he could with, notwithstanding his eager impatience to take advantage of the disorders of the enemy. He therefore was obliged to make some motions in order to turn their left towards the Kamp Monastery and, on the 12th, he caused some detachments to advance to dislodge the enemy from two villages, where they had taken post with a considerable number of men, as being places of the utmost importance in covering their flank. The attack was made with bayonets fixed, and the French were driven from thence with great loss. The proper dispositions were then made for attacking their main army in form the next day. They did not, however, think proper to wait, but on the night between the 12th and 13th they abandoned their boasted impregnable camp at Rheinberg, retiring with the utmost precipitation towards Moers and Uerdingen. Prince Ferdinand immediately took possession thereof and sent several detachments in pursuit of them. His Highness thought proper on the 14th of June to give a new position to his army, by occupying the heights commonly called Sankt Tönis's Mountains, having the town of Moers in front at two full leagues' distance from the camp, the right opposite to the village of Tönisvorst in which 300 grenadiers were posted as an advanced guard, with 12 pieces of heavy cannon, which were more than sufficient to cover the extremity of our wing against any attack. On the 15th, about 5 o'clock in the morning, His Serene Highness was informed that the enemy was advancing in four columns upon our right. His Highness immediately ordered three guns to be fired, as a signal; and the whole army was under arms in order of battle a quarter of an hour later. He went afterwards, himself to reconnoiter, and saw distinctly that at about two leagues' distance from our right flank, a considerable body was coming over the Hüls Plain, and marching towards Krefeld.

NOT knowing whether this body was followed by the whole army, or whether it was only a detachment of it that was marching that way, His Serene Highness halted 'till towards the evening, when he received certain information that the French army had marched towards Neuss, and that Prince de Clermont had detached this corps, under the command of Lieutenant General Comte de St. Germaine, in order to take post at Krefeld.

UPON this information His Highness sent his light troops and hussars to Kempen and Wachtendonk and ordered the army into their camp again.

ON the 16th, he changed the position of the army, in consequence of the motions he had seen the corps of M. de St. Germaine make: he ordered the right to the village of Altenkirchen and continued the left on the heights of Sankt Tönis.

ON the 17th, His Highness went himself to reconnoiter towards Kempen, the position of the enemy's detachment at Krefeld; but could not guess at their reason for fixing this detachment at such a distance from their army. In order, therefore, to be better informed of it, and to see the countenance this corps would hold, he ordered the Prince of Holstein, with, ten Prussian squadrons, the five squadrons of hussars, and the three battalions of Spörcken Guards, and Prince Charles, to march early in the morning of the 18th towards Kempen. He further ordered General Wangenheim to pass the Rhine at Duisburg with four battalions, viz. Scheither, Halberstadt, Bückeburg, and Hanau, and the four squadrons of Bock's Dragoons, and the light troops of Luckner, and Scheither, and to advance that day towards Moers.

General Spörcken, who when the army left Rheinberg had been ordered to keep his post there as long as the enemy should remain in camp at Moers, received orders likewise the next day to join the "army with five battalions and six squadrons, and to leave only General Hardenberg with the two battalions of Gotha and Stolzenberg at Büderich, and that of Diepenbroick at Orsoy. This being regulated, His Highness communicated his designs and orders to the Crown Prince of Brunswick relating to an expedition he proposed; viz. that His Highness should march next day very early in the morning with a considerable corps towards Kempen, whilst the Prince of Holstein should advance with his corps towards Hüls, whereby it would clearly appear whether M. de St. Germaine would retreat towards the army, or whether the army of the Prince de Clermont would advance towards Krefeld in order to encamp there. Agreeable to this plan. His Highness the Crown Prince of Brunswick set forward, on the 19th, from the camp with the 12 following battalions; viz. Block, Spörcken, Hardenberg, Wangenheim, Post, Dreves, Bock, the two battalions of the Brunswick Life Guards, the Hessian Guards, the Hessian Life Guard Regiment, and Prince Charles's Regiment; accompanied with 12 squadrons of Hessians, viz. four of the Dragoon Guards, two of the Life Regiments, two of Prince William's, and two of Meltiz; with three mortars, four twelve-pounder cannon and four of 6-pounders. He marched directly towards Kempen, from whence he could perceive no alteration in the position of Count St. Germaine.

BY a secret order the Prince was directed, in case he perceived no change in the position of the army and of the flying camp of the enemy, to march the next day directly towards Ruhrmond, to endeavor to possess himself of the magazine, as well as of 600 militia who were in garrison there. At 6 o'clock in the morning His Serene Highness Prince Ferdinand in person followed the Crown Prince to Kempen. He perceived some movements in the flying camp, which were of a nature to induce him to believe that M. de St. Germaine designed to march against the Prince of Holstein, who was encamped near Hüls. Soon after he was positively informed, that the whole of the French army had quitted Neuss and were advancing on this side Krefeld: on which, having taken his measures, and formed a plan as the case required, the expedition to Ruhrmond was then first countermanded. Major General Wangenheim was ordered to advance early the next day with this corps towards Hüls, and Lieutenant General Spörcken was directed to march after midnight with the army, and to advance likewise to the plain between Hüls and Kempen. On the 20th of June all the troops His Serene Highness could dispose of were, by this means, re-united in his camp; the right of which extended towards Kempen, and the left towards Hüls. The headquarters were fixed at Kempen; and, in order to prevent any useless movements, His Serene Highness ordered the Quartermaster General not to regard the rank of the different corps, nor the order of battle, but to place the regiments as a great part of them were actually posted[9].

IN this manner the above mentioned 12 battalions and 12 squadrons under the command of the Crown Prince formed the right; next to them the four battalions and four squadrons under the command of General Wangenheim on their left; and the whole

9. Often in 18th century battles, regiments were drawn up in battle line by seniority and honor – the right flank being the highest honor. In this case that would have required re-positioning units that he did not want to waste time on.

army which advanced under Major General Spörcken from the camp at Altenkirchen formed the left wing; which, together, made an army of 35 battalions and 58 squadrons, including the six squadrons of hussars. His Highness had expected that Prince Clermont would advance that day to give him battle, but however no considerable event happened.

ON the 21st, there was observed a great movement in the advanced corps of Count St. Germaine; and about ten in the morning, after decamping, we saw them filing off to their left, and marching towards Anrath, where they joined their grand army.

IN making this motion they abandoned the town of Krefeld, which was on the front of their right wing. Our chasseurs possessed themselves of it directly; and His Highness also went himself to reconnoiter the position of their camp, which was clearly discovered from the steeple at Krefeld. He did not think either to keep the same post, or to make any change in the position of his army; in consequence of which he ordered the chasseurs and hussars away from that place, and the enemy repossessed themselves of it in an hour afterwards.

ON the 22d, His Highness went again to reconnoiter the camp of the enemy, particularly on the side of Sankt Tönis, on the heath which led towards their left; and although he found many diffi-culties, principally on account of the country's being very woody, and having enclosures surrounded by large and deep ditches, he resolved to march the next day to, the enemy, and attack them in their camp.

IN consequence of this resolution, the army was ordered to be under arms on the 23d of June at one in the morning, and not to change anything in the camp, but to leave all of its baggage in it, and wait there for further orders.

THE general officers were assembled in the center of the army where His Highness declared to them his intentions of going to attack the enemy and that he had formed his plan for that purpose. He assigned the command of the whole left wing, consisting of 18 battalions and 28 squadrons, to Lieutenant General Spörcken, having caused the battalion of Zastrow of the Wolfenbüttel troops to enter into the town of Hüls in order to cover our rear. He gave the command of the right wing, composed of 16 battalions and 14 squadrons, to the Crown Prince and Major General Wangenheim, which by the addition of the two regiments of Prussian dragoons, Holstein, and Finckenstein, of five squadrons each, made a corps of 24 squadrons, to be commanded by the Prince of Holstein, as the infantry was by the Crown Prince. As for the light troops, the three squadrons of Black Hussars were given to Lieutenant General Spörcken; the two squadrons of Yellow Hussars to the Prince of Holstein, and the squadron of Major Luckner, with Scheither's corps, were to observe the flank of the enemy's right, being posted in a village called Papenteich. This was the first general disposition of the army.

By, the second, the lieutenant generals who commanded the two wings were ordered to form three battalions of grenadiers out of their regiments of infantry; that is to say, the Crown Prince two, and General Spörcken one; the two first of 500 men each, under the command of Lieutenant Colonels Schulenburg and Schack; and the other of 600 men, under Major de Cram.

AT four in the morning the army began to move; the right advanced in two columns as far as Sankt Tönis, and the left at the same distance on the plain leading to Krefeld, a half league short of it; where they halted to receive fresh orders. Prince Ferdinand went up the steeple of Sankt Tönis; and sent for the two Princes of Holstein and Brunswick. There they observed at leisure the position of the enemy's camp, where all was very quiet. He also sent for several persons thither who were acquainted with the country to learn from them by what route we could advance towards the enemy; and being informed of many other points necessary to the success of a plan His Highness resolved to march to the right, and endeavor to come up with the enemy by the villages of Vorst and Anrath on the flank of their left wing. But, in order to raise doubts in the enemy as to the side on which the real and principal attack would be made, he gave orders to Lieutenant General Spörcken to send Lieutenant General Oberg, with six battalions of the second line, vis. Oberg's, Druchtleben's, Kielmannsegg's Scheel's, Redens' and the fusiliers of Hodenberg's and Bremer's Regiments of Horse, and that of the Body Guards, towards Sankt Tönis, and to give them 12-pounders. Besides this, His Highness gave them the following orders: that, when the action should begin on the enemy's left, M. von Spörcken by way of Krefeld, and M. von Oberg by Sankt Tönis, should do their utmost to advance and penetrate into the enemy's army; but, however, not to venture too far, unless they should be well-assured that our attack succeeded to our wishes. His Highness chiefly recommended it to them to make good use of their heavy artillery, in order to oblige the enemy to employ their attention as much upon their right wing and center as on their left, and to engage and divide their attention equally in three different places; which would prevent them sending any reinforcement to the real attack, for fear of weakening themselves in some part or other where we might make an impression.

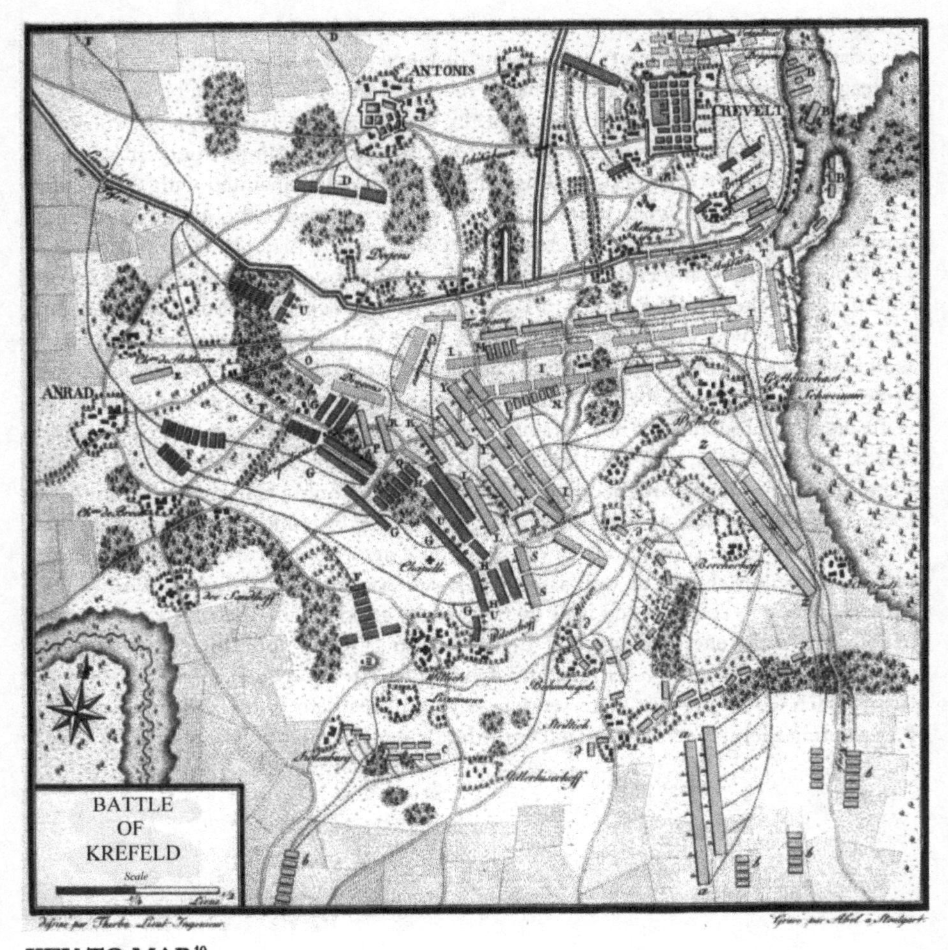

BATTLE OF KREFELD

KEY TO MAP.[10]

A Detachment of de Voyer, consisting of grenadiers, dragoons, and volunteers to observe the Hanoverians.

B Position of Voyer (after his retreat behind the Landwher lining the hedges) at the approach of the left column.

C Under orders of General Sporken, who made a false attack.

D Column under Oberg, which pierced the Landwehr and reinforced Crown Prince of Brunswick.

E Royal Legion, which occupied Anard, and which retired on the left of the French Army after approach of principal column.

10. Editor: The maps used in this work are drawn from Roesh, J.F., *Collection de quarante deux plans de batailles, sieges, et affaires les plus mémorables de la guerre de sept ans* (Frankfurt am Main: Jaeger, 1790). The town names and the "Key to Map" have not been altered to maintain consistency. The town names may differ from those in the rest of the text.

F	Led by Crown Prince of Brunswick, who afterwards probed the woods in several places, successively attacked the French army by four designated debouches
GGG	A part of this column moved along the woods to Willik.
H	Hanoverian Army, which after deposting the French infantry from the woods, deployed in the woods where it was attacked by the French cavalry.
I	French cavalry folds at the beginning of the action, then it moves constantly to the left (to the measure that the Allies move along their right) to avoid the French army being cut off from Neuss.
K	Location where the Tourraine Brigade fought.
L	Attack of the Carabiniers.
M	The Navarre Brigade cannot arrive until after the attack of the Carabiniers.
N	Brigade of Grenadiers de France and Royaux find themselves in the same situation.
O	1st position of Lochmann and Brancas Regiments.
P	2nd position position of Lochmann and Brancas Regiments where they were attacked.
Q	1st position of the Marine Brigade.
R	2nd position of the Marine Brigade.
S	Attack of the Royal Roussillon and Aquitaine Cavalry Regiments.
T	French batteries.
U	Hanoverian Batteries
X	Debouches by which the French retreated on Neuss.
Y	1st position of the French cavalry.
Z	Final position of French cavalry, where it rallied after the battle.

THESE dispositions being made, His Highness put himself at the head of the grenadiers of the right wing at eight in the morning and taking the road that leads to the village of Vorst, which we left on our right, we advanced towards Anrath, where there was a detachment of 400 of the enemy, half horse and half foot, who after a discharge of musketry on each side, fell back towards their camp, which was not above half a mile distant from them, and there gave the alarm. His Highness then caused the troops to advance and double their speed to get out of the defiles. He ranged them in order of battle in the plain between the villages of Willich and marched directly towards the wood which covered their left.

IT was at 1 o'clockin the afternoon, when the enemy began to act. The Duke caused his artillery forthwith to advance, which being a great deal superior to that of the enemy, facilitated the means of our infantry forming themselves over against the wood and of our cavalry's extending upon our right towards the village of Willich, making a show as if they designed to turn the enemy's left flank, to take them in their rear. After a cannonade as violent as it was well supported, His Highness saw plainly he must come to the point of endeavoring to force the enemy out of the wood by small arms: wherefore the Crown Prince put himself at the head of the first line; specifically, two battalions of Schulenburg and Schack Grenadiers, and of the Block, Spörcken, Hardenberg, Wangenheim, Post, and Dreves Regiments, and advanced with the whole front directly towards the wood. The fire then became extremely hot on both sides, and neither discontinued nor in any degree diminished for two and a half hours. In the meantime, all the other battalions likewise entered the wood; so that there were but eight squadrons, which formed a corps of reserve upon the plain, ready to be employed where circumstances should require.

THE other 15 squadrons, which were upon our right, never could penetrate on the other side of the wood, on account of two batteries which the enemy had placed there, and which were sustained by above 40 squadrons. In short, about 5 o'clock in the afternoon, the Crown Prince, assisted by Major Generals Kielmannsegg and Wangenheim, gave orders for an attack to be made by the grenadiers upon the two ditches that were in the wood, that were lined with the enemy's infantry. They were forced one after another. The two regiments of infantry did the same all along their front. Then that part of the enemy's infantry was entirely thrown into confusion and retired out of the wood in the utmost disorder, without ever being able to rally. Our foot followed them, but without venturing to pursue them on account of the enemy's cavalry; which, notwithstanding the terrible fire of our artillery, not only kept the best countenance possible, but even covered their infantry that was flying, in such a manner as to protect them from our cavalry, that between five and six in the evening, had found means to gain the plain. The Hessian dragoons and a regiment of cavalry of the same nation, had two shocks with the Royal Provence Carabiniers and the Rousillon Regiment, and broke them. This was all that the cavalry had to do on that day. A squadron of the carabineers attempted to penetrate through our infantry, and attacked the battalions of Post and Dreves, but with a considerable loss; and though about 40 of them did indeed force their way, they were never able to join their corps, and were all killed either by shot or bayonet.

THE enemy did not then think it proper, or find themselves in any condition, to dispute the ground longer with us, but retired towards Vischell, and from thence took the road that leads towards Neuss. We continued to follow them with our artillery and took a great number of men and horses.

DURING the whole of this affair the fire of the artillery of Generals Spörcken and Oberg did great execution; but as their distance from us made them uncertain as to the turn what affairs had taken on our side, they never ventured to attack the enemy's front opposite to them so that the enemy's right wing and center retired in the greatest order towards Neuss, leaving us masters of the field of battle, after a loss on their side of between 7,000 and 8,000 killed, wounded, and taken prisoners.

SUCH was the end of this action, which cost the Allied Army between 1,200 and 1,300 men, killed and wounded.

THE trophies gained were two kettle-drums, five standards, two pair of colors, and eight pieces of cannon.

THE light troops were sent to harass the enemy's retreat; and at nine in the evening all our three-different corps joined each other in the field from whence the enemy had been driven, and remained there that night under arms.

We thought it might not be amiss to insert the following relation of the above battle as given by the Count de Clermont, as it may serve to throw an additional light upon it:

On the 22d, His Serene Highness the Count de Clermont, having received advice that the enemy, who were encamped from Kempen to Hüls, were preparing to come and attack him, made the proper dispositions for their reception. On the 23d, at 10 o'clock in the morning, His Serene Highness was informed that several columns of the enemy were in sight, marching up to his camp. He immediately put his whole army under arms. The right extended to the wood at Fischeiln, from whence it was lined by the Landwehr as far as the farm of Hückelsmay. A little farther, in the same line towards Anrath, (in which was the Royal Legion), he posted four battalions. He also placed, opposite to the farm of Am Stock, a reserve consisting of carabiniers and dragoons. On the right was another service, composed of the Grenadiers of France, and the Royal Grenadiers, and the brigade of Navarre. Behind the foot, in the center, were two lines of horse. Krefeld was occupied by a detachment of 800 infantry, horse, and hussars.

"Such were our dispositions when the enemy presented themselves, approaching insensibly to Krefeld on the right, to Anrath on the left, and to the farm of Hokelamy in the center! His Serene Highness, after some skirmishes made the detachment at Krefeld, which was posted there only to watch the motions of the enemy, fell back upon the line. He also made the Royal Legion join the left wing.

"ABOUT noon the enemy made their dispositions for attacking in three different parts. They fell on Anrath first, which could not be defended, because it was too for distant from the left of our line. From thence the enemy advanced to the plain between the Niers and a small wood that runs parallel to that river. His Serene Highness had lined this wood with 15 battalions, composed of the Marine and Touraine Brigades, and the detached Bruncas and Lockman Regiments, and 30 squadrons, in order to oppose the enemy if they should attempt to advance that way.

"THE enemy began their three attacks at one time. His Serene Highness soon perceived that their real attack was that in the wood on the left. He sent for the reserve, which consisted of the Grenadiers of France, the Royal Grenadiers, and the Navarre Brigade; but by an inconceivable fatality, the officers whom His Serene Highness ordered to bring up three brigades, mixed them, and this reserve did not come up soon enough. The 15 battalions, after sustaining a fire of three hours, and repulsing the enemy three times, were at last obliged to fall back, after suffering great loss, and causing the enemy to suffer greater casualties. Finding the fire of our infantry slacken drew up in the plain, His Serene Highness ordered the carabineers, and the two battalions of horse of the Royal Rousillon and Aquitaine Regiments, to charge them. The enemy was driven back to the wood; but as they had their principal force in that part, and could bring up fresh troops every minute, they again poured into the plain in greater numbers, and it was no longer possible for the cavalry to attack them with advantage.

"As the reserve which His Serene Highness sent for did not come up, he gave orders for a retreat, which was made in the greatest order, the enemy not daring to follow us, and our army arrived at Neuss without being annoyed the least on its march. We brought off our wounded. His Serene Highness, judging his position at Neuss to be improper, either for waiting for the enemy or for marching to them, is come, after halting there one day, to encamp at Worringen."

THE French lost in this action a considerable number of officers; and among the wounded were the Count de Gisors, son to the Marshal de Belle-Isle; the Chevalier de Muy, lieutenant-general; the Count de Maille, colonel of the Condé Regiment; the Duke de Montmorency, colonel of the Touraine Regiment; the Count de Lauraguais, Colonel of that of Royal Rousillon, Colonel Lockman, Lieutenant Colonel Escher, with four captains, and 17 other officers of the same regiment. Six or eight of their regiments were entirely ruined. On our side there was no officer of note either killed or wounded.

ON the 24th, His Serene Highness encamped in the neighborhood of Krefeld, and Major General Wangenheim was advanced with four battalions and four squadrons to Osterath, where he encamped, in order to be at hand to sustain the light troops, who were in pursuit of the enemy. On the 25th, a Te Deum was sung on the field of battle, with a feu de joie, and a general discharge of all our artillery. His Serene Highness this day made a present to the Hanoverian artillery of a pair of kettledrums, which were taken from the enemy, for their gallant behavior on the day of action. On the 26th, Major General Wangenheim advanced with his detachment to Neuss, and the army also marched, and encamped near Osterath, where the headquarters were established. The Crown Prince was left behind at Krefeld with a corps of six battalions and 10 squadrons. The enemy had in part destroyed the great magazine which they had at Neuss, but the hussars pursued them so closely, that they prevented its entire destruction; and a considerable quantity of flour and oats were abandoned by them, all fit for service. Our advanced parties sent in hourly great numbers of prisoners, exclusive of the many wounded who were unable to keep up with the main body.

THE Count de Gisors died at Neuss, universally regretted, of the wounds he received in the engagement.

ON the 27th, the headquarters were at Neuss; the Crown Prince marched to Ruhrmond, and the Prince of Holstein to Gladeback[11].

ON the 28th, four batteries were completed and opened against the city of Düsseldorf. Both the cannon and mortars were admirably served, and the shells did considerable damage in the town. The French sent their sick and wounded in boats up the Rhine to Andernach and were at the same time hard at work in constructing bridges over the Rhine between Deutz and Mülheim: and having forced the arsenal of Cologne, took out such cannon as they wanted for the defense of them. The Crown Prince made

11. Editor: In 1888 Gladeback became Möchengladbach in order to distinguish it from Bergisch Bladenbach.

himself master of Ruhrmond. Bocard, who commanded in that city, with a battalion of the Marche Regiment, two battalions of the militia, and some Volontaires de Hainault, obtained the honors of war, and were permitted to retire to Liege. His hussars and light troops pushed forwards as for as Tirlemont and Louvain.

JULY 2, the French advanced to the Erss River, fixing their headquarters at Carter; and His Serene Highness established his at St. Nicholas.

JULY 7, the city of Düsseldorf surrendered on capitulation, and the garrison was not to serve against the Allies for the space of one year. An immense quantity of forage and provisions were found in that town, as also a fine train of French artillery and ammunition. A garrison of three battalions took possession of it. About this time, the corps of Fischer's Jägers in the service of France made an excursion in order to plunder some of the villages of the country of Hesse-Kassel, but the militia, having had intelligence of their march, lay in ambush behind some rocks, from whence they suddenly sallied out, and killed and wounded a great number of them; the rest endeavored to save themselves by flight, but they suffered considerably in their retreat, and many were made prisoners.

JULY 14th, Prince Ferdinand having information, that the French army was in motion, resolved to meet the enemy, and endeavor to surprise them on their march. The Allied Army accordingly passed the Ersst in three different places and advanced as fast as the roads would admit of; for the abundance of rain which had fallen for some time before had almost rendered the roads impracticable. The enemy perceived him too soon and made all possible diligence to make themselves masters of the rising grounds; but that did not hinder our army from advancing to form in order of battle within cannon shot of the enemy. However, as we could not get possession of the necessary ground to attack the enemy upon equal advantage, the two armies passed the day in sight of each other without attempting anything. We marched the next day at daybreak and repassed the Ersst without the least disturbance in our retreat, and encamped, on the 16th, near Neuss.

JULY 18th, the troops of the Allies evacuated the town of Ruhrmond about three in the afternoon and marched towards Dülken.

JULY 19th, the Allied Army again advanced, and fixed its headquarters at Bedburdyck, on the eminences on the right side of the Ersst, and the enemy continued near Fravenweller in their old camp, on the other side of the river which separated the two armies. A smart engagement passed between the advanced guard under the command of the Crown Prince, and a large detachment of the enemy. The troops on both sides behaved with great bravery, but the French were in the end obliged to retreat, with the loss of five pieces of cannon, four standards, and a great many officers taken prisoners. His Serene Highness reinforced the garrison of Düsseldorf with a corps of 2,000 regulars, and some light troops. About this time, M. de Clermont returned to France, and was succeeded in the command of the army by the Marshal de Contades.

PRINCE Isenburg, who commanded in Hesse, having notice that the French in the neighborhood of Hanau, under the command of the Prince de Soubise, were in motion, retired from Marburg to Kassel, leaving a garrison in that place. The French, being assembled about Friedberg, advanced by flow marches to Gros Leuedem, where their headquarters were fixed on the 16th of July; the Duke de Broglio, who was at the head of the vanguard, sent forward a large detachment of Royal Nassau's and Fischer's Corps, with the intent to surprise the garrison of Marburg; but they had abandoned it on the 17th, just before their arrival; and the French army encamped in the neighborhood of that place on the 18th, from whence it moved forwards towards Kassel.

ON the 21st of July, the Prince d'Isenburg, with a body of troops under his command, passed the Fulda about a league from Kassel, destroying the bridge after him, and took post near the village of Sondershausen, to observe the motions of the French, Fischer's Corps, which formed the enemy's van, arrived on the 22d on the eminences near Kassel, and next morning two battalions of French troops entered that city. About noon, a body of about 6,000 infantry hastily passed through it, and the horse, to the number of 4,000, having at the same time forded the Fulda, began soon after to skirmish with the Hessian jägers, whom they followed as far as the eminences of Sondershausen. The Prince d'Isenburg, who was posted there with between 6,000 and 7,000 men, supported the jägers; about three the battle began, and lasted with a very brisk firing on both sides 'till sunset when the Hessian troops, seeing themselves on the point of being surrounded by the French horse, retired to Landwehrhagen in good order: but as they found themselves too weak after this action to be able to face again the superior force of the enemy, they proceeded towards Hameln.

THE LOSS of the French was much more considerable than that of the Hessians, and it is imagined they had about 1,500 killed and 3,000 wounded; but a better idea may be formed of their loss by the following account of the action published by themselves.

"MONSIEUR. the Duke de Broglio, commanding a corps which formed the vanguard of the army commanded by the Prince de Soubise, having learned at Kassel that the Hessian troops under the Prince d'Isenburg were retiring towards Münden, marched on the 23d of July to the village of Sondershausen, and reaching the top of the hill perceived the enemy drawn up in order of battle, their right covered by a great rock in the Fulda, and their left by a wood which had a communication with the rock. This post was so extremely advantageous, that the Duke de Broglio found the affair required the best dispositions possible. He had left at Kassel and Sondershausen, for the security of the defiles in case of an unfortunate event, to the amount of 2,500 men, which reduced our corps of the army to near an equal force with our enemy's, whom we computed at about 7,000 effective men, including a regiment of cavalry of 600, and one of dragoons of 800.

M. de Broglio put his infantry in the first line, his cavalry and dragoons composed the second, and he placed the ten pieces of cannon of the brigade of artillery before his right, to annoy the Hessian cavalry which extended to the wood. This cavalry advanced in order to attack our infantry: but the Duke de Broglio instantaneously doubled a part of our infantry, and brought forward, by the openings which that motion formed, a part of his cavalry, which charged that of the Hessians; but they were repulsed, and we began to fear that this circumstance would have disordered our infantry, when, at the moment the enemy's cavalry was going to fall upon the Royal Bavarian Regiment, that regiment made a discharge so very apropos as to make great havoc among them, insomuch that they did not appear again throughout the action.

"DURING this time, Field-Marshal von Waldener, with M. von Diesbach, of the Swiss brigade, and the three companies of grenadiers of Royal Deux Ponts, attacked the wood with great vigor, and found there a pretty obstinate defense. The infantry of the enemy's right briskly engaged our left: the fire was hot on both sides, and the enemy fell back some hundred yards, but they soon returned by favor of the rock, which partly covered them. This advantage was so great, that our left was obliged to give way; and as the enemy were endeavoring to gain our backs in winding around by our left, the Duke de Broglio caused the Apchon Dragooons to advance, with some cavalry behind them. The briskness of the fire continued, and we suffered greatly; when at length the Duke de Broglio sent the Royal Bavarian Regiment, the Royal Deux Ponts, and those of Rohan and Beauvois, to the rock, where they were ordered to make their attacks with their bayonets fixed. This desperate maneuver succeeded, and the enemy was put to flight. We followed them to a great ditch. They threw themselves into the wood on the borders of the Fulda, and some got to the edge of a steep rock, from whence upwards of 300 plunged into the river, where most of them perished.

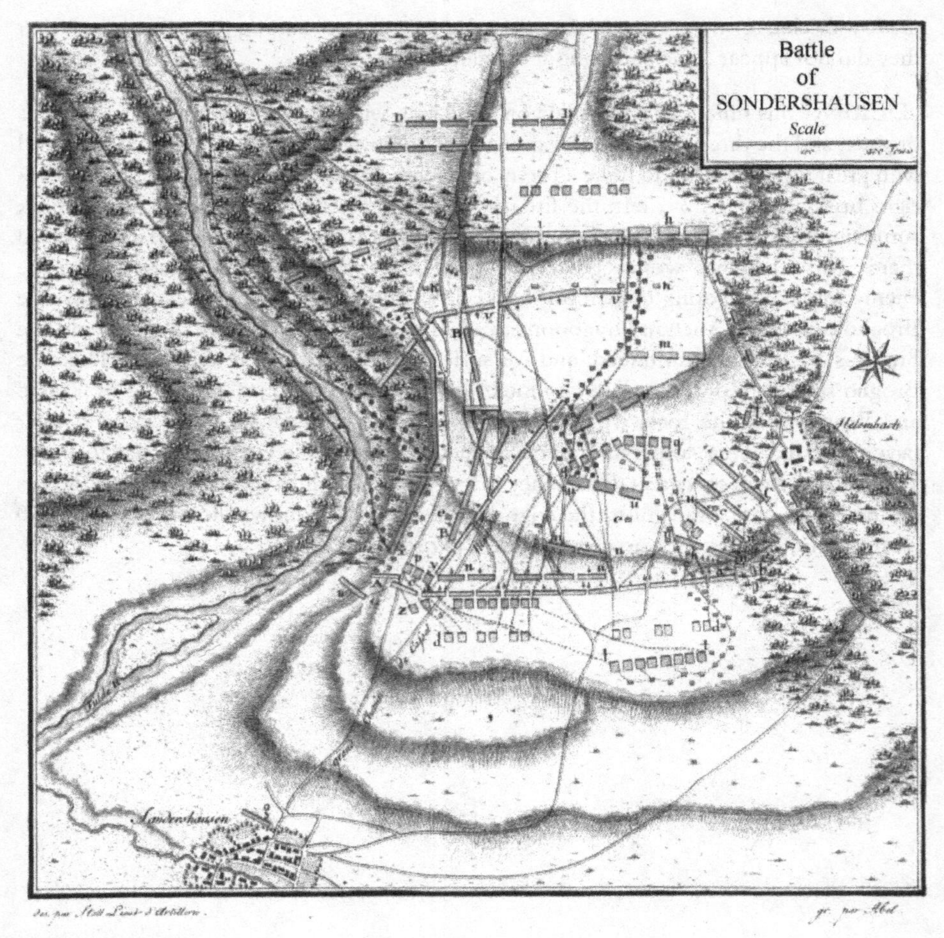

KEY TO MAP.

a	French infantry.
b	3 companies of grenadiers covering the right of the army.
c	Volunteers covering the left flank.
d	Cavalry and dragoons.
e	Grenadiers exchanging fire with Hanoverian advanced posts.
f	Battery of 10 4pdrs.
g	Battalion for the guard of Sondershausen.
h	Hessian cavalry.
i	Hessian infantry.
k	Hanoverian advanced posts.
l	Hanoverian jägers in woods by pelotons.

m Hessian cavalry marching forward to charge the French infantry.

n 2nd position of the French infantry where some regiments doubled on the other to let the cavalry pass.

o Volunteers attacking the right of the Hessian infantry.

p Three squadrons replace the volunteers.

q French cavalry charging Hessian cavalry.

r Movement made by cavalry at m. to reach the left flank of the cavalry q.

s Battalion shooting the cavalry q. at the moment of the shock while the jägers l. fire by the right, which obliged it to fold.

t French cavalry rallying.

u After this attack, the Hessian cavalry march directly against the French infantry, but the latter, standing firmly, gave them a folley at 30 paces that put them out of condition to rally during the action.

v Hessian infantry which had advanced to support the cavalry action, and which by its fire oblived the volunteers (o.) to fold.

w Rallying of volunteers.

x Hessian infantry moves along the escarpment by its right to take the French infantry in the flank.

y Chanage of front by the French infantry to face the Hessian infantry.

z Two squadrons covering the right flank.

A The volunteers attack the right flank of the Hessian infantry.

The French infantry comletes a quarter conversion

B And marches against the enemy with bayonets. The Hessian infantry was broken and thrown from the escarpment, part trying to cross the river and downding, the rest moving through the woods.

C Attack by the Swiss brigade, which encountered much resistance; but finally four cannon decide the victory infavor of the swiss ahd the jägers retire by the woods.

D Ground over which the French army advanced after the action.

"IT was now seven in the evening, very bad weather, a woody country, and the troops had marched seven leagues; all these reasons determined M. de Broglio to remain on the field of battle, but he sent the Baron de Travers with 700 volunteers in pursuit of the enemy. We have hitherto made above 200 soldiers prisoners, and 50 officers; amongst whom are the Count von Kanitz, who commanded under M. d'Isenburg, the first aide-de-camp to that prince, and several lieutenant colonels and majors. We took upon the field of battle seven pieces of cannon, and eight at Münden, where the enemy had abandoned them; so that they have only one 16-pounder left. The day after the action the enemy seemed to be totally dispersed, most of them having thrown down their arms, and retired into the woods. They must have suffered much: we had 785 men killed, and 1,392 wounded. The Duke de Broglio had a horse was shot under him, as well as M. de la Rosière, one of his aides-de-camp; and M. de Mazange, his equerry, who is wounded in the cheek by a pistol shot. The Prince of Nassau was dangerously wounded; the Field Marshal Marquis de Puysequer wounded in the head the Marquis de Broglio, nephew to our general, shot in the thigh; and the Count de Kolen has several wounds. M. de St. Martin, Lieutenant Colonel of the Rohan Regiment, and M. de Roufette, major of that of Beauvois, were killed."

ON the 24th, the French hussars took possession of the town of Münden and from thence proceeded to Göttingen, which they also seized, and the partisan Fischer took post at Northeim with 800 men. Prince Isenburg retired to Einbech, where he made a stand, 'till he should be recruited and receive some small reinforcements which were to be sent to him from Hanover. His Serene Highness, having altered his plan, suddenly filed off towards the Meuse, and encamped at Wasenberg, on the 25th, between three or four leagues from Ruhrmond, having an advanced guard between two thick woods which covered his camp.

THE French army on the 26th marched to Garzweiler near Fitz; on the 27th, to Keyenberg[12] at the source of the Niers; on the 28th, they encamped near Erkelen, and the Count de St. Germaine was detached with 30 companies of grenadiers and some cavalry to observe Prince Ferdinand's motions. The Duke de Chevreuse marched to Neuss with the corps de reserve; and M. de Chevert with 12 battalions and four squadrons of dragoons, which were to guard the bridges near Cologne, was on his march on the other side of the Rhine to invest Düsseldorf; and on the 31st, M. de Contades fixed his headquarters at Dahlen[13].

THE succeeding operations of the Allied Army to their passage over the Rhine are related in the following account given by Prince Ferdinand.

"FROM the time His Highness received the news of Prince Soubise having entered the country of Hesse-Kassel with his army, it appeared either that the French army under M. de Contades must be reduced to the necessity of calling Prince Soubise to their assistance, or that His Highness would be obliged to retreat.

"IN the hopes that Prince Isenburg would have been able to stand his ground, for some time at least, in Hesse-Kassel Prince Ferdinand of Brunswick resolved to carry the scene of action to the Meuse, in order to draw the enemy from the Rhine; and had formed a plan which would have effectually answered the purpose above mentioned, and been productive of the greatest consequences for the public Service: and it was in execution of this plan that His Highness marched to Ruhrmond towards the latter end of July; but the long and heavy rains, which had happened in those parts, had so broke the roads that his march was greatly retarded; and in the meantime His Highness was informed of the defeat of Prince Isenburg's corps near Kassel, where the enemy had opened to themselves the possession of the Weser in case they pursued their advantage, and consequently might act in Westphalia on any side they pleased. In this situation His

12. Editor: Today Keyenberg is part of the town of Erkelenz.

13. Editor: In 1878 Dahlen became Rheindahlen and later became part of Mönchengladbach.

Highness had no other option but a victory over the French, or to repass the Rhine. In the first he was repeatedly disappointed by the backwardness of the French to stand an engagement; and as it was dangerous to remain long in a position where he had the French army on one wing, and on the other the fortress of Gueldres, (of which the garrison had been considerably reinforced), as well as several other posts within reach of obstructing the convoys and subsistence of the army, besides the possibility of the English troops from Emden being prevented from joining the army, in case time should be left M. Soubise to think of intercepting them, His Highness resolved to march back to the Rhine, which was accordingly executed with the greatest success in the following manner: On the 28th of July, the army moved still nearer the Meuse, and encamped between Ruhrmond and Schwalm. The headquarters were fixed at Hallenrad. On that day, advice was received there of the action which had passed the 23d in Hesse-Kassel, the enemy having shown the Prince of Brunswick with orders to dislodge them from thence, and to make himself master of the town, which was done with success the next day. No doubt was made but that the enemy would move towards us; but the so well covered the motions of their army by detachments of light troops, that we had but imperfect notions thereof. In part, however, we were informed of them, and the Duke guessed at the rest, insomuch that, having marched in the night between the 1st and 2d of August towards Dülken, he found the enemy likewise on their way to the same place from Dalhelm. M. de Contades, who probably did not expect His Highness there, chose rather to go back, and take up his former camp at Dalhelm, than to give battle. It was the general opinion, that there would have been an engagement the next day. The Allied Army was under arms on the 3d very early in the morning and made a motion for advancing towards the enemy; but it appeared from the motions we saw them make upon our coming on, that they would endeavor again to avoid an action. His Serene Highness had reasons which induced him to lose no time in pursuing an enemy that was determined not to fight. He made, therefore, at eight in the morning, dispositions for the march to Wachtendonk: the Prince of Kolstein with the Prussians composed the rear guard; the Crown Prince of Brunswick marched with the vanguard to force the post of Wachtendonk. That place, as is well known, is an island surrounded by the Niers, of a very difficult approach, though without fortifications. The Crown Prince, not being able immediately to get down the bridge the enemy had drawn up, without giving them time to recollect themselves, entered the river, and passed it with some companies of grenadiers who followed his example, and drove the enemy away with their bayonets. Afterwards, at sunset, all the army passed the bridges of Wachtendonk, excepting only the baggage, which marched on during the whole night, with the rearguard which covered their march. The army marched on the 4th to Rheinberg, so little harassed by the enemy that not a single soldier of them appeared in the fight. That evening news was brought, that M. de Chevert had passed the Lippe with 12 or 14 battalions and several squadrons, to join the garrison of Wesel, and then fall upon the corps encamped at Mehr[14] under Lieutenant General Imhoff. There was not a moment's doubt, but that that attack would be made the next day. His Serene Highness could have wished to reinforce General Imhoff; but the men were too much fatigued to begin another march the same evening; and the extraordinary overflowing of the Rhine, which rendered the bridges at Rees impassable, was an ad-ditional difficulty: So M. Imhoff had no resource

14. Editor: Mehr is today part of Hamminkeln. There was earlier a "Battle of Meer."

but in his own good conduct, and in the inexpressible bravery of his troops, consisting of six battalions and four squadrons, much weakened by different detachments made from them. But the hand of Providence so visibly seconded the efforts of that handful of men, which after a sharp engagement they gained a complete victory over an enemy who was triple their number. The enemy was driven under the cannon of Wesel, and the field of battle was covered with their dead. Ten pieces of cannon were taken from them, and numerous prisoners of the most considerable rank captured. On the 6th of August, General Wangenheim passed the Rhine with several battalions and squadrons to reinforce M. Imhoff and put him in a condition to make the utmost advantage of a victory as complete as it was glorious to the arms of His Majesty and of his allies. The army marched the same day to Xanaten, where they pitched their camp."

WHEN the army arrived at Rheinberg His Highness intended to have passed the Rhine there, which would have been attended with several advantages, but the prodigious flood in the river, occasioned by the continual rains, had made it overflow to such a degree that the shore was inaccessible, and the same reason made it impossible to make use of the bridges at Rees. It was, therefore, found necessary to march further down, and in the night between the 8th and 9th a bridge was laid over the river at Greithausen[15].

THE enemy had prepared four boats of a particular invention to destroy it, which were coming down the river from Wesel; but they were all taken on the morning of the 9th, by some armed barks we had upon the river, before they could put their design into execution. The same morning about daybreak, the army began to pass, and the disposition His Serene Highness was pleased to make for passing it was as follows: four squadrons of dragoons, the baggage of the headquarters, the sick of the army, the heavy artillery; the army in four divisions, the baggage of the army, and the rearkhguard, which upon this occasion was very strong. The passage was entirely completed on the 10th, the last of the rear guard passing over about 10 o'clock, without any interruption from the enemy. Prince Ferdinand received a letter from the Duke of Marlborough, acquainting him, that His Grace with all the English troops, except Lieutenant General Campbell's Dragoon Regiments, was at Lingen the 8th instant in their way to Coesfeld; and Lieutenant General Imhoff with 11 battalions and ten squadrons was arrived at Bocholt, which being but one forced march from Coesfeld his junction with the corps of English troops became certain.

BEFORE the passage of the Rhine, His Highness received from Lieutenant General Imhoff the following relation of his engagement with M. de Chevert. The consternation of the French in that affair was so great, and their flight so precipitate, that 2,000 muskets were gathered from the ground over which they fled.

"ON the 4th of August, at 6 o'clock in the evening, I received advice from a good source, that the enemy, who were to pass the Lippe over three bridges, would march that night with much artil-lery towards Rees, so as to possess themselves of that place, and burn the bridge. As he might go thither by turning my camp, I took the resolution to decamp with the four battalions and four squadrons under my command, in order to cover Rees, and join the battalions of Stolzenberg and of the Crown Prince of Hesse,

15. Editor: Today Greithausen is part of the town of Kleve.

that were marching under the command of General Zastrow from Spich, where they had passed the Rhine in boats. Having perceived nothing of the enemy and believing that the accounts I had received might be false, I resolved to return to my advantageous post at Mehr. I set forward at six in the morning; and after I had reached my old camp, the advanced guards were no sooner posted, but they found themselves engaged with the enemy, who advanced towards me from Wesel, under the command of Lieutenant General de Chevert, and Messrs. de Voyer, and de Chavigny, major generals, with the whole corps of troops, which were designed to make the siege of Düsseldorf.

"MY front was covered by coppices and clinches, with a rising ground on my right, from whence I could see the whole force that was coming against me. Perceiving, then, that the enemy was marching into this difficult ground, I resolved to attack them as soon as they entered it. I therefore ordered my infantry to advance about 200 paces from the first hedges, and took the Stolzenberg Regiment from my right to post it on the coppice to be in position to fall upon the left of the enemy, whom I saw quite uncovered; and gave orders to the other regiment to march with drums beating up to the enemy, as soon as they should hear the fire of the Stolzenberg Regiment, and attack them with bayonets fixed. This, being executed with the greatest spirit by the whole six battalions, had so great an effect, that, after a resistance of about half an hour, the enemy was put into confusion, and fled towards Wesel, leaving on the spot 11 pieces of cannon, with a great many wagons and other carriages with ammunition.

"THE LOSS on my side consists of no more than 200 men killed and wounded; that of the enemy is not exactly known. We have taken 354 prisoners, among whom are 11 officers. General Zastrow, who was perfectly well, seconded me in this action, and all the officers fought with the greatest courage. The names of these brave regiments are the Stolzenberg, Saxe-Gotha, Crown Prince of Hesse, and Imhoff of Brunswick, and the four squadrons of Von dem Bussche's, which could not go in the manner they wished on account of the enclosures."

IMMEDIATELY after the passage of the Rhine, His Serene Highness gave orders for the evacuation of the town of Düsseldorf, and the garrison accordingly joined the main army.

ON the 1st of August, arrived at Emden from England the following British regiments, under the command of his Grace the Duke of Marlborough, to reinforce the army of the Allies; viz. Napier, Kingsley, Welch Fusiliers, Home's, and Stuart's, infantry; and Horse Guards Blue, Bland, Howard, Inniskilling, and Mordaunt Cavalry. By the 3d, they were all disembarked about six miles above Emden. On the 5th, they marched and encamped by Leer, where they were joined by Brodenel's Regiment of Foot, who had been in garrison at Emden about 16 weeks but were now re-lieved by a party of 400 invalids. On the 6th, they halted; on the 7th, they marched and encamped by Meppen, on the 8th, they were by Lingen; halted the 9th; on the 10th, they marched again, and encamped by Bentheim; on the 11th they halted; on the 12th, they marched to Ahaus; and, on the 17th, they marched and encamped by Coesfeld, where they joined General Imhoff's detachment; and, on the 20th, they were reviewed by His Serene Highness, who expressed the greatest satisfaction at their appearance. The North British Dragoon

Regiment, on the 31st, also joined the army at Coesfeld; they had been detained at sea by contrary winds.

THE French army passed the Rhine about the middle of the month, and by the 18th were encamped on the heath near Wesel; and Prince Ferdinand, having marched by Bork and Gemen, fixed his headquarters at Coesfeld, having an advanced guard at Dülmen. The Prince de Soubise detached a large body to Warburg, and another to Hofgeismar, and at the same time Fischer's Corps quitted Göttingen. On the 21st, M. de Contades marched to Schermbeck, where he fixed his headquarters. The next day he halted there, and on the 23d proceeded to Dorsten, where this contingent passed the Lippe over three bridges, and marched to Recklinghausen, where they encamped;

ON the 31st, a most obstinate skirmish happened near Dorsten between a detachment of Hanoverian jägers and a body of French hussars, in which the latter were entirely dispersed. Each party suffered considerably on this occasion.

ON the 3d of September, Prince Xavier, at the head of 10,000 Saxons who were on their march to join M. de Contades, encamped at Gestorp, within three leagues of Recklinghausen; September 4th, the Allied Army marched', and the headquarters were fixed at Dülmen, with their advanced guard: at Haltern-am-See, September 5th, Captain Scheither with 50 Hanoverian jägers passed the Lippe in the night a little above Gahlen, in order to carry off a million thaler which was going to Dorsten, but it arrived there the day before. He, however, did not entirely lose his labor; for having met with a party of 100 French horse, he defeated them, and made several prisoners. He then proceeded towards Wesel, destroyed a convoy of 30 wagons loaded with wine and flour, took 60 oxen, with watches, rings, etc. to the value of 30,000 livres besides three couriers with their dispatches.

GENERAL Oberg was sent to Lippstadt with a large detachment, to be near at hand to support M. Isenburg, and observe such detachments as might be made from the French army to that quarter.

SEPTEMBER 12, the Grenadiers of France were advanced towards Hamm, and another body of 2000 French infantry were ordered to take post at Altena on the road to Lippstadt. His Serene Highness at the same time pushed forward an advanced corps of the Allied Army as far as Kallenberg[16]. On the 15th, the Duke of Fitz-James, and Count de St. Germaine, were detached from the French army with four brigades to Castorp, and on the 16th, the Duke de Loval was also sent to Lünen with another large detachment.

ON the 15th, the two armies remained still in their former headquarters; but Prince Holstein was detached by His Serene Highness to take post at Werne on the Lippe with a considerable detachment.

ON the 24th, the Bellsunce Infantry Brigade, and a brigade of cuirassiers, were detached from the French army towards Ham; and on the 25th, Lieutenant General M. de Chevert, M. de Voyer; and M. de Grollier, followed them with a large detachment.

---

16. Editor: This may be Calenberg, which is part of the town of Selm.

SEPTEMBER 29, M. de Peru, who commanded a considerable body of troops at Lünen, attacked the Duke of Holstein, who, with three battalions of foot and two regiments of dragoons, occupied an advanced post at Bork; the particulars of which action are as follows: The French, having made themselves masters of two bridges over the Lippe at Lünen and at Beedeburg, took advantage of this, and marched in the nighttime with a very superior force to the advanced posts of the Prince of' Holstein, where they arrived at daybreak. One of our posts upon the road to Lünen stopped them some time and retreated in very good order. The enemy who advanced their infantry through some thicket, whilst their cavalry kept the high road, were stopped by a battalion which we had thrown into Bork, and which made good use of two pieces of cannon they had with them. In the meantime, the enemy got up their cannon, and placed four battering pieces upon an eminence, from whence they charged us very briskly, whilst their muskets fired upon us on both sides. Our orders were to retire towards Olfen, where His Serene Highness the Duke of Brunswick had doubtless very good reasons to draw the enemy. Accordingly we prepared for our retreat, which was performed in the best order imaginable. The enemy, who followed us very closely through the thicket, did not show the same ardor when our rearguard drew up over against them on the plain: on the contrary, they never came out of the wood; and we perceived soon after, that their body, which consisted of 8,000 men, retreated with great precipitation towards Lünen, and repassed the Lippe there. Our whole loss amounted to but 6 killed and 12 wounded. The enemy carried off their dead and wounded. One of our posts, consisting of an officer and 30 men, having lost their way in the wood, had the misfortune to fall into the hands of the enemy; and another post, which we had at Dalhelm[Datteln] was surprised the same day by a detachment which passed the Lippe at the same time. We retook all our posts the same night and pushed some of them to the gates of Altlünen.

AFTER the defeat of Prince Isenburg all possible methods were taken at Hanover to reinforce that general. The jägers in the King's service received orders to assemble at Uslar, under the command of M. Ouenhausen, Grand Huntsman of the Court. They were in number about 1,000 men, who did duty some on horseback, some on foot. They also formed another new regiment and exercised their militia with the greatest diligence.

ON the 9th of September, the Prince of Soubise moved forward to Göttingen, and again took possession of that town. General Prince Isenburg, who had advanced towards that place with his headquarters at Moringen, being greatly inferior to him in numbers, was obliged to fall back to Uslar. On the 14th, the French marched on Northeim, and on the 14th, to Einbeck. Colonel Fischer's Corps made incursions into the Electorate and pushed forward even to the gates of Hanover.

ON the 16th, General Zastrow marched from Warendorf towards Hameln to join Prince Isenburg with the corps under his command. On the 19th, General Oberg, who was at Paderborn, sent a detachment of four squadrons of dragoons, the grenadiers of his seven battalions, and Luckner's Corps, towards Warburg, where the enemy had a camp of five battalions, eight squadrons, and the hussars of Nassau Saarbrücken, commanded by M. Dumesnil, who immediately upon their approach decamped, passed the Diemel, and marched about three leagues beyond it. The next day some of Luckner's Corps, having also passed that river, he retired to Kassel. On the 24th, General Oberg marched from Warburg, and on the 25th, attacked a very large detachment under the command of M. de Waldener, who had been advanced from Kassel, cut off about 200 of his light troops, and on the 26th in the morning, appeared before Kassel. When the French had marched towards Hanover, they left in that city all their baggage, etc. besides a large magazine. General Oberg had formed a scheme to surprise it, and would certainly have affected it, had not M. de Soubise by forced marches arrived the same day in the very crisis; and having reinforced the garrison with seven battalions, encamped in the vicinity of that town, with his right to the gardens and his left to the cascade. On the 27th, Prince Isenburg, who had followed the French in their retreat, joined General Oberg,

INTELLIGENCE being received that the Saxon troops, joined by a large body of French, were on their march to reinforce the enemy, General Oberg, not being able to bring them to an action without attacking them at a great disadvantage in their camp which they had strongly fortified, and fearing not only to be put between two fires, but also to have his communications cut off from his magazines, determined to change his position, and draw nearer to Minden. He accordingly decamped on the 3d of October at ten in the morning with drums beating and trumpets sounding. The French detached a large body of cavalry, with all the grenadiers of their army, to an eminence above Niedervellmar towards Kassel. Their light troops skirmished with ours: Fischer's Corps followed our rear, which had already quitted the village of Obvervellmar. This body of French advanced no farther than the Tannewäldchen: they continued on the eminence, and we quietly took possession of the camp between Hohenkirchen and Rotwesten. On the 4th, they continued their march; on the 5th, they passed the Fulda, and encamped at Landwehrhagen, possessing themselves of Wiltzenhausen and Göttingen. The French were encamped between Wehlheiden and Oberzwehre; they also occupied Battenhausen.

OCTOBER 12, the succor sent by M. de Contades to the Prince de Soubise encamped the 8th instant under the cannon of Kassel, near the French army. General Oberg, who ever since the 25th past, viz. from the time he arrived near Kassel had been desirous of attacking the French, but had been prevented from doing it from the difficulty of the ground they occupied, and which they had made stronger by all possible care, could not doubt but that the French army, thus reinforced, would endeavor immediately to enter upon action. He would have wished to avoid standing upon the defensive; but the superiority of the enemy, joined with the advantage of their position, did not allow him either to pass the Fulda above Kassel, and so to separate himself from the Weser and from his subsistence, or to risk the loss of all by a hazardous attack: he resolved, therefore, to keep the advantageous post which he had taken near Sondershausen, and take advantage of the least motion the enemy might make. In the meanwhile, the Prince de Soubise marched his army, on the 9th in the morning, on the side of Neuenmühle, leaving all his tents standing. He made different motions all that day, and in the evening, took possession of the camp near the Waldau, from Kassel to Oberkaufungen, towards which place his right extended. General Oberg, whose army was under arms, was in hopes of being attacked; but the motions of the French were made at a distance upon eminences divided by hollow ways and as the superiority of the Prince de Soubise enabled him to send a large detachment towards Witzenhausen, and to get around us by the road of Münden, which would have been of very dangerous consequences, General Oberg's care was to prevent being turned. He decamped the 10th at four in the morning and passing by the village of Landwehrhagen intending to encamp behind Lutterberg. The march was unmolested; but the French were preparing to follow us, and instead of encamping General Oberg formed his troops in order of battle. The right was to the Fulda, the left to a thicket upon an eminence, where five six-pounders were placed; the cavalry supported the wings in a third line; the village of Lutterberg was behind us, and a strong rising ground on the side of the village was furnished with four 12-pounders.

By seven in the morning the head of the French army, which had followed us by the way of Landwehrhagen, cannonaded our troops without effect, at the time they were forming. Immediately afterwards we saw a considerable body of troops file off at a distance from our left, which body, marching towards Sichelnstein, might be able to get possession of an eminence, covered with wood, and take us in the flank and rear, or pass by Nienhagen to Münden. Our jägers were on that side and routed them: and as General Oberg had detached Major General Zastrow of the Brunswick troops with two battalions of the second line, sustained by four squadrons, the French, whom our people attacked with their bayonets, were obliged to quit the wood again, and retire to some distance: but they pushed forward still more troops, infantry as well as cavalry, and having passed by Landwehrhagen, they posted their left towards the Fulda, their right extending far beyond our left, and they planted in their front more than 30 pieces of cannon.

GENERAL Oberg made every possible disposition for opposing the enemy vigorously in every part. The whole second line was employed both in reinforcing Major General Zastrow with four battalions and four squadrons, and in supplying two battalions, supported by two squadrons of dragoons, which were placed behind a thin wood, lying between our left and Major General Zastrow, through which the enemy might have come and attacked us; besides that, that little body of troops might fall upon the French flank which outlined our left.

THE day was spent in these dispositions, when at four in the afternoon the French began a very brisk cannonading, which, however, because of their situation, did but little execution; and, in the same instant, they fell with a strong body upon Major General Zastrow. Their first line was composed of infantry, which Major General Zastrow attacked with bayonets and routed, but it was supported by a considerable line of cavalry, which taking our infantry in the front and flank, broke it the moment that it had repulsed the French infantry. Our eight squadrons attacked the enemy's cavalry, and broke some squadrons of it, but their number increased, and came upon us from the wood. The French infantry, which had not been engaged, came on; our's had been partly broken, the remainder was obliged to retreat, but it did in good order. The French then came out almost upon the back of our first line; they placed the cannon, which they had with them, at the same time that all the rest of their army was in motion towards us. The moment was critical: General Oberg, who had constantly given his directions with admirable composure, commanded a retreat, which was made in excellent order quite up to the wood, where the defile that leads to Münden begins. The French, instead of pushing us with their cavalry, which was so greatly superior, continued firing upon us with their artillery, which they brought on very briskly under the conduct of the Duke de Broglio, some of the shot falling among our troops near the defile the horse threw themselves into it precipitately. The artillery and ammunition wagons, coming down in haste, were broken down and overturned. The battalions filed off; three or four of them formed themselves before the opening of the defile. Night came on as the whole passed the defile, marched through Münden, and lay all the night under arms on the other side of the Weser, in a little plain. In our retreat through the defile we were followed by the hussars only, who were driven back by the Bückeburg Battalion. The whole army had passed Münden, by midnight. The sick and wounded were carried from Münden in the night; only 150 were left behind who were in no condition to be removed. There remained at Münden, but a very small quantity of hay and straw. General Oberg withdrew the garrison, and the following day, the 11th, at daybreak, we marched and encamped near Guntersheim, without having our rear at all molested.

Our loss in wounded and slain was not very considerable, as it did not exceed 1,000 men. The d'Isenburg and Kanitz Regiments suffered the most and were almost ruined. The French had the advantage of a very great superiority; for though their officers whom we had taken talked of 50,000 men, it is certain they, at the lowest computation, exceeded 30,000, the Saxon troops having been augmented by the detachment under M. de Chevert, and afterwards by the troops of Mssrs. Fitz-James and Chabot. It appeared by all their maneuvers, that their capital point was to get between us and Münden; for besides the unsuccessful attempt to do it, which they had made on the 9th of October, they detached, on the 10th in the midst of the action, a body of 5,000 or 6,000 men to this side of the Fulda, to try the forces behind us, which we had kept guarded.

M. de Soubise after the action marched to Lutterberg, there he fixed his headquarters. On the 5th of October, M. de Contades marched to Lünen [Lünen?], and on the 6th to Hamm. The Duke de Chevreuse, who was at Dorsten, took post at Recklinghausen, in order to support M. de Lorges at Hamke. On the 8th of October the army under His Serene Highness marched to Nottuln in three columns, where he was joined by the two detached corps of Generals Imhoff and Wutgenau; and, on the 9th, they marched to Münster: at the same time the Crown Prince and the Duke of Holstein marched to Telgtee, and the next day to Warendorf. Lieutenant Colonel Luckner attacked a party of the enemy, composed of same infantry, and the hussars of Nassau Saarbrück, in the neighborhood of Mellingen. He defeated them and took three officers and 56 private men prisoners.

OCTOBER 14, the Allied Army marched from Münster to Telgtee, leaving a garrison in that city. The Crown Prince advanced to Rheda-Wiedenbrück, and on the 17th to Cappel near Lippstadt, where bridges were immediately thrown over the Lippe. The Crown Prince with the vanguard passed it and encamped at Bönninghausen. On the 18th, that prince proceeded towards Soest, in order to dislodge the Duke de Chevreuse, who was posted there with a strong detachment. The attack was made at 7 a.m., and the French were obliged to retire to Werl. On the 18th, the army began to file off by the bridges of Cappel and encamped at Soest; and the Crown Prince advanced to dislodge the enemy from Werl, who retired towards Unna, and then returned to Soest.

On the 20th, Mr. de Contades marched to Werl, where he fixed his headquarters. Here he was joined by the Saxons, and the detachments he had lent to Hesse under the command of the Duke Fitzjames and M. de Chevert, and on the 23d, returned to Hamm. On the 22d, Prince Ferdinand's army made a motion by its right from Soest to Hovestadt, with its right to that place and its left to Ostinghausen. Here he was joined by General Oberg, who was so posted as to cover the right flank of the army. The light troops were all this day engaged with the enemy with great success. His Grace the Duke of Marlborough, who had been left behind sick at Münster, died there about this time, and was succeeded in the command of the British troops by the Lord George Sackville. On the 24th, M. de Contades detached M. d' Armentières with 17 battalions and 26 squadrons towards Münster, with orders to endeavor to take that place by surprise. On the 25th, he approached Steinfurt, where Lieutenant General Kielmannsegg was posted with three battalions and two regiments of horse. This detachment fell back upon the toll house into the town and shut the gates. The French appeared within the reach of the cannon of the rampart, which were well served. They continued in motion the whole day of the 26th, and on the 27th they retired to Hamm, on information of the march of His Serene Highness towards Münster. Colonel Scheither's corps was sent in pursuit of them.

ON the 23d, the Allied Army marched to Lippstadt.

ON the 24th, to Rheda-Wiedenbrück.

ON the 25th, to Warendorf, and halted the next day.

ON the 27th, to Telgtee,

AND on the 28th to Münster.

THE Prince de Soubise altered the position of his army, establishing his headquarters at Hohenkirchen, and cantoned his troops, leaving a garrison in Münden. On the other hand, General Isenburg put some troops into Göttingen, and cantoned his troops in that neighborhood.

ON the 16th and 17th of November the French army separated at Bochum and marched off in three columns; one to Wesel, another to Düsseldorf, and the third to Cologne, where they passed the Rhine to go into winter quarters. They put 40 battalions and 3,000 cavalrymen into those three places, leaving M. de Chabot with the Légion Royale on the left of the Rhine to maintain the post at Hattingen. Their quarters extended from Cleves up to Koblenz along that river, over which they had constructed six bridges. Their headquarters were fixed at Krefeld.

ON the 22d, the Prince de Soubise abandoned Münden; and the 23d, the French also evacuated the city of Kassel, and went into their winter quarters, which were on the left of their main army, and extended from the mouth of the Lahn, inclining upwards along that river and the Main. Their headquarters were at Hanau, and their hospital at Marburg.

WHEN they quitted Kassel, they seized on Giessen, into which they put a garrison of 3,000 of their best troops. They also took possession of Friedberg in the Wetterivia. At both of which places they employed some hundreds of peasants in the repair of the fortifications.

THE Saxon troops filed off towards Wetzlar, where they took up their winter quarters.

ON the separation of the French army, our troops likewise marched into winter quarters, which were regulated in the manner following:

IN the city of Münster where Prince Ferdinand established his headquarters, were four battalions of English troops, two of Hanoverian guards, with two squadrons of Life Guards and Horse Grenadiers; an English battalion in Reinen, and another in Steinhorst [17]; a battalion of the Rheda-Wiedenbrücken Regiment was distributed at Telgtee, Wolbeck, and Alberstock[18]; and a battalion of Saxe-Gotha took post at Warendorf.

FOUR battalions of the Brunswick troops, ten battalions of Hessians, and one of Bückeburg, with seven squadrons of English, horse, eight of Hessian, four of Hanoverian, and 13 of Prussian horse, were repartitioned in the Bishopric of Paderborn, where the Crown Prince established his quarters. This body was commanded by ten general officers.

THOSE which were posted in the Bishopric of Osnabrück, and along the Ems River, consisted of nine battalions and 18 squadrons of Hanoverians, with nine squadrons of, English horse, under the command of seven general officers. There were only one battalion of fusiliers, and two squadrons of the Dachenhausen Dragoon Regiment, quartered in the Bishopric of Hildesheim.

MAJOR General Hardenberg was at Lippstadt, with two battalions of Hanoverians, four of Hessians, and some thousands of militia and light troops.

BESIDES this, the Crown Prince of Brunswick and four other general officers formed a chain composed of eight battalions and 10 squadrons of Hanoverians, two battalions of the troops of Wolfenbüttel, and Scheither's body of jägers, which was repartitioned at Stadtlohn, Gescher-Loberg, Coesfeld, Lette[19], Dülmen, and Hamm, and were posted so as to be assembled in a very short time, if circumstances required it.

BESIDES these, there were in the country of Hesse, under the Prince d'Isenburg, and five other general officers, four battalions of Hanoverians and Hessians, and one of Brunswick, with seven squadrons of Hessian horse, and some companies of hussars and jägers. The Bishopric of Hildesheim was taxed to furnish 6,000 recruits for our army, which they had already begun to raise.

PRINCE Isenburg, who had established his headquarters at Kassel at the time the French had quitted it, caused a part of his troops on the 1st of December to march to Fritzlar, and the rest into the Bailiwick of Gudensberg, where they cantoned.

---

17. Editor: Today Steinhorst is part of Delbrück.
18. Editor: This may be Albersloh, part of Sendenhorst.
19. Editor: Lette is currently part of Coesfeld.

THE French General M. le Marquis de Castreis appeared on the 1st of December at 5 o'clock in the morning, before the gates of St. Goar, with the St. Germaine Regiment, and some detachments scaled the walls, and made prisoners a party of 50 men who guarded that place; and about 8 o'clock he summoned the fortress of Rheinfels. The garrison, consisting of 700 men, surrendered the place without making any defense, and were all made prisoners of war.

THE CAMPAIGN OF THE YEAR 1759

DURING the recess of winter quarters, the armies on both sides took all necessary precautions to avoid being surprised, watching each other's motions with a careful eye, and, far from being inactive, embraced every opportunity of harassing one another where the least view of advantage offered itself. This of course occasioned several different movements and brought on frequent skirmishes. Their attention, however, was not at the same time diverted from making the necessary preparations for the approaching season, nor from using their utmost efforts to enable them to open the campaign with vigor, each endeavoring to be before-hand in the field. For this purpose, reinforcements were sent from England, with requisite stores, some thousands of recruits were raised in Germany for the Allied Army, and though forage and provisions were extremely scarce in those parts, yet proper magazines were furnished, and everything provided which could alleviate the unavoidable fatigues of the ensuing year. No money was spared, and our generals on that occasion displayed the greatest prudence and humanity. The King of Prussia had an interview with His Serene Highness, wherein they had concerted measures and formed a plan of operation; which by the steps taken in the very beginning of the year, appeared and seem highly probable to be in part, that the Allied Army should endeavor to drive the French to the Rhine, and at the same time get between them and the combined armies of the Empire and the Austrians, while His Majesty on the other side should send a considerable detachment into Thuringia and Franconia. By this means the countries of Hanover, Hesse, etc. would be covered, and the army of the Circles and Imperialists would be either forced to retreat or suffer themselves to be enclosed between the two armies without being able to receive any succor from the French, while they, on the contrary, could mutually support each other.

ON the other hand, the Courts of Vienna and Paris had also regulated and drawn up a scheme, pursuant to which the army of the Circles, supported by a body of the Imperial troops, should occupy Thuringia and Franconia, whence they might be able not only to make incursions into the countries of Hesse, etc. but also to support, and be supported by, the French; and a chain would be thereby formed from the Lower Rhine to the Grand Imperial Army enabling them to reinforce and act in conjunction with each other.

THE Prince de Soubise cast his eye on the city of Frankfurt as post of the utmost importance, both to facilitate his own schemes and frustrate those of the Allies; a post that would enable him to keep the concerted communication open with the Austrians; a post that would make him mailer of the Rhine and Main Rivers, by which he might receive supplies, even as far as from Alsace, a post, also, that would serve him as a safe retreat on any occasion. He therefore resolved to make himself master of it at any rate, which he effected by the following unprecedented piece of treachery. On the 2d day of January, the Nassau Regiment presented itself before one of the gates, demanding permission to pass through the city. This liberty was granted, and they were accordingly conducted by a detachment of the garrison, as is the customary ceremony on such occasions, as far as the Sachsenhausen Gate. When they arrived there, instead of proceeding forward, they halted, seized on the grand guard, and took post. Immediately after, five regiments more viz. Beauvoisins, Rohan, Rochfort, Bentheim, and Royal Deux Ponts, entered and took possession of the principal places in that city. Thus, was that free and Imperial town, contrary to all laws seized on by the French, and made the headquarters of their general.

JANUARY, the French partisan Madelet with 300 foot and 60 horse from Wesel, attempted to surprise a Hanoverian post, but was himself surprised in an adjacent village, on the night before he proposed the attempt, by a party lent for that purpose from Coesfeld.

His Serene Highness, having intelligence that a body of the French were in motion on the Ruhr, and had passed that river, reinforced his posts, and ordered out same detachments, who soon forced them to repass that river with the utmost precipitation, abandoning at the same time the important post they had at Hattingen. Another body of about 6,000 French also passed that river some time after, but were in like manner speedily obliged to retire, having without any effect made a forced and fruitless march in this severe season through bad roads, and harassed their men to no purpose.

THE army of the Circles and a party of the Austrians began to advance into Thuringia and Franconia by several different bodies; one whereof entered on the 13th of January into Erfurt, where they took post, formed magazines, and collected a vast quantity of palisades for the repair of the fortifications. This was a very important place, as it was the key both to Saxony and Hesse and was also absolutely necessary to secure their communication with the French. The rest extended themselves into the Duchies of Saxe-Eisenach, Saxe-Coberg, Saxe-Gotha, and the district of Fulda. In the month of February, General d'Arberg, at the head of 12,000 of those troops, suddenly entered the country of Hesse, seized on the Bailiwicks of Schmalkalden, Vacha Friedewald, and Landeck, as also the Principality of Bad Hersfeld, taking post between the Fulda and the Werra. At the same time Colonel Fischer's Corps was sent into the neighborhood of Marburg.

PRINCE Isenburg had an interview near Kassel with the Crown Prince, who came for that purpose from Paderborn. Some light troops were sent towards Bad Hersfeld, as also a detachment to Allendorff[20] on the Werra, to observe the enemy in both these places. Reinforcements were sent from the Bishopric of Paderborn, and the general's headquarters were moved from Fritzlar to Homberg. Preparations were also made at Kassel for the reception of a body of troops, and a bridge was thrown over the Fulda above that city.

AT this juncture, Prince Henry detached General Knobloch from Saxony, with a body of troops into Thuringia, who attacked and made himself master of Erfurt, on the 28th

20. Editor: Today part of Sonden-Allendorf.

of February. He then sent Colonel Kleist forward with his green hussars, who, on the 2d of March, arrived at Eisenach; another detachment marched towards Schmalkalden and Vacha; and, on the 4th, Lieutenant Colonel Wunsch, with 300 men, attacked and dislodged a party near Frauenwald. Several prisoners were made by these parties. On the other hand, General d'Urf, with a body of 4,000 men of the Allied troops, which had been collected near Rotenburg an der Fulda, was to have attacked the enemy's quarters in three different places at once but the hussars and light troops on the preceding day having given the alarm, and also being informed of the reduction of Erfurt, they, in the night, retired with the greatest expedition towards Meiningen, into the country of Bamberg, entirely evacuating the country of Hesse, and abandoning all the ports they had taken possession of. Several prisoners and a great deal of their baggage fell into the hands of our light troops, who closely pursued them. The Prussians, at the end of this expedition, returned into winter quarters.

MARCH 14, the French, in the neighborhood of Frankfurt, detached some squadrons of horse and dragoons to take post near Friedberg, they also sent a corps of 3,000 men into the districts of Hackenberg[21], Dillenburg, and Herborn, where, on occasion, they might be supported, and be ready to co-operate with the army of the circles, who, being reinforced by a large body of Austrians, were again advancing in much greater numbers towards the frontiers of Hesse with surprising celerity, having left a large body in the neighborhood of Erfurt to observe some small parties of Prussians, who had taken up their quarters on the frontiers of Thuringia. Our detachments were obliged to retire everywhere before such a superior force, and the enemy once more seized Schmalkalden, Salzungen, and Vacha: here they seemed to make a halt, but soon after they suddenly rushed into the Principality of Bad Hersfeld, and had like to have surprised the small garrison of that capital, who very narrowly escaped. Another body of their troops were likewise advanced to the Werra.

MARCH 22d, his Serene Highness Prince Ferdinand, on advice of those motions of the Austrians, set out from Münster in the morning, with a design, as was thought, of visiting the posts of Hamm, Lippstadt, and Paderborn, but having drawn some troops out of that neighborhood, he marched directly to the country of Hesse, through roads no army had ever passed before, and encamped, on the 26th, at Rotenburg an der Fulda, on the 27th, he advanced to Bad Hersfeld, where his vanguard surprised about 100 of the enemy, who were now retreating everywhere; and from thence he marched to the town of Fulda. By this march he gained the flank of the French and cut off their communication with the Austrians.

MARCH 31st, the Crown Prince, with only two squadrons of Black Hussars, defeated, near Mellrichstadt, the Hohenzolleren Cuirassier Regiment, and entirely dispersed them; numbers were killed, and 55 made prisoners. The Würzburg Infantry Regiment, which was along with them, being thus deserted by their cavalry became a sacrifice to the hussars, who took 130 of them prisoners, and cut the rest to pieces. The next day he marched to Meiningen, with two battalions of grenadiers and some light troops, where he made the garrison prisoners, consisting of two battalions of the Elector of Cologne's troops, and found a considerable magazine. He thence proceeded to Wasungen and

21. Editor: May be Hachenburg.

made the Nagel Regiment prisoners. General d'Arberg, who was on his march with one battalion and some grenadiers to support that place, came up after the affair was over. A brisk cannonading however ensued, but he was obliged to retire with such precipitation that the light horse could not come up with him in their pursuit. The same time the Duke of Holstein dislodged a party of the French from Freiensteinau[22], making two officers and 56 men prisoners. Colonel Stockhausen also with a detachment of some Hessian hussars and light troops, attacked the Savoy Dragoon Regiment with such vigor that they cut the major part of them to pieces, and took two rich standards from them, which they brought to the headquarters.

ON the side of the Prussians, Major General Knobloch, with his detachment, also dislodged a party of the army of the Circles from Saalfeld on the 26th of March; and, on the 26th, General Linstadt also forced another from Hof.

THUS, the Austrians were everywhere repulsed, and, flying in the utmost disorder and confusion, were pursued beyond Sühl and Schleusingen, in their retreat towards Bamberg.

APRIL 7, the several detachments of the Allied Army returned this day to the headquarters at Fulda, where there were assembled all the Hessian infantry and cavalry, all the Brunswick battalions, 20 squadrons of Prussian dragoons, three regiments of English horse, and seven battalions and six squadrons of Hanoverians, amounting in the whole to about 30,000 men.

THUS far the scheme proposed had been put into execution. It now remained to force the French over the Rhine. This was the grand view, and the object which fixed His Serene Highness 's particular attention; the time now seemed to offer itself, the Austrians could not support them, as they were found employment sufficient by several Prussian detachments which Prince Henry had made expressly for that purpose, neither were they yet joined by their troops from the Lower Rhine; the attempt was, therefore, determined on, and for that purpose His Serene Highness began to move forward with the above corps towards the Duke de Broglio, the rest of the Allied Army being left to cover the Electorate of Hanover, and protect the Bishopric of Münster.

APRIL 10, His Serene Highness, having called in his detached parties, decamped from Fulda and marched to Freiensteinau.

11th, marched to Büdingen.

12th, marched to Windecken[23].

13th, marched towards Bergen[24], a village situated about two leagues from Frankfurt on the road to Hanau, where the French, having had intelligence of His Serene Highness's march, took post the preceding day in a camp which they had strongly fortified some

22. Editor: The original says "Freiensteinau", but no such town exists. This is the most probable correct town.
23. Editor: This village was absorbed by Nidderau.
24. Editor: Bergen today is part of Frankfurt am Main, constituting its easternmost quarter of Bergen-Enkheim.

time before. The French general, the Duc de Broglio, kept this village on his right, put therein eight German battalions, and in the rear of it placed several French brigades. His center and left flank were secured in such a manner, that the Allies must necessarily attack that village before they could come at his line. At 9 o'clock in the morning the army came in sight of the enemy; and notwithstanding the advantage of their situation was so great, His Serene Highness determined to endeavor, if possible, to force them, and accordingly made the proper dispositions, under cover of a rising ground, for the attack of that village. At 10 o'clock the grenadiers of the advanced guard made the assault with great intrepidity, sustaining with surprising firmness and resolution a most severe fire from the enemy in the village; but though they were supported by several brigades under the command of General Isenburg, and exerted themselves with the greatest vigor imaginable, taking three batteries from the enemy in the village, yet there were so many batteries behind one another that they were obliged to retreat in some confusion behind a body of Hessian horse, where they immediately rallied. The troops which defended the village behaved with uncommon spirit, and made so obstinate a defense, that the Allies were repulsed in three different vigorous attacks made in the space of two hours, and never were able entirely to dislodge the enemy, or force them from that important post, which covered the main body of the French. His Serene Highness, perceiving his troops were in some disorder, brought up his artillery, and a most furious cannonading began on both sides. He likewise made new dispositions behind the above rising ground, dividing his infantry into two bodies; one of which he placed on his right, and the other on his left, with his cavalry in the center, covered by a small column of infantry, which was for that purpose posted before it. The army then appeared in the plain, as if it intended to renew the charge, and attack the enemy at the same time both in the village and on the left. By these movements, he amused the French the remainder of the day, for His Serene Highness, ever watchful and attentive to the safety of his troops, had determined to retreat while his loss was yet not very considerable. He judged it imprudent to hazard all to the doubtful issue of a fresh attack, on the success of which the operations of the ensuing campaign so much depended. Accordingly, he gave orders to bury his dead, and remove the wounded; and when night came on made a safe and honorable retreat, without any interruption or molestation from the French, who were so effectually deceived by this maneuver of the Prince, that they kept close in their posts, every moment expecting a fresh attack. The loss of the Allies on this occasion amounted to about 2,000 men in the whole, with five pieces of cannon, which were left behind in the village. Prince Isenburg was among the number of the killed, and Generals Gilsa and Count Schulenburg were wounded. The following circumstance is related of that prince's death. Just as he was going to lead his grenadiers to the assault he said with great composure: "Come, my friends, whoever has courage let them follow me." Scarce had he expressed these words, when he received a musket ball in his breast, and instantly expired.

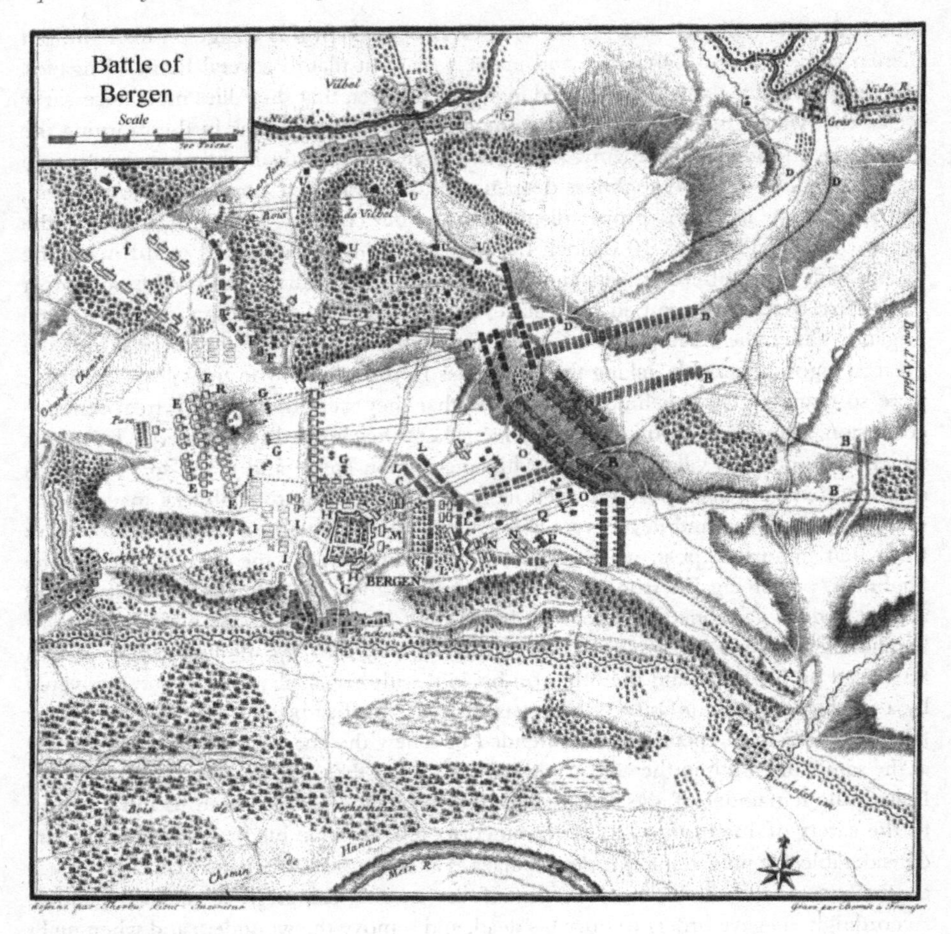

KEY TO MAP.

A Left Allied column, under the orders of the Crown Prince of Brunswick, consistin of the grenadiers coming by Bischofsheim and marching at the same level as those of the center

B commanded by Prince Isneburg, who moved along the Arfeld Wood and who came to support the column of the Crown Prince of Brunswick, these columns attacked on arriving at 10:00 a.m., the village of Bergen in

C the columns

D of the right under the orders of the Princes of Anhalat, Holstein, and Milord Grandet, debouching by Grosgrunau, and advancing to support this attack.

E Position of the French army.

F Position of the Saxons

£ Apcheon Regiment.

G Artillery deployed by Chevalier pelletier.

H 8 battalions defending Bergen.

I 15 Battalions in column to support them.

K St. Germaine Regiment placed in the tower's ditches.

L Allied infantry, which had advanced successfully, near the sunken road.

M Infantry (L.) repulsed in three different attacks and vigorously in the last by the 15 battalions in columns behind the village, which were successively brought to the attack, part passing by the village nad part by the orchards on the right, these troops ursued the allies until they rallied.

N Point where Allied infantry rallied.

O.P. Hanoverian cavalry advances to block the progress of the French troops, who then rtired upon the order of the Duc de Broglie, into the orchards of Bergen, the French infantry retired, the Allies advanced their left

Q causing the French to believe that they wished to attempt a new attack. De Broglie advanced

R two battalions from the reserve as a precaution,

S as well as ten squadrons

T of cavalry, which moved forward from the sunken road.

M The Allies in their final position

Q making some movements to their right to support, with some infantry, the attack of their light infantry

U who were unsuccessful because of the defense of the volontaires

X of the French army; the Allies a bit before night fall moved much infantry towards Bergen, as if to resume a new attack, and proved their position by their right and left and found a firm resistance everywhere. They executed a heavy fire from their artillery

Y and retreated about 11:00 p.m.

THE LOSS of the French was by no means inferior to that of the Allies in the number of the killed and wounded; among the latter was Baron Dim, lieutenant general and commander of the Saxon troops in the absence of Prince Xavier. He not long after died of his wounds.

THE Allies retreated no farther on the night of the battle than to Windecken, a village about a league and a half distant from Bergen, where they halted the next day.

APRIL 15, the wounded being removed from Windecken[25] to Büdingen the army marched to Marienborn, where it halted the day after.

25. Editor: The village of Windecken apparently no longer exists.

APRIL 17, decamped and marched to Bingenheim[26].

APRIL 18, marched to Grimburg. The French, who never quitted their posts while our army was nigh enough to return to the attack, appeared this day with their light troops, under the command of M. de Blaisel, and attempted our rear, but were quickly repulsed with considerable loss.

APRIL 19, marched to Alsfeld, where the army remained 'till the 23d; this day an officer, who was dispatched to a detachtment consisting of one battalion of grenadiers, and two squadrons of the Finckenstein Regiment, with orders relative to their march, was unfortunately taken prisoner by the French; in consequence of which accident, they did not set out in due time, nor kept the proper route, and were by that means surrounded by the enemy, who entirely dispersed or made prisoners the two squadrons of cavalry, but the grenadiers made a brave defense, and kept them at bay until they rejoined the army, which they effected without any material loss except that of their baggage. This day M. de Broglio returned his troops into cantonments but they were so posted as to be able to unite and form themselves into a body in two days' time.

APRIL 23, marched from Alsfeld to Ziegenhain[27], a village about six leagues from Fritzlar, situate in the midst of a marshy ground.

ABOUT this time Prince Ferdinand, by his situation, having no reason to be apprehensive of any movements the French could make, sent from Bad Hersfeld a large detachment under the com-mand of General Urf into Franconia, to act against the combined armies of the Empire and Austrians, in concert with Prince Henry, who had just entered into that country in three columns.

THE French with the greatest diligence fortified their post of Bergen, as also the village of Sachsenhausen one of the suburbs of Frankfurt, on the other side of the Main, where they had a considerable magazine; they also sent all their heavy baggage, etc. over that river, and took every necessary precaution to avoid being surprised, so greatly were they alarmed at the rapid progress of the Prussians, who were advancing towards the Main with great expedition, the Austrians and Imperialists everywhere flying before them.

ON the 7th of May, Prince Henry moved towards Reichenbach, and encamped near Oelsnitz, while General Finck filed off to Adorf, in order to make the enemy believe he had a design to direct his march towards Eger; on the 8th he attacked General M'Guire near Hof, who was posted there with eight battalions and some cavalry; His Serene Highness forced them after some resistance to retire. Upon this occasion one battalion of Marschal, one of Salm, and the battalion of Darmstadt Grenadiers suffered considerably: the Prince of Salm was taken prisoner. General M'Guire retired by Aschau[28]. General Knobloch at the same time also advanced towards Saalfeld, and passed the Saal near Saalburg: General Ried, afraid of being surrounded by this motion,

26. Editor: Today Bingenheim is part of Echzell.
27. Editor: Despite the authors assertion, Ziegenhain is the main Renaissance fortress of Hessen-Kassel. Today it is part of the city of Schwalmstadt.
28. Editor: May be Aschau, in Thuringia, which today is part of Allendorf.

fell back behind Nordhalben[29], where he was attacked on the 8th, and forced, after a smart action, to retire to Steinwiesen; he was again attacked there, and obliged to fall back to Wallenfels[30]; during this time the Austrian General Haddick quitted his camp near Munchsburg, where he had entrenched himself, and marched in the night between the 9th and 10th to Kulmbach, where he arrived in the morning; here the bulk of the enemy assembled, and immediately sent their baggage away by the route to Bamberg, and in the evening marched to Gasmansdorff[31], about a league and half from Kulmbach, where General Palffy remained with their rearguard. Prince Henry's corps arrived on the 10th near Munchsburg, where his headquarters were fixed: on the 11th he marched to the neighborhood of Bayreuth, with his headquarters at Himmelkron. The Prussian General Platen, on the 11th in the afternoon, attacked the Kronegk and Palatine Dragoon Regiments, under the command of General Riedesel, which, after a brave resistance, were made prisoners of war. The Combined Army of the Imperialists retired to Nürnburg.

ON the other hand, Gen. d'Urff, with his detachment from the Allied Army advanced as far as Königshofen; Col. Weysy retired before them, and their vanguard had pushed their patrols as far as Scheinfurt.

On the 16th, Prince Henry entered the city of Bamberg; in this place the enemy had a very considerable magazine, part of which they had destroyed; there was found, however, 400,000 rations of bread, and 100,000 rations of oats, which had received no damage. General Knobloch made himself master of the castle of Kronach after a brisk cannonading. Here Prince Henry received notice that General Gemmingen, with a large body of Austrians, was entering into Saxony; and also that the Russians were in full march: this laid him under the necessity of returning towards Hof, having first raised large contributions, and destroyed most of the enemy's magazines; for which purpose, on the 21st of May he caused his artillery and heavy baggage to file off towards Saxony, and on the 22d began his march, leaving 1,000 men in the city to cover his retreat; this party also on the 25th followed the main body. This expedition of General Gemmingen not only saved the remainder of the army of the Circles, but also freed the French from the alarms they were under from the vicinity of his Royal Highness. On the 30th a smart engagement happened in which the vanguard of the army of the Empire under the command of General Palffy, who was sent to harass the rear of the Prussians, was defeated between Berneck and Gefrees, at a little distance from Hoff; they had a great number killed and wounded, and several were made prisoners, among whom was General Klefeld they lost a great part of their baggage, together with several pieces of cannon, and were pursued as far as Bayreuth.

IT was absolutely necessary to mention the above expedition of the Prussians into Franconia, as it entirely frustrated any schemes the French and Combined Army might have formed with regard to the allies at that juncture.

---

29. Editor: The original text calls this town "Nordelhen", but Nordhalben appears the most likely proper spelling.
30. Editor: The original text calls this town "Waldenfeldt."
31. Editor: Probably Gössmannsreuth, part of Kulmbach.

MAY 14. About this time the French on the Lower Rhine were everywhere in motion. M. de Contades headquarters were at Düsseldorf, where he began to form a camp; they were likewise forming one at Wesel, and another at Büderich, and on the 25th he removed them to Mülheim, where their main body was assembling. M. d'Armentières was left behind on the Lower Rhine with a body of about 20,000 men.

MAY 18, Prince Ferdinand removed his headquarters to Lippstadt, bringing with him the greatest part of the troops from the left. General Imhoff was left in the country of Hesse with a body of 10,000 men. General Hardenberg took post at Hamm with those battalions and squadrons which he had under his command at Lippstadt. The troops likewise at Münster, and in that neighborhood, were everywhere in motion on their march towards the Lippe, in order to canton along that river.

MAY 24. The headquarters of the Allied Army were transferred from Lippstadt to Hamm, and on the 28th to Recke; General Spörcken with the troops from Münster was at Dülmen. The Crown Prince was at Unna to which place General Hardenberg had marched from Hamm with the detachment under his command. Lieutenant General Wangenheim was at Dülmen and Haltern-am-See to observe M. d'Armentières. Luckner's and Scheither's corps were at Dorsten, where they had frequent skirmishes with the light troops of the French army.

JUNE 3, the British infantry quitted their cantonments, and encamped near Lünen.

JUNE 5, His Serene Highness's headquarters were removed from Recke to Werl, and the army remained posted along the Lippe and Ruhr. General Imhoff was encamped near Fritzlar: the magazine at Münster was removed to Lippstadt, and that at Osnabrück was transported to the banks of the Weser: the corps under M. d'Armantières remained at Wesel and Düsseldorf.

M. de Contades marched through Siegburg, passed the Dill, and arrived, on the 1st and 2d of June, at Giessen with 57 battalions and 40 squadrons. M. de Noailles, who commanded the vanguard, was at Marburg with 25 battalions and 14 squadrons, and M. de Broglio was at Friedberg with the corps de reserve, consisting of 18 battalions and 31 squadrons: the Duke de Brissac also joined him with his corps. The French army being thus assembled, encamped on the 4th and 5th at Niederwalgern[32], from whence it marched on the 6th in two columns, the right passing through Marburg, and the other keeping a little to the left of that town, and on the 7th, it arrived at Frankenberg. On the 8th, it marched to Lassenburg, and on the 10th, it encamped at Korbach, where its headquarters were established. Its corps de reserve, under M. de Broglio, marched on the 6th from Guntershausen to Homberg; on the 7th, it proceeded to Fritzlar, and on the 8th, to Ubersdorff: his vanguard, composed of the de Clermont Volunteers took post the evening of the 6th at Ziegenhain, from which place the garrison belonging to the Allies retired towards Fritzlar.

THE Crown Prince of Brunswick passed the Ruhr with a large detachment. A party of his light troops unexpectedly appeared on the 5th before the town of Elberfeld, attacked the Provence Regiment who were posted there, and dislodged it. The loss of

32. Editor: Today this is part of the community of Weimar (Lahn).

the enemy was considerable in killed and wounded. They had 83 private men made prisoners, together with their commanding officer M. le Chevalier de Montfort, and eight other officers. On the 6th the prince entered Kaiserswerth, and on the night between the 6th and 7th, surprised a body of 1,000 of the enemy at Duisburg, the greatest part of whom were made prisoners. From thence he proceeded, on the 8th, to Dortmund in the country of Mark. In short, he traversed with great rapidity all the French quarters in those parts, insulted Düsseldorf, alarmed Cologne, and ruined several of the enemy's magazines. By this expedition he not only greatly annoyed the enemy, but also, by amusing M. d'Armentières, concealed the real designs of His Serene Highness, and at the same time covered the march of the Allied Army.

GENERAL Imhoff perceiving the French intended to cut him off, retreated from Fritzlar on the 8th towards Kassel, in the neighborhood of which place he encamped; and having caused the pontoons, artillery, hospital, and heavy baggage, to be removed from that city to Minden, he proceeded to Lichtenau, leaving behind him General Zastrow with three Hanoverian battalions and one regiment of dragoons. M. de Broglio made a forced march with a view to surprise this small corps; but they being apprised of his approach, and finding themselves too weak to defend that city, prudently retreated by the way of Münden towards Hameln and Minden; and the French entered that defenseless capital early on the morning of the 10th, and sent immediately a detachment in pursuit of von Zastrow as far as Münden, of which place they also took possession. Both here and at Kassel the enemy found some magazines, which the Allies were not able to remove at the time they were forced to retire.

THE Allied Army was all assembled by the 11th of June in the neighborhood of Werl and Soest. Six companies of English grenadiers were formed into a battalion, the command of which was given to Major Maxwell.

ON the 13th, they marched to Anröchte.

ON the 14th, they proceeded to Büren, where they encamped and the headquarters was established at the castle of Brenken near Erpernburg. The army extended along the heights of Büren, having the Alme Rivulet with a large valley in its front: the left was covered by a wood, and on the right was a steep descent: both the flanks were, likewise fortified with entrenchments and artillery.

M. de Contades, on advice that the Allies were in motion, and having called in all their out parties were advancing towards Büren, where General Imhoff had taken post with his corps, imagined that his Serene Highness intended to dispute the defiles of the Diemel; in order, therefore, to prevent his designs, he immediately decamped from Korbach, on the 13th marched to Stadburg[33], and the light troops which had been posted there advanced to Essentho, within a league of Büren; and he, at daybreak on the 14th, followed them with the whole army; passed the Diemel and the defiles of Essen without any obstruction, encamping on the eminences of Essen and Meerhof, at the latter of which places he fixed his headquarters. M. de Chevreuse, with a large detachment, was advanced in his front at Fürstenberg[34], at the entrance of the valley. A smart action

33. Editor: This may be Padberg.

34. Editor: Today part of Bad Wünnenberg.

passed before daybreak between the light troops of both armies. The Hanoverian hussars, supported by the jägers on foot, attacked between Leiberg and Wünnenburg the Volontaires de Château, Theirri, Turpin, and Dauphiny. The success was nearly equal on both sides: M. de Theirri was wounded, and several of the Volunteers were made prisoners.

M. de Contades, before he quitted Korbach, had sent orders to M. de Broglio to join him with all possible diligence, which orders he received at Kassel on the 13th. He immediately prepared everything for his departure, and in three forced marches arrived on the 16th at Lichtenau, within two leagues of Meerhof[35]. When he quitted Kassel, he left a detachment of four battalions and two squadrons under the command of M. de Waldener to keep possession of that place.

HERE the two armies remained inactive for some time in sight of each other, their advanced posts not being above a mile and half asunder, without making any attempt to attack, as the position of each was equally strong, and inaccessible, both by art and nature. M. de Contades did not think it advisable to quit his advantageous camp to attack the Allies, though he was greatly superior in numbers after the junction of M. de Broglio; but in order to take an advantage of this superiority, he formed a design of turning their left. For this purpose M. de Broglio was ordered to proceed from Lichtenau to Atteln[36]. On the 18th, a large detachment under the command of M. de Xavier was advanced to Nordborchen[37], and their light troops seized on the town of Paderborn. This party was ordered to proceed by forced marches around the left of the Allies, with an intent to cut off their communication from the Weser, and that part of the Bishopric of Münster situate along the Ems River. This maneuver of the enemy determined His Serene Highness (who could not spare a detachment to observe Prince Xavier) to change his position and march to Reitburg. The Allied Army accordingly on the 19th struck their tents, and marched to Lippstadt, in the neighborhood of which place they encamped; and on the 20th, they passed the Lippe River above and below the town, and retired towards Reitburg, pitching their camp near to that town in an advantageous situation, having the Ems River in their front, with their right extending to the village of Windenbrück, and their left to that of Neukirchen They were not in the least molested in this march, nor was there any attempt made on their baggage, which was covered by all the grenadiers of the army and the light troops. A party of the enemy commanded by M. de Murel, indeed, appeared at the bridge of Bee after the whole had passed the river; but they were soon repulsed, and obliged to retire with great precipitation.

GENERAL Wangenheim still remained encamped near Dülmen with 11 battalions and seven squadrons, in order to cover the right of the Allied Army, and observe the motions of M. d'Armentières' corps, who had marched from Wesel and took post at Schermbeck. The grand hospital which was at Münster, as also that of Kassel, which had been before sent to Minden, were both transferred to the city of Verden; and the heavy baggage and hospital of the army, which had been removed from Paderborn to Osnabrück, were now removed to Nienburg,

35. Editor: Today Meerhof is part of Marsberg.
36. Editor: Today Atteln is part of Lichtenau.
37. Editor: Nordborchen is part of Borchen.

ON the 24th of June, M. de Contades marched from Meerhof in six columns towards Paderborn, in the neighborhood whereof he encamped with his right extending towards that town, and his left towards the village of Weyer[38], having an advanced corps at Neuhaus[39]. The Duke de Chevreuse took post at Büren with the corps which he had under his command at Fürstenberg.

ON the 29th, the French army changed its position, and marched from Paderborn, directing their march towards Reitburg, encamping within about three leagues of that place, on the heaths between Lippspringe and Ost Schlangen[40].

ON the 30th, His Serene Highness quitted Reitburg, and proceeded to Marienfeld, where the headquarters were established, the army being encamped between that place and the village of Harsewinkel: the enemy's light troops followed our rear, and a smart action passed between five squadrons of the Prussian hussars, commanded by Colonel Narzinsky, and a party of the French, consisting of the Turpin and Béréchiny Regiments, and a detachment of hussars, in which the latter were entirely dispersed with the loss of 60 killed and wounded, and 70 taken prisoners, together with 160 horses.

A party of 300 French chasseurs, headed by a captain of the Enghien Regiment, seized on Reitburg Castle by a coup de main; the garrison, consisting of 130 men, were made prisoners, besides a few sick; they pushed forward their light troops as far as Bielefeld.

ON the 3d of July, the Allied Army decamped and marched to Dissen, where the headquarters were fixed; and their light troops were advanced in their front as far as Halle.

ON the 4th, the French also decamped, and proceeded to Bielefeld, where they fixed their headquarters, with their left to that place, and their right extending to Herford; by this step they proposed to intercept the Allies from the town of Minden, towards which place His Serene Highness Prince Ferdinand was directing his march in order to secure the passage of the Weser.

As the advanced posts of the two armies were very near to each other, their light troops had several severe skirmishes. Our hussars, which were posted at Halle, were attacked by a party of the French, consisting of about 1,000 of the Volontaires de Clermont, and Grenadiers Royaux, and some hussars. They were obliged to give way and fall back upon the castle of Ravensburg, where the Hanoverian jägers and the Prussian light infantry were posted. The enemy came up to the castle with spirit but were soon forced to retire with the loss of about 20 of their men. A detachment of five battalions of grenadiers and four squadrons of dragoons were sent to reinforce the light troops; and the French immediately abandoned the village of Halle. The Black Hussars and some Hessians had also a smart skirmish with Turpin's Regiment, in which they killed and made prisoners above 100 men. The Hanoverian jägers likewise surprised a party of the enemy who were posted at Neukirchen[41], killed a captain and 17 men of the Volontaires de Clermont, and brought prisoners into the camp one captain, one lieutenant, and 46 private men.

---

38. Editor: Weyer may be Wewer, now part of Paderborn.
39. Editor: Neuhaus is a palace in Paderborn.
40. Editor: Today Ost Schlangen is part of Schlangen.
41. Editor: Neukirchen is part of Melle.

ON the 8th of July, the Allied Army decamped from Dissen, and marched to Osnabrück: the heavy baggage, etc. which were in this place, were removed to Bremen. Major General Wangenheim, who, as was said before, had been left to observe M. d'Armentières, receiving orders to join the army, marched on the 3d of July from Dülmen to Münster, and, having left General Zastrow with a garrison of about 3,000 men in that place, proceeded by the way of Stadburg[42], and joined the army in this camp.

M. de Chabot sent a summons on the 7th to Lieutenant General Zastrow to surrender the town, to which he gave the following reply: "Sir, in answer to the summons you sent me, I cannot fail to acquaint you that I am not placed here to give up the town of Münster, but to defend it in form, in order to merit your esteem and that of M. d'Armentière." It was accordingly invested in form on the 19th; and on the night between the 11th and 12th, M. d'Armentières made an attempt to surprise the garrison, attacking it at the same time in five different places; but he was everywhere repulsed with considerable loss, having had 900 men killed and 1400 wounded on that occasion.

LIEUTENANT Colonel Freytag having passed the Weser made an incursion into the frontiers of Hesse and advancing towards Münden fell in with the Volontaires d'Alsace Regiment near that town. He immediately attacked them, and either killed or took prisoners the whole corps. Some of the private men, to avoid the fury of the jägers, threw themselves into some boats they found on the side of the Weser; but the greater part were drowned, and scarcely any arrived on the other side.

M. de Broglio, who had been posted at Engeren[43], marched from thence in the evening of the 8th of July towards Minden with a considerable detachment, consisting of 16 battalions and 1,400 infantry of different corps, together with the carabineers of his reserve, the Schomberg and Nassau Regiments, and Fischer's Corps. They arrived before Minden at daybreak and summoned it to surrender. Major General Zastrow, who commanded in that place, refused to comply with the summons, and the town was immediately invested. The French general determined to attemptto take it by assault; but the weakest part was on the other side of the Weser, and he had neither boats nor pontoons to affect the passage of that river. A reconnoitering party, however, found by chance a float of timber, by the help whereof Fischer's Corps with 300 volunteers immediately crossed over, and attacked the head of the bridge, while M. de Broglio favored the attack by a brisk cannonade on this side. They at last forced that port, and entered the town about 9 o'clock in the evening. General Zastrow with the garrison, consisting of a Hessian battalion and some piquets of different corps, amounting in the whole to 1,500 men were made prisoners of war. The enemy found there a considerable magazine. The taking of this town was of the greatest importance to the French, as they thereby secured the passage of the Weser, and opened to themselves a free inlet into the country of Hanover. M. de Contades removed his headquarters, on the 10th, from Bielefeld to Herford, having a part of his army at Gohfeld.

ON the 10th, His Serene Highness decamped also from Osnabrück, and marched to Bohmte. Here he received the account of the loss of Minden. He immediately

42. Editor: Stadburg is probably Landbergen.
43. Editor: Engeren is probably Enger.

determined to halt there the next day, and sent forward a detachment of about 10,000 men, together with all the light troops, under the command of the Crown Prince, in order to secure the post of Stolzenau. The light troops of this party, commanded by M. Fredericks, on their march thither fell in with a party of 500 French infantry, headed by M. de Villars, between Diepenau and Stolzenau. He immediately at-tacked and defeated them, killed and wounded a considerable number of them, and made 200 prisoners. When they had advanced somewhat farther, they perceived another party of 600 French cavalry filing off through a hollow way near the village of Holzhausen. M. Fredericks immediately gave orders to the Prussian hussars to attack them in front, while he should attack them in the rear with his jägers and cut off their retreat from the village. These dispositions succeeded so well, that 200 of the enemy were killed, and the remaining 400 made prisoners, together with the Count des Salos, their commanding officer.

COLONEL Freytag continued his incursions with great success and being reinforced with some light troops advanced farther into Hesse; they even proceeded as far as Kassel surprising the little town of Wiltzenhausen in the neighborhood of that place, making the garrison prisoners of war. The French who were posted in Münden, finding themselves too weak to defend that place, abandoned it, and retired to Kassel. A reinforcement of two battalions was sent into that country from the main army of the French.

THE Allied Army marched on the 13th to Rhaden, and on the 14th, proceeded to Stolzenau, where the headquarters were fixed. On the 14th, that part of the French army which was at Gohfeld[44] marched to Minden, and on the 16th, M. de Contades arrived there with the remainder. M. d'Armentières remained before Münster; the Duke de Chevreuse was sent to invest Lippstadt with three battalions, three squadrons, and some light troops. M. de Broglio passed the Weser, taking a position on the road to Bückeburg; Fischer's Corps made incursions into Hanover, and their other light troops extended as far as Osnabrück, of which place the French had possessed themselves.

His Serene Highness, having received notice that the French had a design of seizing on, the town of Bremen, determined to be beforehand with them, and accordingly sent four battalions under the command of General Dreves to garrison that place, who arrived there on the 15th.

JULY 16, Prince Ferdinand was informed that M. de Contades was this day filing off towards Minden, and that M. de Broglio was posted on the other side of the Weser. Having, therefore, well considered their situation, he imagined that with diligence and secrecy he might be able to attack and force them before their junction. For this purpose, he ordered the army to march on the night between the 16th and 17th, in three columns, from the camp of Stolzenau to Petershagen Heath. When he came there, he found the enemy posted behind the Minden morass, with their right descended by the town of Minden, and their left extending to a mountain near the village of Hartenhausen. As this position would not permit him to attack them with any prospect of success, he encamped the army with its right to Bruninghogstede, and its left inclining to the Weser, taking up his quarters at Offenstede in the rear of the left wing.

44. Editor: Today Gohfeld is part of Löhne.

THE body of troops commanded by Prince Charles of Bevern, consisting of five battalions of grenadiers and eight squadrons of Hessian dragoons, together with General Wangenheim's corps composed of eight battalions and ten squadrons of Hanoverians, formed the vanguard of the whole army under the orders of the Crown Prince of Brunswick. This vanguard formed the head of the center column (which was composed of the heavy train of artillery); and after it had passed the village of Eldhausen, drew up in order of battle near the Petershagen Wood, where it also encamped the same day.

THE 17th, Prince Ferdinand being informed that a large body of the enemy were encamped on this side the morass, gave orders for the troops to hold themselves in readiness to march; and early in the morning a detachment of the enemy, consisting of some grenadiers and horse, was driven out of a wood in the front of the Prince of Bevern's camp; the Crown Prince ordered the whole vanguard (which was supported by the piquets of the army) to advance into the Minden plain, where they formed in the front of the villages of Todtenhausen, Kutenhausen, and Stemmer[45]; the infantry in the rear of the cavalry, and the hussars upon the left.

THIS motion obliged a body of the enemy posted in the front of Minden to retire under the cannon of the town.

His Serene Highness Prince Ferdinand went forward to examine the position of the enemy, whilst the whole Allied Army was ordered to advance in nine columns towards the Minden plain.

THE first column was composed of the cavalry of the right wing; the second, of the brigade of heavy artillery of the right wing; the third and fourth, of the infantry of the right wing, the fifth, of the brigade of heavy artillery of the center, the sixth and seventh, of the infantry of the left wing; the eighth, of the brigade of heavy artillery of the left wing; and the ninth column, of the cavalry of the left wing.

THE army formed its line of battle behind the village of Todtenhausen, with its right to the village of Südfelde, and its left to the wood near the Weser. In this situation it remained 'till 4 o'clock in the afternoon, when orders were given to march back into the old camp, as the position of the enemy was different from what it had been the evening before.

THE enemy had information of the above march of the Allied Army by 11 o'clock at night, and in consequence thereof had, in the night, struck their tents, entirely altered their position, and withdrawn all their troops that were on this side the morass, excepting some advanced parties, and by 4 o'clock were in order of battle, excellently posted in an advantageous situation behind the morass: the Duke de Broglio, who had received orders to pass the river with all diligence, had also joined them; but he again re-passed the river the same night when all was quiet, encamping with his right to Meussen, and his left to the Weser. The same day the enemy altered the position of their left wing, extending it to the foot of the mountains near Uphausen.

45. Today these towns are part of the city of Minden

As soon as Prince Ferdinand had brought his army back to their camp, General Wangenheim's corps took up its old position; but that of the Prince of Bevern encamped behind Todtenhausen; a battalion of grenadiers was posted in that village, whilst the hussars took post between Kutenhausen and Stemmer, and the grand guard was advanced before Todtenhausen.

THE 18th, Wangenheim's corps took post before Todtenhausen: the headquarters were transferred to Petershagen, and a detachment of 500 foot, and 50 horse, were posted at the village of Friedewaldee.

THE same day a smart skirmish happened near Lippstadt, between the Karabiniers of Bückeburg and a party of French *volontaires*, in which the latter were dispersed.

THE 19th, the piquets of the army were posted in the village of Stemmer and Holzhausen; and the same night they attacked the enemy's hussars, who had taken post at Hille, and made 40 prisoners.

THE 20th, His Serene Highness Prince Ferdinand ordered openings to be made through the dyke of the Landwehr, from Holzhausen to Todtenhausen, in order to facilitate the army's entering the plain of Minden by squadrons and grand divisions.

M. d'Armentières received this day his heavy artillery from Wesel, and the batteries were opened against Münster; the garrison quit the town on the 22d, and retired into the citadel.

THE 21St, the piquets of the infantry were posted at Nordhammeren, Holzhausen, and Stemmer; those of the cavalry between Friedewaldee and Holzhausen.

THE 22d, Wangenheim's corps changed its position, the cavalry encamped upon the right, and the infantry on the left of the grenadiers under the Prince of Bevern; the brigade of heavy artillery of the left, with Bückeburg's Regiment, encamped near the windmill before Petershagen, in which village Kielmannsegg's remained 'till the 1st of August.

THE 24th, the bridge of boats near Offenstede was perfected, and the two battalions of Hanoverian grenadiers posted in the villages of Wietersheim and Jössen[46], under the command of Colonel Laferd, were ordered to protect it.

ON the 25th of July, the citadel of Münster surrendered by capitulation; the Governor, Lieutenant General Zastrow, with the garrison, consisting of 3,100 men, were all made prisoners of war. M. d'Armentières immediately after the reduction of this place, proceeded to Lippstadt to besiege it in form, and M. de Chevreuse, who had invested the same, returned to the French main army.

THE 27th in the afternoon, the Crown Prince set off from the camp at Petershagen with six battalions, viz. Zastrow senior, Diepenbrock, Behr, Bock, and the two battalions of the Brunswick Regiment du corps, together with eight Hanoverian squadrons of von dem Bussche and Bock, and marched towards Lübbecke: the same day the battalion of

46. Editor: Today Wietersheim and Jössen are part of Petershagen.

Bückeburg with the brigade of heavy artillery of the left, took a camp in the rear of the grenadiers.

THE 28th Gilsa's Regiment joined the army from Stolzenau.

THE French having pushed forward a party towards Vechta, in order to block up the small garrison which defended it, Prince Ferdinand determined to relieve that place, and for that purpose sent M. de Schlieffen with 40 hussars, supported by 200 of Breidenbach's dragoons, who effected the same; General Dreves marched thither from Bremen with the garrison of that town, and was joined by M. de Schlieffen; they then proceeded to Osnabrück, where the Volontaires de Clermont were in garrison. M. de Schlieffen forced one of these gates and made himself master of the place; the *volontaires* lost some men, and two pieces of cannon, in the attack and in their retreat.

THE 29th, the army marched in three columns by the right from Petershagen camp to that of Hille; Prince Ferdinand led the first column, composed of the first line, the heavy artillery, conducted by the Count of Lippe-Bückeburg formed the second column, and General Spörcken led the third, composed of the second line. The army took its camp between Hille and Friedewald, having the villages of Nord, Hemmeren, and Holzhausen in its front; the headquarters were at Hille, and covered by the Napier and Kingsley Regiments. A disposition was made of the piquets of the army; the British were posted in the village of Hartum; the Hanoverians in Sud Hemmeren, the Hessians in the wood between Hartum and Holzhausen; those of Brunswick were in Stemmer, and the cavalry piquets were in the woods, with a detachment upon the road from Hartum to Hahlen.

THE two brigades of light British artillery assigned to the piquets, and the Generals of the day were ordered to Hartum.

IN order to conceal the march of the army, General Wangenheim's corps was formed under arms near the batteries Count Bückeburg had erected before Todtenhausen; and when those troops went back to camp, the Bückeburg Regiment, with the brigade of heavy artillery of the left wing, encamped in the front of the line.

THIS day His Serene Highness desired all the general officers to inform themselves very exactly of the several passages and routes through which the army was to march into the plain of Minden, and to make themselves perfect in them, in case the army should be ordered to advance.

THE 30th in the afternoon, the three battalions (1 each of the Linstow, Prince Charles, and the first of Behr (Brunswick) Regiments) marched from camp, under the command of General Gilsa, to take post at Lübbecke, where they were joined the next day by a detachment of 300 horse of the right wing.

THE 31st in the afternoon, His Serene Highness renewed his orders to all the generals, who were to lead the columns, to examine in person those routes which their respective columns were to take in order to get into the plain of Minden, and particularly to examine the ground between the windmill of Hahlen[47] and the village of Stemmern, where the army was to form in order of battle.

47. Editor: Today Hahlen is part of the city of Minden.

JULY 31st, M. de Contades, who had written to Paris for that purpose, obtained leave to engage the Allied Army, and having considered his situation, judged it to be a convenient juncture to attack the corps under General Wangenheim, which he thought he should be able to effect before it could be supported by the main body, from which it was detached above two leagues; he also knew the Allied Army was weakened by the large detachment under the Crown Prince; he therefore determined to pass the defile at Minden, contrary to the advice of the Duke de Broglio, and for that purpose the enemy were taken up all that day in throwing eight bridges over the rivulets which run between the morass and the town of Minden; about midnight they came out of their camp in eight columns: at the same time the Duke de Broglio's corps repassed the Weser at Minden, and formed the ninth column upon the right of their army.

AUGUST 1ST, the Crown Prince, who had been detached on the 27th, marched that evening towards Lübbecke, and in the morning of the 28th, dislodged the enemy who occupied that post, on the 29th, he marched to Riemsloh[48], where he was joined by General Dreves from Osnabrück; on the 30th, he advanced towards Herford, and on the 31st he took post at Kirchlengern, which lay in the road of the enemy's convoys from Paderborn.

THE Duke de Brissac, who commanded a detachment from the French army consisting of about 8,000 men, had the same evening taken post near Gohfeld, encamping with their left to that village, and their right towards the salt pits, with the Werra River in their front. The Prince determined to attack them the next morning; but as their position was impregnable in front, there was no other way to come at them but by surrounding their left, for which purpose the following dispositions were made: Three attacks were formed, all of which were to depend on the success of that on the right; the troops destined for that attack consisted of a battalion of Diepenbrock, two of the Brunswick Guards, 200 volunteers, and four squadrons of Boch's Dragoons, the four battalions of Alt Zastrow, Behr, Block, and Kanitz, and one squadron of Charles Breidenbach, with all the heavy cannon, composed the center; the left was formed of three battalions, Block, Dreves, and Zastrow, and of four squadrons of Von dem Bussche: the troops of the center were designed to keep the enemy at bay, whilst those of the right should surround their left; those of our left were to march to the bridge near the salt pits, in order to prevent the enemy's retreat to Minden.

THE Crown Prince marched with the right, Count Kielmannsegg was in the center, and M. de Dreves and M. de Bock brought up the left: they set out at 3 o'clock in the morning from their camp at Quernon[49]. The enemy, on their part, likewise intended to attack us: as soon as Count Kielmannsegg had come out of the Beck Defile[50], the enemy presented themselves before him, and a cannonade began on both sides; the right was to pass the Werra, in order to turn the enemy's left at the village of Kirchlengern, upon a very narrow bridge, this difficulty however was in some measure removed by the spirit of the troops, the infantry fording the river partly behind the horsemen, and partly in peasants' wagons.

48. Editor: Today part of the city of Melle.
49. Editor: This may be Quernheim, which today is part of Kirchlengern.
50. Editor: Beck is today called Obernbeck, part of Löhne.

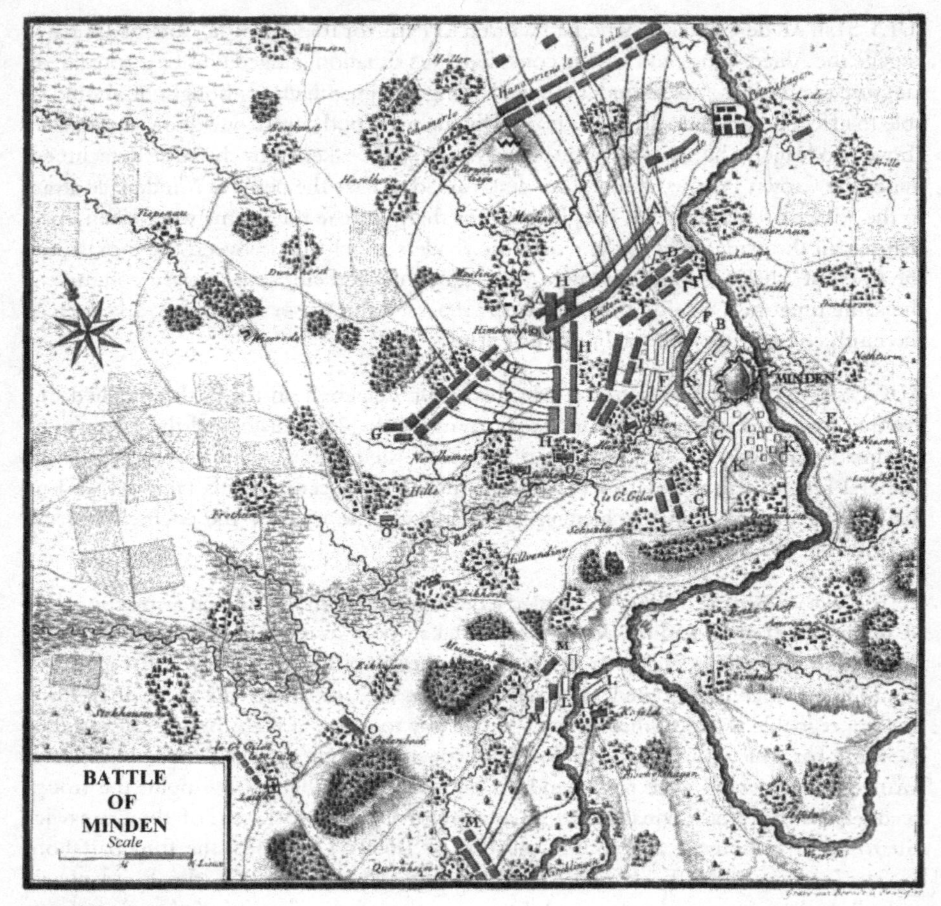

KEY TO MAP.

A Prince Ferdinand's army on 17 July reconnoitering the French army,

B which retired,

C and he cannonaded it in is retreat & returned afterwards to his camp.

D Troops of General Wangenheim to cover Tonhausen.

E De Broglie's reserve, which joined the French army on 31 July at C. The French army debouched on 1 August in eight columns and arranged itself in battle formation with

F The infantry on the wings, and the cavalry in the center in three lines, its right on the Weser and left on Halen, which it captured, then it attacked the posts of Eickhorst, Eickhusen, and Gelenbeck, and cannonaded Hille, headquarters of the Duke of Brunswick.

G Hanoverian army comes out of the Petershagen camp, on 29 July, to encamp at Friedewalde. It debouches in eight columns at 5:00 a.m., on 1 August, and forms

H	between Hemern and Hartum.
I	3rd position of Hanoverian Army, which forced the French to retire to K.
K	New French position.
L	French detachment commanded by the Duke de Brissac, which retired on 31 July from Kirchlingen.
M	Corps of the Herediary Prince, which obliged the Duc de Brissac to retire.
N	Hanoverians after the battle.
O	Detached Hanoverian corps that Maréchal de Contades attacked before the battle.
NB	The action began about 9:00 a.m. and finished at noon.

By the passage of the Werra, the position of the enemy was entirely changed; the fire of the artillery was brisk on both sides, and lasted for two hours, though ours had always the superiority: at last, upon our showing ourselves upon their rear, they immediately gave way, and in their filing off came upon the skirts of M. de Bock, who received them with a discharge of artillery, which was well supported; when, finding themselves entirely surrounded, they had no other resource but in flight. Five pieces of the enemy's cannon, with their baggage, fell into our hands; their losses in killed and wounded was very considerable, and a great number were made prisoners. Lieutenant General Kielmannsegg deserved the highest commendation: M. Otte, Colonel of Alt Zastrow's, distinguished himself greatly at the head of his regiment, and repulsed the enemy's cavalry, that fell upon him, with considerable loss. Our loss was very flight; Captain Wegner of the artillery was wounded in the leg: to him and to Major Storck was owing the good service we had from the artillery.

IN this action, which was of infinite consequence at that juncture, the Crown Prince displayed the talents of an able general in the disposition of the troops under his command; and the whole was concerted and executed with the greatest judgment and spirit. An enemy, at least equal, if not superior, in numbers, was forced from a post so advantageous and strong as to be deemed almost impregnable and obliged to fly with the utmost precipitation. But however shining this action was in itself, yet it was in some measure eclipsed and swallowed up by that glorious and ever memorable victory gained on the same day over the combined armies of M. de Contades and the Duke de Broglio by His Serene Highness Prince Ferdinand, a victory of such importance, as entirely defeated the French views, disconcerted all their schemes, and rescued Hanover, Brunswick, and Hesse, from the rapacious hands of a cruel, ambitious, and elated enemy who, puffed up by their late progress, thought themselves certain of their prey, which they had already in imagination devoured. What a sensible mortification, then must this decisive stroke have given to the insolent pride and vanity of M. de Contades, who, trusting to his great superiority of numbers, publicly vaunted on the day before the battle, that he would in two days' time enclose Prince Ferdinand and his army, and send their capitulation to the Court of Versailles!

ABOUT 5 o'clock in the morning of the 1st of August, the whole French army was formed in order of battle upon the plain. The Duke de Broglio's reserve came close to the Weser: the cavalry occupied the heath in the center, and the infantry of the left extended to the morass near the village of Hahlen; His Serene Highness Prince Ferdinand (who had ordered his army to hold itself ready to march at 1 o'clock in the morning) began to move out of his camp in eight columns about five. The cavalry of the right wing formed the first; the heavy artillery of the right wing the second, the infantry of the right the third and fourth, the heavy artillery of the center the fifth, the infantry of the left wing the sixth and seventh, and the eighth column consisted of the cavalry of the left wing.

GENERAL Wangenheim's corps, having moved out of its camp much about the same time through the openings already made in the Landwehr Dyke, was soon formed in order of battle. The grenadiers were posted upon the right of the batteries of Todtenhausen, the eight battalions of infantry in the hedges of Kutenhausen upon the right of the grenadiers, and the 18 squadrons of ca-valry in the open fields upon the right of the infantry.

AT three in the morning, the enemy began with cannonading the village of Hille, where Prince Ferdinand had his headquarters, from a battery of six pieces of cannon, erected the day before on the Eickhorst Causeway, which led through the morass to Hille. Opposite to this place they had also posted some troops with orders to make a false attack on that side, with an intent to favor their real one on our left, but not on any account to pass the morass until our army should give way. They were, however, disappointed in their scheme of drawing our attention to that quarter; for His Serene Highness, judging their intention, contented himself with sending thither two pieces of heavy cannon, and enjoined the officers of the piquets posted at Hille to defend it 'till the last extremity; and at the same time General Gilsa, who was posted at Lübbecke, was to attack the enemy at Eickhorst.

WHILE the army was in march to form itself, the enemy began to cannonade the batteries of Todtenhausen and General Wangenheim's corps.

BETWEEN six and 7 o'clock, the Allied Army began to take up its ground in order of battle, having its right to the enclosures between the villages of Hartum and Hahlen, and its left towards Stemmer.

THE piquets of the army, under the command of the Prince of Anhalt, as lieutenant-general of the day, were drawn up in the front of the cavalry of the right wing near to Hahlen; and from them were detached the piquets of the infantry, with two howitzers, to get possession of Hahlen, where the enemy had thrown two battalions during the night.

ABOUT 7 O'CLOCK, after the cavalry of the right wing was formed, the French began to fire from a battery, which raked our column of artillery upon its march.

As soon as the infantry of the right wing was drawn up behind a fir wood, the two brigades of British foot, the Hanoverian Guards, and Hardenberg's Regiment, marched forward to attack the left of the enemy's cavalry, having bore for about 150 paces a very smart cannonading from a large battery of the enemy, the fire of which was crossed by another battery at Malbergen[51]: but notwithstanding the losses they sustained before they could get up to the enemy, notwithstanding the repeated attacks of all the enemy's cavalry, notwithstanding a fire of musketry well kept up by the enemy's infantry, notwithstanding their being exposed in front and flank, such was the unshaken firmness of those troops that nothing could stop them; and the whole body of the French cavalry was totally routed.

THE Saxon troops, which were on the left of the French cavalry, near their large battery, made a show of coming down upon these conquering regiments, after the French horse had gone off; but the good countenance of the British foot, and the sharp fire they kept upon them, soon obliged the Saxons to fly. The brigade of infantry, commanded by Major General Scheele, detached from the center of the army by order of His Serene Highness to support the piquets in the village of Hahlen, with Wangenheim's Battalion and Hessian Guards, likewise was detached to support the English, at the conclusion of this attack, which came in near the right of the British infantry, and also fired upon the Saxons.

DURING this attack upon our right one of our batteries silenced that of the enemy which had so much annoyed our infantry, obliging it to be withdrawn. At the same time, the attack upon our left was concluded with like success, and the enemy's batteries at Malbergen were taken. In this attack the Regiments du Corps and Hammerstein (Hanoverian horse), the Holstein Regiment (Prussian), and the Hessian horse and battalions of grenadiers, signalized themselves prodigiously.

GENERAL Wangenheim's corps maintained almost the same position during the whole action.

THE batteries erected under the care of Count von Lippe von Bückeburg, Grand Master of the Artillery, in the front of Todtenhausen, contributed greatly to decide the fortune of the day; he having by that battery which was before the grenadiers, totally extinguished the fire of the enemy's batteries on their right, and made, at the same time, great havoc among the Swiss and grenadiers de France.

ABOUT 9 o'clock in the morning the enemy began to give way, a general confusion soon followed, and about 10:00 a.m., the whole French army fled in disorder, part took shelter under cover of the cannon of Minden, and the rest made the best of their way over the bridges they had thrown over the rivulets between that town and the morass, every one of which they broke down as soon as they had passed over for fear of being pursued.

THE Duke de Broglio covered the retreat; he occupied with his infantry the gardens near Minden, soon after which his cavalry followed the main body of their army.

TOWARDS the end of the battle the artillery of the right was pushed forward as close as possible to the enemy posted near the wood of Dützen, who were part of those

51. Editor: Malbergen has, apparently completely disappeared, but may have been absorbed into Minderheide, a quarter of Minden. If so, the only trace that remains of it is a street named "Maulbeerkamp."

battalions our piquets had drove out of the village of Hahlen, to which, in their retreat, they had set fire.

PART of the French army having retired into its old camp, His Serene Highness commanded the British artillery to advance as near the morass as possible to dislodge them; this order was executed, and the enemy was, in consequence thereof, obliged to retire behind the high ground whereon Hands the windmill of Dützen, with their right extending towards the Weser.

GENERAL Gilsa's corps that had been detached to Lübbecke, pushed forward over the morass by Eickhorst as high as the French camp, driving before it all the posts which the enemy had remaining on that side.

IN this last position they stopped some time, and were beginning to retreat by Wittekindesberg to Herford; but meeting with the shattered remains of the Duke of Brissac's corps flying from Gohfeld over the mountains, and seeing their retreat by that road cut off, they were under the necessity of returning and crossing the Weser over the bridges they had made, under the cannon of Minden. They burnt the bridges as soon as they got over.

THE cavalry which was posted on our right did not engage this day, as they were destined to support the infantry of the left line. When the enemy began to retreat, they were ordered to move forward, to pursue the flying troops of the enemy, but through some mistake they did not come up in time and were thereby prevented from reaping that share of glory which they might otherwise have done.

THE victorious army encamped the same night upon the field of battle, the headquarters being fixed at Suderhimmen. The loss of the Allies in this action amounted to about 2,800 killed and wounded, of which number the British troops alone made 1,394. We lost no officers of distinction. That of the French consisted of between 7,000 and 8,000 killed, wounded, and made prisoners in the action; the Prince de Camille was amongst the number of the slain; the Count von Lutterberg, and the Marquis de Monit, Maréchaux de Camp, with several other officers of principal rank, were among the prisoners. The trophies gained were 43 pieces of cannon, ten pairs of colors, and seven standards. Such was the signal and glorious victory of Minden (also called "Todtenhausen"), where the intrepid bravery of the troops, their resolute and undaunted countenances during the whole action, (not one platoon giving way) gained them immortal honor.

BRITISH TROOPS AT THE BATTLE OF MINDEN

Cavalry	**Infantry**
Bland	Napier
Inniskilling	Stuart
Blues	Welsh Fusiliers
Horse Grenadiers	Kingsley
Howard	Brundenell
Mordaunt	Holme
Greys	British Grenadiers

HANOVERIAN TROOPS AT THE BATTLE OF MINDEN

Cavalry	Infantry
Von dem Bussche	Hanoverian Guards
Bredenbach	Hardenberg
Gardes du Corps	Linstow
Hammerstein	Reden
Bock	Scheele
Bremer	Wangenheim
Eltheim	Saxe Gotha
Regiment du Corps	Alt Zastrow
Reden	Diepenbroeck
Heise	Behr
Hodenberg	Brock
Grothhaus	Stolzenberg
	Brunck
	Hanoverian Grenadiers
	Spörcken
	Jung Zastrow
	Halberstadt
	Schulenburg
	Oberg

HESSIAN TROOPS AT THE BATTLE OF MINDEN

Cavalry	Infantry
Prince Wilhelm	Hessian Grenadiers
Regiment du Corps	Prince Karl
Prussian	Dolle
Miltiz	Gilsa
Dragoons du corps	Marshsbach
Prince Friedrich	Hessian Guards
	Erbprinz
	Prinz Wilhelm (Hanau)
	Bischhausen
	Anhalt
	Leib Regiment
	Hessian Grenadiers

PRUSSIAN TROOPS AT THE BATTLE OF MINDEN

Cavalry	Infantry
Holstein	Behr
Finckenstein	Regiment du Corps
	Brunswick
	Imhoff
	Brunswick Grenadiers
	Bückeburg Regiment

LIST OF THE FRENCH OFFICERS WOUNDED AND TAKEN PRISONERS IN THE BATTLE OF AUGUST 1, 1759, AT MINDEN

Staff Officers: Marquis de Monti, *Maréchal de camp.* Count de Bouflers, Marquis de Coudray, *Brigadiers of the King's Armies.* M. de Segur, *Aide-de-camp.*

Grenadiers de France. Prince Chimelle, *Colonel* de Monjene, Count de la Faget, de Monjene, de Barche, *Captains.* Count de Villers, Chevalier de Freta, de Beussen, de Serting, de Cara Mentran, Bute, la Bocassière, de Cretini, de la Varenne, Richard, Villars, de Sotomajor, de la Palomnière, *Lieutenants.* Comeias, *Aide major.*

Gens d'Armes. Count de Fougières, Count de la Hage, Marquis de Murinais, *Colonels.* Count de la Rivière, d'Eschoisy, de Mamesville, de Grally, *Lieutenant Colonels.* Marquis de Tracy, *Captain-Lieutenant and Colonel.* Marquis Canisy, *Lieutenant and Colonel.* Marquis de Cannesis, Chevalier de l'Argle, Count de Custinière, *Sous-lieutenants and Colonels.* Count d'Egreville, *Coronet and Colonel.* Marquis de Crenol, Count de Noé, de Lambersye, *Ensigns and Lieutenant Colonels.* Count de Herbouville, *Captain-Lieutenant and Brigadier of the Army.* Count d'Eselignac, *Brigdier of the King's Army, and Coronet.* Count de Lannnoi, *Captain and Brigaider.* Dauvent, Ensign and Brigadier. du Moulet, *Ensign.*

Carabiniers. Marquis de Beauvet, *Brigadier.* Chevalier de Commbeaut, de Mogazin, de la Plance, Olier, *Captains.* Chevalier de Foix, *Lieutenant.* d'Ulle Pedrix, d'Orcet, du Beautie, de Musi, *Coronets.*

Régiment d'Aumont. St. Tour, Chevalier de Carrière, *Captains.* de Montfort, de Bonnemore, Lagobertie, Chevalier de Page, La Jaubertie, de Chali, Descombes, de Salos de Jone, Chevalier Aulmman, *Lieutenants.*

Régiment d'Aquitaine. de Mondomin, Chevalier de la Rousslet *Captains.*

Régiment de Vatan. Marquis de Vatan, *Colonel.* Chevalier de Madron, Captain. de la Rocque *Aide-major.*

Régiment de Touraine. St. Julien, de Villemontes, de Mongion, Dutrat, Delaier, Dubrat, Maillard, Chevlaier Denvie, de Senasse, *Captains.* Casaut, Duvents, Corbier, Gerat *Lieutenants.*

Régiment de Gotha. Boserne, Burgsdorff, *Lieutenants.* Gorsehen, *Ensign.*

Régiment de Marcien. de Massillon, Marquis de Montiers, *Captains.* de la Brassière, *Lieutenant.*

Régiment de Rochefaucault. de Varcourt, de Cardliac, *Captains.* De Toulongon, *Cornet.*

Régiment Royal Deux-Ponts. de Neuland, *First Captain.*

Régiment Colonel général. de Montière, Chevalier de Perignat, *Captains.* Chevalier du Four, de Clapion, *Lieutenants.*

Régiment Mestre de Camp. de Burville, *Major.* Vicent, *Lieutenant.* Lamagier, Marschil, *Cornets.*

Régiment Rovergue. de Perrin, de la Baissiene, Darbois, Caussiers, de Lerubard, du Petit, Thouar, de St. Cirque, *Captains.* de Montagne, *Lieutenant.* Chaubon, *Aide-major.*

Régiment Enghien. Lantin de Moncois, *Captain.* de Trouril, de Sablaunet, *Lieutenants.*

Régiment de Charite. du Mazon, *Captain.*

Régiment Royal Italien. de Senesi, *Captain.*

Régiment du Rochau [Saxon]. von Hayne.

Régiment de Tournassis. de Richeburg, de Lenel, de Pierraul, *Captains.*

Régiment de Walder [Swiss]. François de Milliet, *Major.*

Régiment Richemont. Chevalier de Bitune, *Captain.*

Régiment Belsunce. de Vanquet, *Lieutenant.*

Régiment de la Marche. La Chassaine, Chevalier de Perrat, *Lieuteuants.*

Régiment de Condé. Chevalier de Villson, *Captain.*

Régiment de Bouillon. Marquis de Foudrass, *Captain.*

Régiment de Champagne. Cunion, *Lieutenant.*

Régiment de la Dauphine. de la Tour, *Captain.*

Régiment de Planta. de Wesby, *Captain.*

Régiment de Piémont. Cati, *Captain.*

Régiment de Poli. Boischarrant, *Lieutenant.*

Régiment du roi. de Lanoi, *Captain.*

Régiment de Schomberg. Flacke, *Cornet.*

Régiment de Massel. de Condale, *Captain.*

Régiment de Montier. Limon, *Lieutenant.*

Artillery. Chevalier de Tacher, *1st Lieutenant.* Dangers, *Lieutenant.*

Prince of Saxony Regiment. Vittinghoff, *Captain,* Hauche, *Lieutenant.*

Régiment de Tallerand. Chevalier de Tallerand, *Captain.* Bricaul, *Lieutenant.* de Staaga, Graville, *Cornets.*

Régiment de Planta. Nesmy, *Captain.*

Régiment de Salle. La Vogere, *Cornet.*

Régiment d'Auvergne. La Borde Albuse, Dupra Duamac, *Lieutenants.*

Régiment des volontaires du Dauphine. La Brelinaière, *Lieutenant..*

Régiment Royal Etranger. Delut, *Lieutenant.*

Nassau Hussars. Karl Sperber, *Cornet.*

Régiment des Chevaux légers de la reine. Marquis de Marray.

Non-Commissioned Officers

Gens d'Armes	6	Gens d'Armes de la reine	5
Scotch	33	Chevaux léger de la reine	3
English	7	Gens d'Armes de Dauphine	2
Burgundy	1	Chevaux léger de Dauphine	6
Light Horse of Burgundy	14	Gens d'Armes de Berry	3
Gens d'Armes	4	Chevaux léger de Berry	4
Light Horse of Acquitaine	3	Gens d'Armes de Orléans	3
Gens d'Armes of Acquitaine	1	Chevaux léger de Orléans	10
Gens d'Armes of Burgundy	3		
Total Non-Commissioned Officers			79

LIST OF THE KILLED, WOUNDED, AND MISSING IN HIS MAJESTY'S SIX REGIMENTS OF BRITISH INFANTRY AND ARTILLERY IN THE BATTLE OF MINDEN

12th Regiment; Major general Napier. Killed, FalkingHamm, Probyn, Townshend, Lieutenants; 4 Sergeants, 1 drummer, 77 rank and file. Wounded, Lieutenant Colonel Robinson; Murray, Clowdesly, Campbell, Captains; Dunbar, Captain Lieutenant; Fletcher Barlow, Lawless, Freeman, Campbell, Rose, Lieutenants; Forbes, Parkell, Kay, Ensigns; 11 Sergeants, 4 drummers, 175 rank and file. Missing, Chalbert and Ackland, Captains; 11 rank and file.

20th Regiment, Major General Kingsley. Killed, Frierson, Stewart, Cowley, Captains; Brown, Norbury, Lieutenants; Crawford, Ensign; 1 Sergeant, 79 rank and file. Wounded, Grey, Parr, Tennnent, Captains; Parry, Captain Lieutenant; Luke, Nugent, Thompson, Denshire, Boswell, Lieutenants; Erwin, Dent, Renton, Ensigns; 12 Sergeants, 212 rank and file.

23rd Regiment, Lieutenant Colonel Huske. Killed, 4 Sergeants, 31 rank and file. Wounded, Pole, Lieutenant Colonel; Fowler, Fox, Captains; Bolton, Captain Lieutenant; Barber, Reynell, Patterson, Groves, 1st Lieutenants; Ferguson, 2nd Lieutenant; 6 Sergeannts, 3 drummers, 153 rank and file. Missing, 10 rank and file.

25th Regiment, Lieutenant General Earl Home. Killed, 1 Sergeant, 18 rank and file. Wounded, Gore, Captain; A. Campbell, Sterrop, Wilson, Lieutenants; Pintard, Edgar, Lockhardt, Ensigns; 4 Sergeants, 115 rank and file. Missing, 9 rank and file.

37th Regiment, Lieutenant General Stuart. Killed, Green, Lieutenant and Adjutant; 1 Sergeant, 42 rank and file. Wounded, Cliffe, Bayley, Blunt, Greme, Parkhurst, Lord Viscount Allen, Captains; Smith, Barbutt, Spencer, Slorach, Hamilton, Lieutenants; Elliom Ensign; 4 Sergeants, 4 drummers, 180 rank and file. Died of their wounds, Hutchinson, Captain Lieutenant; Brome, Lieutenant. Missing, 22 rank and file.

51st Regiment, Colonel Brundenell. Killed, Widdows, Lieutenant and Adjutant; 20 rank and file. Wounded, Furey, Lieutenant Colonel; Montgomery, Blaire, Donnellan, Walker, Captains; Gordon, Knollis, Green, Lieutenants; Peake, Ensign; 3 Sergeants, 75 rank and file. Missing, 1 Sergeant, 4 rank and file.

Royal Regiment of Artillery. Killed, 2 rank and file. Wounded, Rogers, Harrington, Lieutenants; 1 Sergeant, 9 rank and file. Missing, Carden, Lieutenant; 2 rank and file.

TOTAL

Killed	3	Captains	Wounded	3	Lieutenant Colonels
	7	Lieutenants		23	Captains
	2	Ensigns		28	Lieutenants
	22	Sergeants		12	Ensigns
	2	Drummer		41	Sergeants
	269	Rank and File		11	Drummers
				919	Rank and File
Missing	2	Captains	Dead of wounds	1	Captain Lieutenant
	2	Lieutenants		1	Lieutenant
	1	Sergeant			
	58	Rank and File			

ONE of the consequences of the victory gained over the Duke de Brissac by the Crown Prince was, the preventing the French from making their retreat by the way of Paderborn, as was their intention, where they had considerable magazines; and they were forced to retreat through countries in which they had no subsistence but such as they could pick up upon the road.

IT is the custom in Germany the morning after a battle to draw out all the troops. Accordingly, His Serene Highness Prince Ferdinand, on the 2d of August by 6 o'clock in the morning, had all the army drawn up on the field of battle, with the artillery in the center, which, by way of rejoicing, fired, and the soldiers in rank followed; after which the following orders were issued out.

THE army to be under arms at 6 o'clock this afternoon to fire a *feu de joie*. The brigades of heavy artillery are to take their posts on the wings and in the front: the three brigade troops of light artillery are to join the heavy, viz. Captain Drummond's brigade, with Major Hasle's upon its right; Bückeburg's brigade on the left of the center brigade of heavy artillery; Captain Foy's brigade on the right of Colonel Hutte's. When the order is given for firing it will be continued for three rounds, beginning upon the right, first the artillery, then the army; the order of firing as follows: 1st, the Saxe-Gotha Regiment a volley, 2d, Captain Phillips's brigade, 3d, Major Hasle's, 4th, Captain Drummond's brigade, 5th, the heavy and light artillery of the center brigade, 6th, Captain Foy's brigade, 7th, Lieutenant Colonel Hutte's brigade, 8th, Bückeburg Regiment and grenadiers, a volley then the first line from right to left, followed by the second from left to right; the cannon taken from the enemy to be placed with the center brigade of heavy artillery, and to fire with it.

His Serene Highness orders his greatest thanks to be given to the whole army for their bravery and good behavior yesterday, particularly to the British infantry, and to the two battalions of Hanoverian Guards; to all the cavalry of the left wing; and to General Wangenheim's corps, particularly the Holstein Regiment, the Hessian cavalry; the Hanoverian Regiment du Corps, and Hammerstein's; the same to all the brigades of heavy artillery: His Serene Highness declares publicly, that, next to God, he attributes the glory of the day to the intrepidity and extraordinary good behavior of these troops, which he assures them he shall retain the strongest sense of as long as he lives; and if ever, upon any occasion, he shall be able to serve these brave troops, or any one of them in particular, it will give him the utmost pleasure. His Serene Highness orders his particular thanks to be likewise, given to General Spörcken and the Duke of Holstein, Lieutenant-Generals Imhoff and d'Urff; His Serene Highness is extremely obliged to the Count de Bückeburg for all his care and trouble in the management of the artillery, which was served with great effect; likewise to the commanding officers of the several brigades of artillery; viz, Colonel Brown, Lieutenant Colonel Hutte, Major Hasle, and the three English Captains, Phillips, Drummond, and Foye: His Serene Highness thinks himself infinitely obliged to Major-Generals Waldgrave and Kingsley for their great courage and good order in which they conducted their brigades, His Serene Highness further orders it to be declared to Lieutenant General the Marquis of Granby, that he is persuaded that if he had had the good fortune to have had him at the head of the cavalry of the right wing, his presence would have greatly contributed to make the decision of that day more complete and more brilliant; in short, His Serene Highness ordered, that those of his suite whose behavior he most admired be named, as the Duke of Richmond, Colonel Fitzroy, Captain Ligonier, Colonel Wattson, Captain Wilson, Aide-de-Camp to Major General Waldgrave, Adjutant Generals Erstoff, Bülow, Derendolle, Count Tobe, and Mellerti, His Serene Highness having much reason to be satisfied with their conduct; and His Serene Highness desires and orders the generals of the army, that upon all occasions when orders are brought to them by his aides-de-camp, that they be obeyed punctually and without delay."

I think myself obliged in justice to mention, that on discovering a mistake in the order of thanks published by Prince Ferdinand of the 2d of August to the officers of the British artillery, in which Captain Macbean was omitted to be mentioned, His Serene Highness was pleased to write a letter with his own hand, of which the following is a translation, to Captain Macbean, which was delivered by His Excellency the Count von Lippe-Bückeburg, Grand Master of the artillery in the Allied Army:

To CAPTAIN MACBEAN *of the* BRITISH ARTILLERY.

"SIR,

"IT is from a sense of your merit, and a regard to justice, that I do in this manner declare, I have reason to be infinitely satisfied with your behavior, activity, and zeal, which in so conspicuous a manner you made appear at the battle of Todtenhausen (Minden) on the 1st of August. The talents you possess in your profession did not a little contribute to render our fire superior to that of the enemy; and it is to you, and your brigade, that I am indebted for having silenced the fire of a battery of the enemy which extremely galled the troops, and particularly the British infantry.

"ACCEPT then, Sir, from me, the just tribute of my most perfect acknowledgment, accompanied with my most sincere thanks. I shall be happy in every opportunity of obliging you, desiring only occasions of proving it; being; with the most distinguished esteem,

"Your devoted, and entirely affectionate Servant,

(Signed) FERDINAND, Duke of Brunswick and Lüneburg."

AUGUST 2d, His Serene Highness caused the town of Minden to be summoned at 9 o'clock in the morning, which surrendered at discretion by noon; the garrison consisted of 2,500 regulars, and 300 light troops, who were made prisoners of war; there was moreover found in the town a considerable number of wounded officers, besides 1,533 private men which were in the hospital. The quantity of baggage, provisions, and warlike stores which the French left behind them here, was almost incredible.

AUGUST 4th, the Allied Army marched from the neighborhood of Minden to Gohfeld: His Serene Highness detached this day Lieutenant General d'Urff with seven battalions and 20 squadrons, with orders to proceed by Lemgo, Detmold, and Lippspringe, from thence to join the army at Paderborn. The Crown Prince also passed the Weser at Hameln with 16 battalions and about 23 squadrons, including almost all the light troops of the army, in order to pursue the enemy who were retiring with the greatest precipitation towards the country of Hesse.

M. d'Armentières, who, after the capitulation of Münster, had, on the 3d of July, formed the blockade of Lippstadt, raised the siege thereof this day, on information of the loss of the battle of Minden, sent away his heavy artillery and baggage to the Lower Rhine, together with a detachment of ten battalions to reinforce the garrisons of Wesel, and the city of Düsseldorf; he, with the remainder, marched by the way of Paderborn to Warburg, where he arrived on the 7th of August. The French garrisons that were in Münster, Dülmen, and Warendorf, destroyed the magazines they had formed there, and evacuating those places, fell back towards the Rhine.

M. de Contades arrived this day at Olendorp[52], with the broken remains of his army.

AUGUST 5th, the Allied Army decamped and marched to Herford. General d'Urff on this day came up with the whole of the enemy's heavy baggage at Detmold; he surrounded the escort of 800 cavalry and infantry, whom he made prisoners: the booty taken here was immense, as it consisted of the Saxons' military chest, the baggage of M. de Contades, Count de St. Germaine, Prince de Condé, and Duke de Brissac, as also that of most of the principal officers of the French army. There was likewise on this occasion found in one of M. de Contades's coaches, a box containing some papers of the utmost consequence; amongst which in particular were some letters from M. de Belle-Isle, who was at the head of the Department of War in France, to M. de Contades, extracts of which are here inserted, as they immediately relate to this campaign, and were written at a time when they thought themselves already secure of the possession of Hanover, etc. They likewise will serve to give a just idea, not only of the necessities of the French, and the difficulties they labored under to defray the expenses of the war, but also of the humanity of their intention, in case they had actually rendered themselves masters of those provinces belonging to the Allies, and indeed with regard to the whole of the German princes.

M. de Contades sent a trumpet to His Serene Highness, desiring he would have the goodness to take care of the wounded he was obliged to leave behind him at Minden, and also to save what private papers might be found in the baggage that was taken belonging to the principal officers.

52. Editor: This may be Oldendorf, but there are three such towns and it is uncertain which one is meant.

Extracts from some ORIGINAL LETTERS *of* M. the Duke de Belle Isle
To M. le Marshal de Contades.

"I am still afraid that Fischer set out too late; it is, however, very important and very essential that we should raise large contributions. I see no other resource for our most urgent expenses, and for refitting the troops, but in the money we may draw from the enemy's country; from whence we must likewise procure subsistence of all kinds, (independently of the money) that is to say, hay, straw, oats, for the winter; bread, corn, cattle, horses, and even men to recruit our foreign troops. The war must not be prolonged; and perhaps it may be necessary, according to the events which may happen between this time and the end of September, to make a downright desert before the line of the quarters which it may be thought proper to keep during the winter, in order that the enemy may be under a real impossibility of approaching us; at the same time reserving for ourselves a bare subsistence on the route which may be the most convenient for us to take, in the middle of winter, to beat up, or seize upon, the enemy's quarters. That this object may be fulfilled, I cause the greatest assiduity to be used in preparing what is necessary for having all your troops, without exception, well clothed, well-armed, well equipped, and well-refitted in every respect, before the end of November, with new tents, in order that, if it should be advisable for the King's political and military affairs, you may be able to assemble the whole, or part of your army, to act offensively and with vigor from the beginning of January, and that you may have the satisfaction to show your enemies, and all Europe, that the French know how to act and carry on war in all seasons, when they have such a general as you are, and a minister of the department of war that can foresee and concert matters with the general.

"You must be sensible, Sir, that what I say to you may become not only useful and honorable, but perhaps even necessary, with respect to what you know, and of which I shall say more in my private letter.

"Versailles (Signed) M. Duke de Belle Isle.
"July 23, 1759"

"AFTER observing all the formalities due to the magistrates of Cologne, you must seize on their great artillery by force, telling them that you do so for their own defense against the common enemy of the Empire, that you will restore it when their city has nothing farther to fear, etc. After all, you must take everything you have occasion for, and give them receipts for it. —

"You must, at any rate, consume all sorts of subsistence on the Upper Lippe, Paderborn, and Warburg. You must destroy everything which you cannot consume, so as to make a desert of all of Westphalia, from Lippstadt and Münster as far as the Rhine on one hand, and on the other from the Upper Lippe and Paderborn as far as Kassel, that the enemy may find it quite impracticable to direct their march to the Rhine or the Lower Ruhr: and this with regard to your army, and with regard to the army under M. de Soubise, that they may not have it in their power to take possession of Kassel, and much less to march to Marburg, or to the quarters which you will have along the Lahn, or to those which you may occupy, from the lower part of the left side of the Ruhr, and on the right side of the Rhine, as far as Düsseldorf and at Cologne."—

"You know the necessity of consuming or destroying, as far as it is possible, all the subsistence, especially the forage, betwixt the Weser and the Rhine on the one hand, and on the other betwixt the Lippe, the Bishopric of Paderborn, the Diemel, the Fulda, and the Werra, and to make a desert of Westphalia and Hesse."—

"ALTHOUGH the Prince of Waldeck appears outwardly neutral, he is very ill disposed, and deserves very little favor. You ought, therefore, to make no scruple of taking all you find in that territory: but this must be done in an orderly manner, giving receipts, and observing the most exact discipline. All the subsistence you leave in his country will fall to the enemy's share, who will by that means be able to advance to the Lahn, and towards the quarters which you are to occupy on the left side of the Ruhr. It is, therefore, a precaution, become in a manner indispensably necessary, to carry it all away from thence." —

"THE question now is what plan you shall think most proper for accomplishing, in the quickest and surest manner, our great purpose, which must be to consume, carry off, or destroy, all the forage and subsistence of the country which we cannot keep possession of."—

"THE upper part of the Lippe, and the country of Paderborn, are the most plentiful; they must, therefore, be eat up to the very roots."—

"You did mighty well to talk in the most haughty tone with regard to the necessaries Racrouth and Diusburg must furnish our troops with. It is necessary to speak in that tone to Germans; and you will find your account in using the same to the regencies of the Elector of Cologne, and still more to that of the Palatine."—

"AFTER using art becoming ceremony, as we have the power in our own hands, we must make use of it, and draw from the country of Burgues which shall be necessary for the subsistence of the garrison of Düsseldorf and of the light troops, and reserve what may be brought thither from Alsace and the bishoprics for a case of necessity."—

ON the 6th of August, the Allied Army marched from Herford to Bielefeld.

A party of our Hessian hussars, who had been sent to take possession of the city of Münster, appeared before the gates of that town, but were about an hour too late, for the French Volontaires de Clermont Regiment had just re-entered it. M. de Gayon also came thither soon after with a detachment of those French troops which M. d'Armemtières had sent to the Lower Rhine on his raising of the siege of Lippstadt. Colonel Boyd was therefore sent with a party of regulars and some heavy artillery and mortars in order to dislodge the enemy, and endeavor to make himself master of that town. He arrived there on the 7th, summoned M. de Gayon the commandant to surrender, and, on his refusal, he immediately constructed some batteries, and began a bombardment. He was afterwards reinforced by three battalions from Lippstadt; but he was still too weak to invest the town on all sides, or prevent their receiving supplies and reinforcements from time to time, and was therefore obliged to quit the attempt, and retire towards Lippstadt.

ON the 8th, the Allied Army marched to Stuckenbrock, and on the 9th, they proceeded to Paderborn, where they halted on the next day. We made 400 prisoners in that town; and besides the large magazines we found at Minden, we retook those at Osnabrück, which the French had not touched, and also seized on those of the enemy at Bielefeld and Paderborn, which were very considerable. His Serene Highness sent forward from thence several detachments, in order to secure some of the passes into the country of Waldeck. M. d'Armentières had taken possession of one or two of them, particularly that of Warburg on the Diemel.

ON the 11th of August, the Allied Army marched from Paderborn to Dalen, where the headquarters were fixed, and on the 12th, they encamped at Stadburg.

M. de Contades, on the 11th, reached the neighborhood of Kassel, encamping the main body of his army near Lutterberg: the Duke de Broglio encamped with his corps de reserve at Obervellmar. Their troops were greatly fatigued and worn out by the forced marches they were obliged to make, in order to secure the defiles of Münden, where they arrived on the 9th. The Crown Prince followed close at their heels, laying hold of every opportunity of harassing them in their retreat. He attacked their rear six different times with great success, taking a considerable number prisoners, and taking several wagons laden with their baggage; in particular, near Grubenhagen, Einbeck, and the defiles of Münden, in each of which places the enemy suffered considerably. Their loss by desertion during this retreat was incredible; whole companies going off together, especially of the Saxons and German troops that were in French service.

THE barbarity and inhumanity of the French, in the countries through which they retreated, is beyond imagination: they not only pillaged, plundered, and stripped, every place they entered, but the very women were also abused and prostituted without respect to age or quality; numbers of the defenseless and innocent inhabitants were wantonly murdered; and, to complete the whole, they set fire to most of the villages on their quitting them; Einbeck, Northeim, Göttingen, Bisperode, and Latforde, felt the effects of their cruelty in a particular manner; nor did the city and country of Hildesheim fare better than the Hanoverians, though subject to their good friend the Elector of Cologne.

ON the 13th, the Allied Army entered the country of Waldeck, directing its march so as to gain the flank of the enemy, by Hartholtzen, Mengeringhausen[53], to Korbach, where it encamped on the 20th.

THE same day, the Crown Prince passed the Weser at Herstelle[54], so that he could either join His Serene Highness, or act separately, as occasion required; but he had first taken possession of Münden and Witzenhausen, in both of which places he had left garrisons.

ON the 15th, Luckner's Hussars routed a considerable detachment of the enemy at Volkmarsen, and forced them to retire with considerable loss.

ON the 17th, the Crown Prince dislodged a part of M. d'Armentières' corps from Wolfhagen, where he had taken post. On the same day, the Prince of Holstein attacked, sword in hand, a whole battalion of the Grenadiers Royaux at Naumburg, in sight of the enemy's army, and made them all prisoners.

M. de Contades, perceiving that His Serene Highness intended to cut off his communication with his magazines at Friedberg and at Frankfurt, found himself reduced to the necessity of abandoning the country of Hesse; and he accordingly, on the 18th, evacuated the city of Kassel, retiring towards Marburg.

---

53. Editor: Todal Mengeringhausen is part of Arolsen.

54. Editor: Today part of Beverungen.

ON the 19th, Major Fiederichs, at the head of some Hanoverian jägers, summoned that capital, which, after some cannon shot, surrendered. The garrison, consisting of 400 men, were made prisoners of war. There were also found here above 1,500 wounded men, whom the French had left behind, besides a considerable magazine.

ABOUT this time, General Imhoff was detached from the Allied Army with a body of troops, in order to carry on the siege of Münster.

ON the 20th, a detachment of 500 infantry and 30 cavalry was sent towards Frankenberg to observe the enemy's motions, and another party was also detached to Urky for the same purpose.

ON the 21st, His Serene Highness decamped, and marched to Fürstenberg.

ON the 22d, the Allied Army proceeded to Frankenberg, and the Crown Prince with his corps was posted at Heina, where he was joined by the Prince of Holstein and General Wangenheim, with their respective corps.

ON the 23d, the Allied Army halted. This day the French army arrived in the neighborhood of Marburg, greatly fatigued by forced marches. The main body encamped behind the Ohm River, with the headquarters at Grossseelheim; and M. de Broglio with his corps de reserve took post behind the Lahn opposite to Wetter, where Colonel Fischer lay with his corps.

THE same day, Lieutenant Colonel Freytag, with a party of light troops, attacked the castle of Ziegenhain, which after an hour's defense surrendered. The commandant with the garrison, consisting of about 400 men, were made prisoners of war.

ON the 24th, the Allied Army marched from Frankenberg, and encamped at Münchhausen, and the Crown Prince with his corps was advanced to Wohra[55].

ON the 25th, the Crown Prince marched to Schönstadt, where he took post.

On the 27th, M. d'Armentières was detached from the French army with two brigades and 16 pieces of cannon to the Lower Rhine. This day M. d'Estrées, the oldest marshal of France, arrived at the French camp, where he was sent to endeavor by his prudence and wisdom to reconcile the animosities and discontent that reigned in their camp, and to set things on a better footing.

On the night between the 27th and 28th, the Crown Prince marched towards Wetter, and in the morning early surprised Colonel Fischer's Corps consisting of 2,000 men, whom they attacked sword in hand, entirely defeated, and dislodged them, with the loss of 60 killed, many wounded, and 400 made prisoners, besides a great number of horses and their camp equipage: the remainder fled in the greatest confusion towards Marburg. Colonels Harvey and Beckwith, at the head of some British cavalry and grenadiers, distinguished themselves in a particular manner on this occasion.

ON the 29th, the Allied Army marched from Münchhausen , and encamped near Wetter.

55. Editor: Today Wohra is part of Wohratal.

ON the 2d of September, the Crown Prince, who had lain hold of every opportunity of harassing the enemy on their right, suddenly crossed the Lahn, and marched to Linhausen[56] on their left, where he encamped; and on the same day pushed forward with a part of his corps to Niederweimar, where he surprised the enemy, made several prisoners, and took two pieces of cannon, without the loss of one man.

THE Prince of Bevern, also, this day marched towards Marburg with four battalions, four 12-pounders, and 16 light field pieces, and took post on an eminence which commanded the castle of that place, not above 200 yards distant from the glacis.

ON the 4th of September, M. de Contades being closely pressed on his left by the Crown Prince, and judging by his motions that the Allies intended to cut off his communications by seizing on Wetzlar, quitted his strong camp between Marburg and Amöneburg, and retired towards Giessen, encamping that night at Mainzlar.

ON the 5th of September, the town of Marburg was taken possession of by the troops of the Allied Army, but the French garrison, commanded by M. du Plessis, retired into the castle.

ON the 6th of September, the Allied Army encamped near Elnhausen, where the headquarters were established. The Right Honorable the Lord George Sackville set out from the Allied Army about this time on his return to England; and the command of the British troops in Germany was conferred on His Excellency the Right Honorable the Marquis of Granby.

GENERAL Imhoff, who had been detached towards Münster, had prepared with the greatest diligence everything requisite to form the siege thereof; and, though greatly impeded by the rains, opened the trenches on the 29th of August, and by the 2d of September had got ready three batteries, from whence he began to fire on the 3d early in the morning, and prosecuted the siege with great vigor. But on the 6th, he received certain information, that M. d'Armentières was arrived the day before at Coesfeld with ten battalions of regulars, besides some regiments of militia, drawn from the garrisons of Düsseldorf, Cologne, and Wesel. That general not being able to man the trenches, and at the same time make head against a force so superior, found himself under the necessity of raising the siege, which he accordingly did this day, being the 6th of September, in the afternoon, retiring with his small corps to Telgtee, where he encamped; and M. d'Armentières encamped the following day under the walls of Münster.

AT this time four regiments more were sent from the main army of the French to the Lower Rhine to reinforce M. d'Armentières.

SEPTEMBER 7, the French army quitted their camp at Mainzlar, and encamped on the heights of Gros-Buseck[57], with their left at Schiffenburg, and their headquarters at Anroth. The corps de reserve under the Duc de Broglio encamped at Münchholzhausen with its right at Dutenhofen, and its left extending to Wetzlar.

---

56. Editor: This might be Elnhausen, part of Marburg.

57. Editor: Today part of Buseck.

ON the 10th, His Serene Highness marched to Niederweimar[58], where the headquarters were fixed.

ON the 11th, Prince Charles of Bevern and the Count de Bückeburg, who lay before the castle of Marburg, having for some time cannonaded it, were obliged to open the trenches on the 9th in form; and on the morning of this day the commandant M. du Plessis, surrendered by capitulation. The garrison, consisting of 39 officers and 818 non-commissioned officers and private men, were made prisoners of war. The besiegers had not one man either killed or wounded at this siege, which is the more surprising as the trenches were opened in form. A great quantity of provisions and ammunition was found in that town.

ON the 13th, the enemy attacked the advanced posts of the Duke of Holstein, but were quickly repulsed with considerable loss. The same day, a considerable body of horse under the command of the Prince de Beauffremont changed their position in the French camp, and took post at Kleinlinden[59], about half a league from Giessen, where he encamped between that place and the Duc de Broglio's corps, in order to be able to support him in case of necessity.

ON the 18th, M. de Fredericks and M. de Luckner, having intelligence that the French intended to seize on the town of Wetzlar, immediately repaired thither. The jägers passed the Lahn on the bridge, while some squadrons of hussars forded the river. They pushed the enemy back at first with some loss; but M. de Broglio coming up with a considerable reinforcement, they were obliged to give way, and, retreating to Wetzlar, passed the Lahn under a very smart fire both of cannon and musketry, which did not however kill or wound one of their men. The enemy after this burned down the bridge which had been constructed a little below the town, and the next day threw some troops into Wetzlar.

SEPTEMBER 19, His Serene Highness marched to Krofdorf, where he fixed his headquarters, the main army encamping with their right to Rodheim, and their left extending to Wissmar, with its front about two miles from the town of Giessen. The corps of General Wangenheim, and that of the Prince of Holstein, were advanced on their right along the Lahn, opposite to the town of Wetzlar, to observe M. de Broglio's corps.

SEPTEMBER 23, General Imhoff, having received some small reinforcements from Hanover, quitted his camp at Telgtee, and again marched towards Münster; and M. d'Armentières decamped from thence, on the night between the 11th and 12th, and retreated towards the Rhine. That city was once more invested by the Allies; but M. d'Armentières, being joined by the four regiments which had been detached, about the 6th, from the French army, he again advanced by Dorsten to Lühnen, where he encamped the 23d, having an advanced party at Hamm. General Imhoff, at the same time, raised the blockade of Münster, and marched to Telgtee, where he encamped. In this position they both remained for some time, each expecting to be reinforced.

58. Editor: Today part of Weimar (Lahn).
59. Editor: Today part of Linden.

THE 27th, Colonel Count Schulenburg, at the head of a detachment of 200 infantry and 200 cavalry advanced to Neukirchen[60], on the Solmbach, in the District of Westerwald, surprised a party of Nassau hussars, and seized on a large magazine belonging to the French; which they were forced to destroy, not being able to carry it off. They also took a chest containing 12,000 florins.

COLONEL Luckner and Colonel Freytag, at the head of the light troops, being detached on the left of the enemy, proceeded along the Lahn as far as Limburg, where they arrived on the 23d; from whence they made excursions on the rear of the French as far as Frankfurt, harassing the enemy's posts, and intercepting their convoys. They also by their situation cut off the communication between M. d'Armentières, and their main army, or at least rendered it very difficult and precarious, and prevented their receiving any supplies of forage, etc. from the country of Triers.

OCTOBER the 6th, a party of the Allies took post at Homberg, on the Ohm River, which they fortified with redoubts and entrenchments.

THE 12th, the Allied Army remained in their old position at Krofdorf and that of the enemy were also in their old camp around Giessen.

GENERAL Imhoff, being reinforced by a large body of cavalry, again advanced; and M. d'Armentières, having, on the 1st, thrown some supplies of provisions into Münster, retired, on the 3d, to Nottuln, and, on the 4th, to Coesfeld in his way to Wesel. The blockade of Münster was once more formed. General Imhoff's corps formed three camps, one at Dyckburg[61], where the headquarters were fixed; another at Luckenlech; and the third at Kinderhaus[62]: that General also received another reinforcement of five battalions and six squadrons, which had been detached from the Allied Army. M. d'Armentières advanced, on the 9th, to Bochum; and General lmhoff, with a part of his corps, marched to Dülmen, from whence he detached General Bülow, on the 11th, with some light troops supported by some infantry, who marched with all expedition to Dorsten, surprised the guard at the head of the bridge, who were all cut to pieces; and the French had just time to shut the gates: and while the Hessians and Scheither's Grenadiers were endeavoring to force them open, the enemy evacuated the town at another gate, and fled with precipitation towards Wesel. They were closely pursued, and 2 captains, 2 lieutenants, and 80 private men, were made prisoners on this occasion.

ON the 14th, a party of the enemy, consisting of 300 men, attacked our post at the bridge of Oberlimb, which was guarded by 20 jägers and 40 grenadiers of General Wangenheim's corps. The jägers, who were advanced, were forced to give way, and fall back on the grenadiers; but Lieutenant de Thun, who commanded them, attacked the enemy with great bravery, and the jägers at the same time returning to the charge, the French were repulsed with the loss of seven killed and several wounded.

OCTOBER 16, His Serene Highness Prince Ferdinand Duke of Brunswick and Lüneburg was invested with the most noble Order of the Garter. As that investiture was performed in camp, the following account of the ceremony is inserted:

---

60. Editor: Today part of Braunfels.
61. Editor: Today part of Münster.
62. Ibid.

"THE King of Great Britain having constituted the Right Honourabie the Marquis of Granby, and Stephen Martin Leake, Esq. Garter Principal King of Arms, Plenipotentiaries, for investing His Serene Highness Prince Ferdinand of Brunswick with the most noble Order of the Garter, Mr. Leake arrived at the camp, with the habit and ensigns, on Monday the 15th. The next day, the Plenipotentiaries had their first audience of His Serene Highness, at the headquarters, and presented their credentials and the book of statutes and His Serene Highness having agreed to accept the election with the usual reservations, the Plenipotentiaries immediately invested him with the Garter, Ribband, and George, Garter pronouncing the usual admonitions in Latin. The next day was appointed for the public investiture; and for that purpose, a large tent was prepared on a hill in full view of the French camp, and another lesser tent at a little distance from the great one, for His Highness to receive the first part of the investiture. To this tent the Prince came about 12 o'clock, escorted by a detachment of the horse guards blue[63], who were afterwards drawn up on either side upon the slope of the hill before the tent, others doing duty on foot." His Serene Highness was received by the plenipotentiaries in the lesser tent, where the habit and ensigns had been previously laid on a table, and he was immediately invested with the surcoat and sword. A procession was then made to the great tent in the following order:

Gentlemen and officers of His Serene Highness.

Garter's Secretary carrying the book of statutes.

The Marquis of Granby's Secretary carrying the hood.

Colonel Ligonier, Aide de Camp to His Serene Highness,
carrying the cap and feather.

Colonel Fitzroy, Aide de Camp to His Serene Highness, carrying the collar.

Chester Herald in his coat of arms and collar carrying the King's commission.

Garter King of Arms in his proper mantle,
carrying the mantle of the order on a crimson velvet cushion.

The Marquis of Granby, as first Plenipotentiary.

His Serene Highness the Prince,
supported by the Lieutenant General Waldegerve and Moyston.

IN this manner they proceeded to the great tent, where two chairs of state were placed; one for the sovereign, having an escutcheon of the royal arms and titles over the chair; the other for the Prince, having an escutcheon of his arms and titles above his chair. Upon entering the tent, every person made three references to the sovereign's state, and the habit and ensigns were severally laid by the persons who bore them upon a table before the sovereign's stall. The Prince sat down in his chair, the two plenipotentiaries in chairs on each side of him, the music playing. After a little pause, the Marquis of Granby (standing up made a short speech in French, which was answered by the Prince). Garter then presented the king's commission, which was read by the Prince's secretary. The plenipotentiaries then invested His Highness with the habit and ensigns; viz. first,

63. Editor: By this the writer of the document meant "Blues Horse Guards."

the mantle, then the hood, then the collar, Garter pronouncing the usual admonitions. They then placed the cap and feather on the Prince's head, and seated him in his stall, the music playing. Lastly, Garter proclaimed the sovereign's stile in French, and then the Prince's, the drums beating and trumpets sounding. This being done, a procession was made back to the lesser tent in the same manner as before, His Serene Highness having the train of his mantle borne by a page.

His Highness continued in this tent about an hour, 'till the great tent was prepared for dinner, which was given by the Marquis of Granby, His Serene Highness sitting at table in the habit of the order, having his cap held behind his chair, the plenipotentiaries on his right hand, and the Crown Prince of Brunswick on his left. The second course being served up, His Serene Highness stood up, put on his cap, and then taking it off, drank, 1st, the Sovereign's health; 2dly, the rest of the Royal Family; 3dly, the Knights companions of the order: in return, whereof the Marquis of Granby drank, 1st, the health of the Prince; 2dly, the rest of his family; 3dly, the King of Prussia.

THE next day His Serene Highness gave an entertainment in three tents near the headquarters, at which were present (as at the former) all the principal officers of the army; the whole being conducted with as much order and splendor as the circumstances of a camp would admit, and to the entire satisfaction of His Serene Highness.

ON the 21st of October, M. de Contades detached six battalions of infantry and two regiments of cavalry towards the Lower Rhine, to reinforce M. d'Armentières.

ON the 23d, Lieutenant Colonel Luckner, at the head of a party of light troops, advanced to Niederbrechen, where the French had a strong post, in order to cover their convoys of forage. He immediately attacked the enemy, and entirely defeated them with the loss of 1 lieutenant colonel, 1 major, 2 captains, and 50 non-commissioned officers and private men killed, besides 1 officer and 70 private men made prisoners. He also took 100 horses, and 112 wagons laden with forage.

ON the 26th of October, His Serene Highness detached from his camp at Krofdorf four battalions of infantry and four squadrons of cavalry, to reinforce the corps under General Imhoff, who continued the blockade of Münster.

NOVEMBER. The armies on the Lahn remained inactive keeping the same position very nearly in their former camps. Nothing material passed between them, except some skirmishes, which generally terminated to the advantage of the Allies. Both armies caused their camps to be well fortified and entrenched. His Serene Highness ordered his troops to shelter taking every necessary precaution to secure his men from the inclemency of the weather, which at this time was very severe. He also issued out very precise and distinct orders for the forming of the troops, in case of an attack, upon the first signal, and the cavalry was almost constantly kept saddled for the same purpose.

M. d'Estrées and M. de Contades were recalled from the French army, and M. de Broglio, who had been at Paris, returned to the French camp, invested with the full command of the whole, being promoted over the heads of several senior officers, who all resigned and quitted the army: among the number of these were M. de Chevreuse, M. de Noailles, and M. de Brissac.

Messrs. Luckner and Freytag continued their incursions on the French posts in the rear of their army with great success and disturbed their communication with Frankfurt in such a manner, that nothing could pass or repass without a strong escort.

NOVEMBER 11, the garrison of Münster made a sally, but were repulsed with the loss of 100 men.

ON the 14th, the trenches were opened before Münster with great success. The batteries were completed on the 15th, and everything got ready in order to begin the liege in form.

ABOUT this time three companies of Keith's Highlanders joined the Allied Army.

NOVEMBER 18, His Serene Highness sent a body of 1,500 men to Wideleberg[64] on the road to Cologne. This detachment not only alarmed the city of Cologne, and gave umbrage to M. d'Armentières on account of his rear, but also enabled the Allies to draw forage out of the Duchy of Burgues.

THE Crown Prince was likewise detached with a reinforcement of eight battalions to join General Imhoff before Münster.

NOVEMBER 22. The batteries began to fire on the town and citadel of Münster on the 16th, and the siege was carried on with the greatest vigor. Two attacks were formed under the direction of the Count von Lippe-Bückeburg, the one against the town, and the other against the citadel. The attack on the town was a false one, serving only to amuse the besieged, and draw their attention to that quarter. It took in three bastions, and might, on occasion, be converted into a real one.

M. d'Armentières advanced within four leagues of the town making a show as if he designed to attempt the relief of it. On the night between the 19th and 20th, he attacked the village of Albachten[65], and dislodged some of our Hanoverian jägers who were posted there; but that place was soon recovered, and General Imhoff made the proper dispositions for attacking their main body the following morning, but the enemy had retired with precipitation. Had M. d'Armentières, who was superior in number, acted with vigor, the affair might have been doubtful; for General Zastrow who covered the siege with eight battalions being ordered to join General Imhoff, there then only remained 3,000 men to defend the trenches against a garrison of 2,500, and the destruction of part of the besiegers' works by a sally would have caused insurmountable difficulties, on account of the severity and badness of the weather.

M. de Gayon, who commanded in the town, perceiving M. d'Armentières had retreated, sent out a trumpet on the 24th to demand terms of capitulation, which being agreed on, the garrison marched out on the 22d of November when the Allies took possession of that city.

THE Crown Prince, who was in full march to that place, returned to the army at Krofdorf, as soon as he received the account of its reduction.

---

64. Editor: The spelling of this town is too far from the correct spelling for it to be identified.
65. Editor: Today Albachten is a suburb of Münster.

NOVEMBER 23, General Imhoff fixed his headquarters at Münster, and sent strong detachments to Haltern-am-See, Dülmen, Coesfeld, and Olfen, and he cantoned the rest of his troops in the villages around Münster. M. d'Armentières after his retreat from Münster put his troops into quarters in the Duchy of Cleves.

THE Duke of Württemberg with a body of about 10,000 of his troops entered the country of Fulda, and took up his quarters in that capital, in order either to join or act in concert with the French army, according as occasion should require. His Serene Highness determined to send the Crown Prince to dislodge him, and prevent their junction.

FOR this purpose, on the 25th of November, the regiments that had been at Korbach returned with their baggage to the army, and marched on Marburg and its neighborhood; and the same day those that had been with Prince Charles of Bevern, on his expedition towards Cologne, returned likewise to Marburg.

ON the 28th early in the morning, the Crown Prince of Brunswick and Prince Charles of Bevern set out from Marburg with the following regiments, viz, De Bock, Hanoverian dragoons, Prince William, and Prince Frederich of Hesse's cavalry, two battalions of the Guards Regiment, and two of Imhoff of Brunswick's, the Grenadier Regiment, Hessians, and that of Blunsbach, 100 jägers of Trümbach's corps, one squadron of White, and one of Black Hussars. This corps having left their baggage behind, marched the same day to Kirtorf and Heimertshausen, and the following, being the 29th, to Angersbach[66], their vanguard having in their way gallantly repulsed a body of the enemy consisting of the Volonteers of Nassau. The two battalions of the Guards Regiment, and those of the Imhoff Regiment, and Boch's Dragoon Regiment, lay that night at Angersbach; Prince Charles of Bevern with the other regiments at Lauterbach: the hussars and the Trümbach Volunteers were posted further on at Landenhausen, and the Crown Prince passed the whole night at the advanced post of the hussars. At 1 o'clock in the morning of the 30th, the whole corps was again put in motion, and marched directly towards Fulda. As the enemy did not in the least expect this visit, no troops were met on the road. At a little distance from Fulda, the Crown Prince having ordered the whole corps to be drawn together behind the nearest height, and the hussars to march forward, His Serene Highness went to reconnoiter, in person, almost up to the gates of the town.

As the country about Fulda forms a plain of tolerably even ground, the right of which is watered by a river of the same name, the fields on this side being divided by a long hollow way, on one side of which the Württemberg troops had ranged themselves in small bodies on separate spots of ground, our hussars and Yellow Dragoons drew up in front of those troops thus irregularly posted.

IN the meantime, the rest of His Serene Highness's corps, both horse and foot, went around the hill, and proceeded in their march, without interruption, to the other side of the hollow way, in such a manner, that they were soon able to take post upon the flank of the Württemberg Regiment, which by degrees retreated into the town. Our cannon fired on them during the whole time they were filing off.

THE enemy's infantry having made some show of forming themselves; in the square of the town, we played our howitzers upon them to drive them from thence.

66. Editor: Today Angersbach is part of Wartenberg.

THE whole corps of the enemy having then passed through the town, our hussars and Yellow dragoons, led on by the Crown Prince in person, together with the Hessian grenadiers and Boch's Dragoon Regiment, passed it likewise in the pursuit whilst Prince Charles of Bevern went around the outside of it, and passed the river over the bridge.

THE enemy in their retreat shut all the gates of the town after them, but they were forced open by our cannon. Our troops found on the other side of the town the enemy's three battalions of grenadiers, and the Werneck Regiment, formed again in order of battle, as if with an intention of defending themselves; but the rest of the troops of Württemberg had drawn towards the left, and retired as fast as possible.

THE Crown Prince ordered immediately all the hussars and Boch's Dragoon Regiment to advance upon the said four battalions; and His Serene Highness with the rest of the troops filed off along the heights to the right, 'till he found himself able to gain the enemy's flank. It was then that we broke in upon them; and though they fired in the best manner they could, there were but 6 dragoons killed, and 14 wounded, on our side; Count Platen, captain, was killed in the first onset by a musket ball. A considerable number of the enemy were cut to pieces, and the rest, having thrown down their arms were made prisoners of war, together with all their officers. We took from them two pieces of cannon, two pairs of colors, and their baggage.

THE next day, the first of December, 923 prisoners were sent to Hersfeld under an escort commanded by Major Marshall. The rest of these four battalions were either killed or very much wounded.

OUR hussars went in pursuit of those of the enemy who went off before the action, and took the greatest part of their baggage, carriages, wagons, etc.

THE Duke of Württemberg was in person with his corps, which he had just then drawn up for a *feu de joie*; so that these regiments were in their best clothing. The Duke had invited all the ladies in the town of Fulda to his table, and to a ball which he intended to have given that very day, but, upon the unexpected news of the Crown Prince of Brunswick's being at the gates of the town with his hussars, the Duke thought proper to get off. That part of his cavalry which was not taken, was obliged to decamp in haste with the rest of his infantry, and to file off in our presence, on the other side of the Fulda. One of these regiments of cavalry, the grenadiers, and the Werneck Regiment were commanded in a very disorderly manner and this had enabled us to cut them so easily in pieces, and with so little loss on our side.

NOVEMBER 27. Both the armies on the Lahn River remained in their old positions without any material alteration, except that the cavalry of the Allies were cantoned in the neighboring villages, on account of the severity of the weather.

ON the 1st of December, the Crown Prince remained quiet at Fulda the whole day. But he afterwards advanced as far as Ruppertenrod[67], a place situated upon the right flank of the French army. This position, added to the difficulty of subsisting their troops any longer in a country entirely exhausted, probably determined the Duc de Broglio at

67. Editor: Today Ruppertenrod belongs to the town of Mücke.

last to abandon his camp at Giessen, which he did on the 5th of December. In falling back towards Butzbach, on the direct road to Frankfurt, His Serene Highness Prince Ferdinand of Brunswick detached two corps in pursuit of him. A garrison of near 2,000 men was left in Giessen, the commander whereof had been summoned to surrender.

ON the 5th of December, His Serene Highness ordered his infantry to canton in the villages around Krofdorf, where they could be assembled on the smallest notice.

DECEMBER 6, M. de Broglio had his headquarters at Friedberg, and the French army cantoned in the villages between that town and Butzbach. M. de St. Germaine was advanced with 40 companies of Grenadiers at Butzbach, in order to cover their cantonments, and support their light troops upon occasion.

MAJOR General Blaisel, who commanded in Giessen, having refused to surrender, that town was invested by a body of troops under the command of the Duke of Holstein.

DECEMBER 7, General Imhoff took post near Hattingen[68] with his headquarters at that place; and the troops under his command were cantoned in the country of Mark, being advantageously posted on the Ruhr. This day his light troops gained a considerable advantage over those of the French in the neighborhood of Elberfeldt .

THE 11th, a detachment of the Allies surprised a party of 300 French horse, who were quartered in the village of Billersheim, near Heingen, and made the greater part of them prisoners.

ON the 21st, the French commandant M. du Blaisel made a sally in the night with a body of 1,200 men, in order to surprise the Behr Regiment, which was cantoned in Kleinlinden[69], but the piquets giving the alarm, that regiment immediately assembled, and forced them back into the town with the loss of 30 men killed and 20 made prisoners,

THE Duc de Broglio received this day the baton of a marshal of France. This baton, which is sent or delivered to such as His Most Christian Majesty thinks proper to create Maréchaux de France, is 16 inches long, covered with blue velvet interspersed with *fleurs de lys* embroidered with gold, with a gold ring at each end, and this motto *Belli terror* engraved on one end, and on the other, *Pacis decus.*

ON the 24th of December, the French troops which were cantoned in the neighborhood of Cleves, marched to Düsseldorf, leaving only one regiment of foot at Engheim, and one regiment of dragoons at Xanten and Kalkar to patrol along the Rhine,

THE 25th, General Gilsa marched, on the 4th, from the neighborhood of Münster, with the detachment under his command, by the way of Unna, and the country of Waldeck, to the country of Hesse, in order to join the Crown Prince, who, after this junction, marched towards Erfurt, at which place he arrived on the 18th; and from thence proceeded to Chemnitz and Leipzig in Saxony, where he joined the King of Prussia this day.

---

68. Editor: Today Hattingen is in the Ruhrgebiet.

69. Editor: Today part of Linden.

THE Duke de Broglio thinking to avail himself of the absence of the Crown Prince with his detachment, which had considerably weakened the Allied Army, caused the grenadiers of the French army, with the troops placed between Butzbach and Friedberg to advance, on the 24th, towards the Lahn, and on the following day, being the 25th, a large body of the French army appeared before the Allies without coming to any action; a slight cannonade only passed between them on the side of Kleinlinden and Hachelheim[70], without any great effect on either side, when the enemy retired to their old cantonments.

ON the 28th, a detachment from General Imhoff's corps, consisting of five battalions and seven squadrons, arrived at Ober Weimar[71], about three leagues from Krofdorf.

ON the 29th, Colonel Luckner with his chasseurs attacked a party of the enemy consisting of 400 men, the greatest part of whom were cut to pieces: the remainder were all made prisoners, with their commanding officer M. de Muret excepting about 20, who escaped by flight.

ABOUT this time, a party of Colonel Scheither's corps passed the Rhine, surprised a detachment of the French, burned a large magazine, took the whole baggage of the Swiss Jenner Regiment, and made several other captures, without any loss on their side.

DECEMBER 31, the advanced parties of the Allies, which had been posted between Butzbach and Giessen, were, after the 25th, removed to Stauffenberg[72] on the left of the army, and on this day eight battalions and several squadrons of the French appeared before that village: however, they attempted nothing, but after the exchange of a few cannon shots retired the same way they had advanced.

70. Editor: This may be Heuchelheim.

71. Editor: This is apparently part of Wissmar, which is part of Wettenberg.

72. Editor: Stauffenberg is north of Giessen. Between 1977 and 1979 the cities of Giessen and Wetzlar and several smaller communities between them were politically merged into Stadt Lahn. After significant protests by the citizens, this consolidation was undone.

[illegible]

[illegible]

[illegible]

[illegible]

[illegible]

[illegible]

THE CAMPAIGN OF THE YEAR 1760

JANUARY 1. General Imhoff, having made some detachments, which traversed the country of Burgues, one of these advanced this day to Kaiserwerth, and from thence to Uerdingen, where they destroyed one of the French magazines.

ON the 7th, the Duke de Broglio, not having found it practicable to surprise the Allied Army, much less to attack it in front, was obliged, as was observed before, to retire back to Friedberg; but in order, however, to draw some advantage from the weakness of the Allied Army since the march of the detachment under the Crown Prince, and being also desirous to keep open his communication with Giessen, which he had determined to support, he made large detachments to our right and left. In consequence whereof, several corps under the command of M. de Voyer marched by Weilmünster to Limburg and Weilburg, to support their troops that were on their march from Düsseldorf and had actually arrived on the Dill. Several smart skirmishes happened between the advanced parties and light troops of both armies, in which ours had in general the advantage, excepting the following: M. de Voyer had ordered the Marquis de Vogue to attack, on the 3d in the morning, the town of Herborn, where there was an advanced post of General Wangenheim's corps, consisting of a captain and 100 men, who not retiring in time were, after a vigorous resistance, all made prisoners of war. The Picardy and Tour du Pin Brigades cantoned themselves there that night; and the Waldener Brigade with Fischer's Corps made themselves masters of the town of Dillenburg on the same day. The garrison retired into the castle, which they maintained, though severely cannonaded by the enemy; and M. de Voyer cantoned his reunited corps along the Dill.

WHILE the French made these motions on the right of our army, the Württembergers supported by some of the French light troops made incursions into the country of Hesse, by the way of Romrod and Alsfeld, as far as Ziegenhain. By that means the French rendered the arrival of provisions to the Allied Army very difficult from the country of Nassau, as well as from that side where the Württembergers were: moreover, the violent rains which fell at that time greatly retarded the convoys which came from Kassel. His Serene Highness Prince Ferdinand, therefore, thought it most advisable for the convenience of his troops to change their cantonments. For this purpose, he sent off his heavy baggage on the 2d; the artillery on the 3d; the army marched on the 4th, and on the 5th Prince Ferdinand himself followed with the rearguard, fixing his headquarters at Marburg, the main body cantoning in the neighborhood of that place, with the advanced guard at Dillenburg, as was said before, and another on the right of the French. His Serene Highness set out at 1 o'clock in the morning, of the 7th, to relieve the Dillenburg Castle, which was now closely pressed by the enemy; and on that evening the relief thereof was happily provided by M. de Derenthal, one of his aide-de-camps, who forced the town, and threw provisions into the castle. The French, besides a number killed, lost on this occasion 700 private men, and 40 officers, who were made prisoners, among whom was M. de Paravicini; as also seven pair of colors, and two pieces of cannon.

ON the same day, Major Keith's Highlanders supported by Colonel Luckner's hussars, attacked the village of Eyesbach[73], near our quarters, on the side of Dillenburg, where there was an advanced post of the enemy consisting of Beaufremont's Dragoons, entirely defeated them, killed and dispersed the greatest part of that regiment, and made 80 men prisoners; they also took 200 horses, and all their baggage. The Highlanders distinguished themselves in a very particular manner on this occasion.

JANUARY 8. M. de St. Germaine advanced on our left with the French grenadiers, supported by some dragoons, and eight battalions, but the Prince of Holstein, at the head of our grenadiers, supported by some dragoons, and four battalions, came up with them in the neighborhood of Ebsdorf, and: forced them, after a brisk cannonade, to retire with precipitation. Our hussars pursued them and made seven officers and 50 men prisoners of war.

JANUARY 19. The French army being dispersed and gone into winter quarters, the Allied Army also began their march to their respective winter quarters this day, those of the British troops were at Osnabrück, where they arrived on the 29th: His Serene Highness Prince Ferdinand established his headquarters at Paderborn; about 14,000 were quartered in the Bishopric of Münster, under General Spörcken; about 10,000 were quartered in the country of Hesse, and the remainder in the neighborhood of Paderborn, Lippstadt, etc.

THE French placed large garrisons in Düsseldorf, Wesel, etc., and their troops which were on the Lower Rhine extended along that river from Kranenburg to Cologne; the remainder of their army was quartered on the Lahn, the Main, and the Rhine, in the neighborhood of Frankfurt, Hanau, etc., the Saxons and Württembergers were quartered in Franconia.

JANUARY 20. A detachment of the Württembergers advanced towards Hirfchfield, with an intent to carry off, or destroy, a magazine belonging to the Allies in that town; but on information that a party of Hanoverians were in pursuit of them, and not a league off, they immediately retired with the utmost precipitation.

JANUARY 27. The Crown Prince's detachment was cantoned in the villages between Freyburg and Chemnitz, where they remained in perfect tranquility: His Serene Highness continued his headquarters at Freyburg.

JANUARY 28. This day His Serene Highness the Landgrave of Hesse Kassel died at Rinteln, aged 77 years, 10 months, and 18 days.

FEBRUARY 2. A party of the Allies attacked the advanced posts of the enemy at Hackenberg, Wallenrod, and Altenkirchen, made several of their men prisoners, and dispersed the remainder.

73. Editor: This may be Elbach, which today is part of Dillenburg.

COLONEL Scheither carried off two whole companies, and a pair of colors, belonging to a new regiment, which was forming in the Westerwald for the Army of the Empire.

THE detachment under the command of the Crown Prince being assembled at Chemnitz, His Highness came there on the 12th, at which time he began his march towards Hesse; and notwithstanding the severity of the season, arrived by brisk marches on the 18th at Wanfried, where a part of them remained, and the rest proceeded towards the country of Schmalkalden. The Crown Prince arrived on the 29th at Paderborn.

MARCH 1. The French made a show of attacking the chain in the front of the quarters of that part of the Allied Army cantoned in the country of Hesse, with a body of 4,000 or 5,000 men, but without any success; one body of 2,500 appeared by the road of Giessen before the town of Marburg, and after some resistance forced the gates, taxed the town at 100,000 francs, for the payment of which they took two hostages; they also formally summoned the castle, but were only answered from the mouths of the cannon, which soon forced them to abandon the town, retiring by the way they came: our hussars went in pursuit of them, and made several prisoners. Other parties appeared likewise before Homberg, Alsfeld, and Hertzberg, but without attempting to attack them; so their expedition proved ineffectual.

THE French having sent some detachments into the country of Fulda, the Crown Prince at the head of a party of the Allies advanced on their right by the heights of Vogelsberg, while General Gilsa with another body advanced towards the heights of Fulda. This body, on the 14th, came to Bad Hersfeld on the 15th, they then proceeded to Schlitz. The enemy's volontaires under the command of M. de Noue de Vair were driven back from Salmünster, and our chasseurs, under the command of General Luckner, entered Fulda on the 17th, where General Gilsa soon after arrived, but, on the 19th, he marched towards Neuhof, on advice that the French had taken post on the heights between that place and Fulda. The enemy was immediately attacked and dislodged, retiring by the way of Schlüchtern. General Luckner greatly distinguished himself in this affair. General Gilsa afterwards returned to Fulda.

M. le Duc de Broglio, as soon as he had received information of the march of these detachments, caused the *generale*[74] to be beaten. The French army was everywhere in motion and repaired to its headquarters; a large detachment was sent to Gillenhausen, and another on the road towards Fulda: but on notice that the Crown Prince had turned off to his left towards the country of Würzburg, the Duc immediately sent off 16 squadrons to reinforce the Saxons and Württembergers.

THE different objects of this expedition being fulfilled, such as dislodging the enemy from the country of Fulda, ruining several of their magazines, seizing on a number of recruits, which were raised in the country of Hanau for the completing of their German regiments, and alarming the French in their quarters, these detachments returned, carrying off with them 1,036 recruits, several prisoners, and a number of carriages laden, without the least interruption on their march from the enemy,

74. Editor: The generale is a signal beaten on drums to tell the troops to prepare to march.

As soon as the French General had received certain advice that the Allies had marched back to their quarters, he recalled the detachments he had made, and ordered his army to return likewise into their quarters, which they accordingly did on the 28th of March.

APRIL 1. General Imhoff with a brigade under his command marched towards Ziegenhain, in order to be at hand to support the garrison of Marburg in case of necessity.

APRIL 11. This day the Landgrave of Hesse Kassel had an interview with His Serene Highness Prince Ferdinand and the Crown Prince, with relation to the operations of the ensuing campaign.

APRIL 28. There happened this day a smart action at Vacha, a town situated on the frontiers of Hesse, which formed the head of our chain of cantonments upon the Werra. A detachment of the enemy, consisting of the regiment of Mr. d'Apchon, together with some voluntaires, made an attack on that town. Colonel Freytag, who commanded in that place, being overpowered by the great superiority of the enemy, was at first obliged to abandon it; but he only retired to a rising ground that was in the neighborhood, where he took part, and kept the French in play 'till two battalions of our grenadiers, who were quartered not far from thence, came up to his assistance. The enemy immediately retired and were pursued for three leagues and were attacked and driven from Geisa, where they intended to take up their quarters for that night. There were only two companies of jägers on foot, one on horseback, and one squadron of the Black Hussars, that had any share in this affair. Our loss in killed and wounded amounted to about 30 men; that of the enemy was about 120. The French had brought a number of wagons from Fulda, which they designed to have loaded with the plunder they should take from Vacha and Hersfeld[75], but they were forced to make use of them in carrying off their wounded men.

APRIL 29. His Serene Highness removed his headquarters from Paderborn to Nehaus, which is about the distance of half a league from thence; but the Crown Prince still retained his quarters in that town.

Count de St. Germaine, who had been at Frankfurt to concert measures with the Marshal Duke de Broglio for the operations of the ensuing campaign, set out this day from thence to take the command of the French army that was to act on the Lower Rhine.

MAY 5. the British troops who were quartered in and near Osnabrück marched out of their quarters in order to take the field, and, on the 12th, the last division of them arrived at Paderborn and the adjacent villages. His Excellency the Marquis of Granby, likewise, came there the same day. He had been obliged to remain behind some days at Osnabrück on account of illness.

MAY 14. All the Allied troops near Paderborn marched from thence towards Fritzlar.

---

75. Editor: Today Hersfeld is Bad Hersfeld.

MAY 20. His Serene Highness established his headquarters at Wabern, and the army entered a camp which had been traced out for them on the heights near Fritzlar; and, on the 21st, they were reviewed by His Serene Highness. General Imhoff was advanced with a large detachment toward the right at Kirchhain on the Ohm; and M. de Gilsa was likewise advanced with another towards the left at Hersfeld on the Fulda. The headquarters of the Marquis of Granby were at Fritzlar, and that of the Crown Prince and the Duke of Holstein were at Möllrich.

THE three following British regiments from England joined them in that camp, viz. Royal English Dragoons, Mostyn, and Ancram Cavalry, together with 200 light horse.

GENERAL Spörcken also at the head of the troops quartered in the Bishopric of Münster marched this day in order to take post at Dülmen and formed a line from thence as far as Hamm, to observe the motions of the French army on the Lower Rhine under the command of M. de St. Germaine.

ABOUT this time, the troops of the Prince of Württemberg, which had been 'till now in the pay of the French, quitted that service on some disgust, and returned towards Swabia: they were computed to be about 9,000 men.

COLONEL Fischer's Corps, which were to join the corps of M. de St. Germaine, took post on their flank at Elberfeld; and a body of the Hessian hussars, belonging to General Spörcken's corps, were at Dortmund.

MAY 23, General Luckner, who had orders to harass the enemy's convoys between Giessen and Butzbach, set out from his camp near Kirchhain with a detachment consisting of 500 hussars and jägers on horseback, and 500 grenadiers and jägers on foot, and after marching through Heuchelheim, Buseck, and Schiffenberg, he found himself, on the 24th in the morning, on the high road to Butzbach, without having met any of the enemy or their convoys; he thence proceeded in order to surprise that town, and carry off or destroy a magazine which the French had there. Count Waldner commanded in that place, with a garrison of 400 infantry, 100 of Caraman's Dragoons, and 50 of Béréchiny's Hussars.

M. Luckner had scarcely made the proper dispositions for the attack, before a patrol of the enemy of a cornet and 12 hussars appeared on the side of Lich, these were all taken except the cornet and one hussar, who escaped and spread the alarm at Butzbach. A little after another officer and 16 hussars appeared but retired as soon as they perceived him; they were closely pursued by our hussars, who entered the town along with them: M. von Waldner retreated out of the town by another gate, in order to gain a wood which, lay on the road to Friedberg. Our hussars came up with a piquet of Caraman's Dragoons, and took prisoners one officer and 20 men, the rest having dismounted, dispersed, and fled over the hedges and ditches: a piquet of infantry was also overtaken, 25 of whom were made prisoners, the rest escaping over the hedges. M. de Luckner then divided his corps into two parties: the jägers on horseback entered the wood, took or killed all they could find, while the hussars of Brunswick pursued the other runaways towards Friedberg, and brought back a great number of dragoons, hussars, and about 30 carriages.

M. Luckner then entered the town and distributed to the poor inhabitants the magazines and provisions that they could not carry away. On the 25th, he returned back to his camp with four officers and 100 private men prisoners. His whole loss amounted to no more than two hussars killed and five wounded.

THOSE who had fled to Friedberg gave the alarm so strongly there, that the commandant thought proper to set fire to a large magazine in that place, but on advice that M. Luckner had retired, he caused it to be extinguished.

MAY 27. The French army, in consequence of the alarm given by M. Luckner, were all put in motion towards Friedberg, and cantoned in Wetterau; having a large detachment under Prince Xavier of Saxony on their right, in the country of Fulda, and another under the Prince de Camille on their left, on the Lower Lahn.

MAY 29. In a skirmish that happened this day in the country of Fulda, the Black Hussars belonging to the Allied Army made prisoners a company of the Dauphin Regiment.

JUNE 7. M. de Broglio having sent a reinforcement to Prince Xavier in the country of Fulda, His Serene Highness detached the Crown Prince with a body of about 4,000 men to join General Gilsa: on the 9th he arrived at Schlitz, from whence he advanced to Fulda; but the enemy, not thinking proper to wait for him, retired towards their main army, and the Prince returned, on the 14th, to Schlitz.

JUNE 13. The Allied Army remained in their camp near Fritzlar; and the French army continued in their cantonments, having a very considerable corps under the command of the Count de Lusace encamped at Lohr[76], as also another under M. de St. Pern at Gelnhausen, both of which were on their right, they had on their left the Prince de Camilleat Limburg, and M. de Guerchy, who had been advanced to Hachenburg, fell back and joined that corps.

LIEUTENANT Colonel Bülow at the head of some of the Legion advanced to the village of Meyerich, where a part of Fischer's Corps had taken post. He immediately attacked them with great celerity the guard were all either taken prisoners or killed, and the whole party defeated. The enemy had a great number killed; 50 were made prisoners, and the remainder fled in the greatest confusion. A considerable booty was taken on this occasion. M. de Buttlar, who was detached by Colonel Bülow over the Ruhr, also defeated a party of the enemy, and brought in 20 prisoners. The legion lost only two men and three horses in this whole affair. Colonel Bülow returned, on the 15th, to Dortmund.

THIS day the 2d Dragoon Guards Regiment joined the Allied Army. On the 17th, the Hodgson, Bockland, and Griffin Infantry Regiments also came into camp; and on the 20th, the Barrington, Cornwallis, and Kerr Infantry Regiments, likewise joined the army, being part of the reinforcements from England.

THE French army on the Lower Rhine under M. de St. Germaine were all assembled about the beginning of this month near Düsseldorf. On the; 6th, they passed that river,

76. Editor: This may be Lohra.

and encamped at Kalkum; the 17th, they crossed the Ruhr at Mülheim; on the 18th, they encamped at Steyl[77]; on the 19th they marched to Dortmund, from whence General Spörcken's advanced parties fell back to Hamm; and, on the 20th, they marched to Lünen, where M.de St. Germaine fixed his headquarters.

THE French army under the command of M. de Broglio assembled, on the 19th, at Friedberg, on the 20th, it marched to Hungen, and, on the 21st, to Grünberg, where it halted on the next day, and was there joined by the reserve under Prince Xavier of Saxony from the right, and M. de Guerchy from the left; on the 23d, it marched towards Schweinsberg , where it passed the Ohm on the 24th, and on the same day encamped in the neighborhood of that place, M. de Broglio fixing his headquarters in that town.

THE Allied Army quitted their camp at Fritzlar on the 24th and encamped at Freilendorf; on the 25th, they proceeded to Neustadt, with an advanced guard on the heights of Alendorf.

On the 26th, the army was under arms, and formed the line of battle. M. de Broglio, expecting to be attacked, ordered the Count de Lusace, who had remained on the left side of the Ohm, to pass the river and march to Kirchdorff. He also formed the line of battle; but nothing passed except some skirmishing between the light troops. On the 27th, His Serene Highness marched back to Ziegenhain, and encamped on the heights between that place and Treysa[78] on the right of the Schwam, having that river in his front; the light troops being posted on the other side thereof occupied the town of Wallenburg and the woods in the front of Neustadt. The enemy sent out their two vanguards and their light troops to harass our rear in our retreat, but without any effect. These two vanguards joined at Neustadt, where they encamped that night. The next day M. de Broglio marched with the whole army, encamping with his right to that town, and his left to Speckswinkel, fixing his headquarters at Neustadt.

SEVERAL smart skirmishes passed between the advanced guards, piquets, and light troops, of the two armies.

ON the 29th, the Allied Army changed its position, placing their right to the heights of Treysa, and its left to Schonborn. General Imhoff covered its right flank, and its left was covered by the Crown Prince of Brunswick, who joined the army in this camp, having marched thither from the country of Fulda after some successful skirmish with the enemy, particularly on the 18th at Hosenfeld, and on the 23d at Zielbach, where he made prisoner several officers and private men, and took a number of horses, without any loss on his part.

M. de Broglio detached M. de Chabot with the Irish Brigades to lay siege to Marburg, which surrendered on the 30th. The garrison, consisting of about 400 men, under the command of Major Puffendorf, were made prisoners of war.

ON the 30th of June, the Allied Army fired a *feu de joie* on the agreeable news of the French having raised the siege of Quebec.

77. Editor: This may be Steele, part of Essen.
78. Editor: Today part of Schwalmstadt.

THIS day the Carabineer Regiment, cavalry, from England, joined the army.

JULY 4, a body of about 1500 French cavalry attempted a *coup de main* on Fritzlar, but M. de Luckner came up in time enough to prevent them: he immediately attacked and repelled them with loss, pursuing them as far as Freienhagen.

ON the 2d of July, Campbell's battalion of highlanders, infantry, with 300 recruits for Keith's battalion, joined the Allied Army from England.

ON the 3d, M. de Broglio detached M. de Clozen with a considerable body to take post at Frankenberg. He likewise sent another large detachment to Rosenthal under the command of M. de Poyanne, and some other parties marched at the same time towards Heina and Iesburg.

ON the 4th, General Imhoff was detached from the Allied Army to Niederurff, and M. de Luckner also went to encamp at Bad Wildungen.

ON the 5th, Prince Ferdinand ordered a large body of troops to cross the Schwam, who encamped behind some redoubts and works which he had caused to be thrown up on the heights before his camp on the other side of that river. The Crown Prince was likewise sent to Riebelsdorf on his left.

ON the 6th, a considerable body of the enemy, under the command of M. de Vair, advanced above Veirec[79] to dislodge those troops that were posted on this side the Schwam. They also made a show of attacking our right, but they were repulsed with loss.

THIS day M de Luckner attacked the body of the enemy under M. de Clozen at Frankenberg, dislodged them with considerable losses, driving them back upon Rosenthal, where M. de Poyanne was posted.

ON the 7th, M. de Rothe was detached from the French army to take post at Holzdorff with two brigades of infantry and a body of cavalry.

His Serene Highness Prince Ferdinand perceiving the enemy had an intention to out flank his right by the several detachments they had made on their left, and also having advice that their reserve on the Lower Rhine under M. de St. Germaine, which had marched on the 4th from Dortmund to Arnsberg, was directing its route towards Brilon and Korbach, broke up his camp, and marched on the 8th at 3 o'clock in the afternoon, arriving on the morning of the 9th on the heights of Braunau[80], not far from Bad Wildungen, where he encamped. The advanced corps of the Crown Prince, being reinforced by some battalions and squadrons under Major General Griffin, was sent forward the same day as far as Sachsenhausen[81].

M. de Broglio, as soon as he was informed of the march of the Allied Army, judged that His Serene Highness designed to seize on the heights near Korbach, which post he also had proposed to get possession of, and M. de St. Germaine was in full march for that

79. Editor: This may be Wiera, today part of Schwalmstadt.
80. Editor: Today part of Bad Wildungen.
81. Editor: Today part of Waldeck.

purpose. He, therefore, ordered the advanced guard of his Army immediately to push forward for that place, and he followed them with the main body by forced marches, to be near at hand to support them.

ON the 10th, Prince Ferdinand resumed his march in the morning at 2 o'clock, and the Crown Prince likewise marched the same morning from Sachsenhausen towards Korbach. The enemy's, advanced guard and the van of M. de St, Germaine's corps had arrived there before him, and had formed themselves on the heights near that place.

THE Crown Prince judging them not to be so numerous as they really were, and imagining their whole force might not exceed 10,000 foot, and 17 squadrons, determined to endeavor to dislodge them; the attack was accordingly made with great vigor, and the engagement became extremely hot about 2 o'clock in the afternoon; the enemy being continually reinforced with fresh troops as they arrived, and having thereby a great superiority of numbers, with a large artillery, the Prince found it was not possible to drive them from their advantageous post, therefore, as there was no occasion for maintaining that post which he himself occupied, our main army being arrived at Sachsenhausen, and as it was moreover not practicable to bring up a reinforcement in time to sustain the Crown Prince in his post, His Serene Highness Prince Ferdinand sent him orders to rejoin the army, part of which was then formed.

THE Crown Prince accordingly made his dispositions for a retreat, which was attended with some confusion among our battalions and squadrons; the enemy taking advantage of this disorder, pressed very briskly upon our troops, both with their artillery and a large body of cavalry; our battalions would have suffered considerably, had not the Crown Prince at the head of Eland's squadrons, and Howard's Dragoon Regiment with great bravery made a most furious charge on the enemy, and thereby gave our infantry an opportunity of making a safe exit from this affair, as did also Major General Griffin at the head of the two British battalions of Kerr and Brundenell; one squadron of Bland's, commanded by Major Mill, and Howard's Dragoon Regiment, gained great honor; in a word, the troops in general behaved with great bravery and spirit, showing much cheerfulness and alacrity during the whole of the action.

THE Allies were obliged to leave behind them 12 pieces of cannon, four howitzers, and 30 ammunition wagons, which could not be carried off, as we had 96 artillery horses killed and 80 more wounded; our loss in men amounted to seven officers, eight sergeants, and 163 rank and file, killed; 18 officers, 21 sergeants, and 428 rank and file, wounded; two officers, two sergeants, and 175 rank and file, missing; making in the whole 824 men killed, wounded and missing.

The Crown Prince received a slight wound in the shoulder. The loss of the enemy was computed at between 700 and 800 men in their own accounts.

THE French encamped on the heights of Korbach, their reserve, under M. de St. Germaine, was at Canstein[82] on their left, and kept post at Stadtberge[83]; the light troops

82. Editor: Canstein is a village and a castle that today are part of Marsberg.

83. Editor: Stadtberge is the former name of Obermarsberg, which is, Today part of Marsberg.

were encamped between this reserve and their main body at Mulhausen; the French and Swiss Guards, the Grenadiers of France, and the Grenadiers Royaux, with a brigade of cavalry, were encamped at Berndorf[84]; M. de Stainville was at Frankenau with a body of cavalry. On the other hand, the Allied Army encamped at Sachsenhausen, their left not being above half a league from the enemy's right, separated therefrom by a hollow way almost impracticable; General Spörcken was encamped at Mengeringhausen[85] with his corps from Münster, they had also another camp at Twiste[86] between the two; their light troops were posted at Arolsen; frequent skirmishes past between the advanced parties and light troops of both armies while they remained in this camp.

ON the 16th of July, the castle of Dillenburg, which had been for a considerable time besieged by the French, surrendered after a brave and obstinate defense, the garrison, to the number of about 250, were made prisoners of war.

UPON advice that a detachment of the enemy, consisting of six battalions, viz., three of Anhalt, two of Royal Bavière, and one of Turpin, besides Béréchiny's Hussar Regiment, under the command of Major General de Glaubitz, was advancing towards Zeigenhain[87], and was actually encamped at Wasenberg[88], His Serene Highness the Crown Prince was detached from Sachsenhausen the 14th of July at night for Fritzlar, towards which place six battalions of the army had already filed off; viz. one battalion of Behr, one battalion of Marchal, two battalions of Mansbach, and two battalions of the Hessian Guards, he marched early the next morning to Zwesten; where General Luckner, with his regiment of hussars, as also Elliot's Light Dragoon Regiment (who were then just arrived there from England) joined him: they continued their march, and arrived that evening at Treysa, but M. de Gaublitz had already marched from Wasenberg, and encamped at Emsdorf. Our troops being fatigued passed the night at Treysa, and marched the 16th to Speckswinkel[89], where Major Fredericks was posted with his jägers, and to which place Colonel Freytag had advanced with one of his brigades: our infantry did not arrive 'till 11 in the morning.

THE Crown Prince himself went forward and reconnoitered the enemy's position, and found their camp placed at the opening of the mountains, with their left extending to a wood before Emsdorf, with the village of Emsdorf before their right: he took with him five battalions, placed the foot chasseurs, and a brigade of the chasseurs on horseback at the head as an advanced guard, and made a detour of nearly two leagues across the woods, mountains, and the village of Wolfkuler[90], in order to gain the left flank of the enemy, who, thinking themselves very secure, were surprised in their camp, and had only time to place two battalions upon their flank, but these, after the first attack made upon them by the chasseurs, were routed by the 2nd Hessian Guard Regiment, the colonel of which, M. Naurodt, was wounded at the first discharge. Four pieces of

84. Editor: Today Berndorf is part of Twistetal.
85. Editor: Today Mengeringhausen is part of Bad Arolsen.
86. Editor: Twiste is today part of the town of Twistetal.
87. Editor: Today Ziegenhain is part of Schwalmstadt.
88. Editor: Today Wasenberg is part of Willinghausen.
89. Editor: Today Speckswinkel is part of Neustadt in Hessen.
90. Editor: This may be Wolferode, next to Emsdorf, now part of Stadtallendorf.

cannon played from the wood upon the camp, and the five battalions immediately drew out, and wheeling about pushed the enemy who had scarcely formed themselves behind their camp. While this passed, General Luckner, whom the Prince had left in a bottom before Speckswinkel with the cavalry and a battalion of Behr (Hanoverian), got up the heights at the first firing, and attacked the right of the enemy, (where M. de Glaubitz had placed Béréchiny's Regiment), and received a general discharge of all the musketry of those that could get to their arms, as well as from the artillery that was ready to play. The enemy was put to flight, and passed a wood which was behind them, the rearguard only showing some appearance of resistance. All their baggage, artillery, and tents, were taken; they retired by Langenstein, to which place Behr's battalion pursued them; from thence, having thrown themselves into another wood, the same battalion passed through Langenstein, and posted themselves upon the stone bridge that is over the Ohm River. During this time the cavalry had got up to our right, and keeping close to the side of the enemy, had cut them off from the road that leads to Amöneburg, and it being impossible for our infantry to follow them, the Crown Prince took with him the Elliott's Light Dragoon Regiment, got together some hussars, and passed in pursuit of them into the wood which they had reached on the other side of the Ohm; and finding them again on their march in the plain in their way to Niederklein, he charged and broke through them four or five different times, at last separated 500 men from the main body, those were surrounded, and obliged to lay down their arms. Not satisfied with this, he marched against the remainder of the enemy's infantry, which had thrown itself into Niederklein, and had fixed itself near a wood. They were immediately surrounded, and summoned to surrender, which they accordingly did. Béréchiny's Regiment was likewise either entirely taken or cut to pieces by Luckner's Hussars.

AMONG the prisoners, of the greatest note, were Major General Glaubitz himself, and the Prince of Anhalt, who was a brigadier. Count Hessenburg and Count Muschinski were killed by the same cannon ball.

ON our side the brave Colonel Freytag was dangerously wounded; M. Derenthal, Prince Ferdinand's aide-de-camp, received a shot in his thigh, M. Walmsden, major of brigade, had his horse killed under him; and M. Normand, Major General Behr's aide-de-camp, had his head taken off by the last cannon shot that the enemy fired. Our loss on this occasion was 162 killed, 152 wounded, and six missing. The trophies gained were nine pair of colors, (almost all of which we owed to the intrepidity of Elliott's Regiment, under the command of Major Erskine, which for its first appearance in the field did wonders), five pieces of artillery, and a howitzer. Major General Behr and M. de Bischhausen had the honor to command the infantry under the Prince's orders, which showed throughout the whole as much courage as good will to march on and engage, though harassed and almost exhausted with the fatigues of their march. The prisoners were all conducted to Ziegenhain.

THE following is the detail of the above affair as published by the French, which, as it is very circumstantial, and particularizes the whole maneuver, I have inserted here:

THE Anhalt Brigade had been left behind to keep open the communication. It was encamped within a league of Marburg. On the 14th of July, it received orders to draw near to Ziegenhain, in order to form the blockade of that place. It had no cannon but the field pieces of the regiments. This design was laid aside afterwards; for on the 15th, the brigade was ordered to return again, and encamp at the village of Emsdorf, two leagues behind Neustadt, in order to set out on the 16th for Iersburg. The allowance of beef and bread was two days in arrears. These provisions were expected on the 16th from Marburg, that the brigade might b he tents standing and all the equipage. We endeavored to gain the right of the wood that leads to Marburg, but a strong body of the enemy was posted there.

WE then turned to the left to gain the eminences and the woods. It was at this time that upwards of 2,000 English horse, jäger zu pferd and hussars, fell upon the brigade sword in hand, and picked up all that could not follow. We halted to give them a brisk discharge: they retreated: we continued our march cross a rivulet and got to a wood which extended to a kind of a ruined fortress, under which we wanted to retire. We mustered our men, and found we had not lost above a fourth, though we had marched above two leagues. We were greatly surprised to find the openings of the woods filled with chasseurs, who stopped us short. We changed our resolution, and crossing the wood came again to a plain. We imagined the enemy's cavalry would give us some respite, as they had morasses to pass, but scarcely had we marched half a league, when the whole, again united, surrounded us, and fell sword in hand on the brigade and the column. We gave them another sharp fire: upwards of 300 horsemen had broken into the column, who were cutting about them with their swords; above 200 of these were killed on the spot.

"THEY again retired, and we began to march, for the third time, to gain an open wood, and wait for the enemy in order of battle. In this retreat, we left behind above half the brigade who could march no longer. One whole battalion of Anhalt was taken at this place.

"WHEN we got into the open woods, the Crown Prince sent an aide-de-camp to summon us to surrender, which we refused. The Prince then sent General Luckner to M. de Glaubitz, who showed him all the posts, that he was surrounded by upwards of 2,000 horse; that there was no retreat for him, and that he must necessarily surrender.

"M. de Glaubitz consented without consulting any field officer of the two regiments. We were told we were prisoners; and soon after the Crown Prince came up, who highly commended the obstinate defense and the long retreat we had made after being surprised. We were, indeed, completely surprised. The Prince and General Luckner told us that they came into our wood, and into the cornfields, within 500 paces of our camp without seeing any patrol of hussars, or any grand guard; that at eight in the morning they had placed two battalions in the village at a quarter of a league from our camp; that they knew we expected our bread, and waited 'till it should be distributing to fall on us.

"ALL this is inexcusable when it is known we had 600 hussars, and 500 foot chasseurs, who guarded the headquarters. As to Béréchiny's Hussars, after the first attack on the village they fled at full gallop to Marburg, abandoning the foot: they did not lose ten men, and made no show of defense. They arrived at Marburg to the number of 500.

"THE Crown Prince had 8,000 foot and chasseurs, and upwards of 2,000 horse, with 14 pieces of cannon. Above one third of the Royal Bavière was killed or wounded, its colonel and major were both killed; the Anhalt Regiment did not lose so many. This brigade had upwards of 900 men killed or wounded.

"THE enemy owned that they had lost above 1,000 men, chiefly on the first attack of the wood. Our troops must be allowed to have defended themselves with obstinacy, when it is considered they were attacked and surprised at Ebsdorf[91] at 12 o'clock at noon, and that they did not capitulate 'till 6 o'clock in the evening near the village of Niederklein, which is four leagues from Ebsdorf; that they marched those four leagues by crossing fields of corn, swamps and hollow ways, and that the weather was excessively hot, this justice cannot be denied them."

ON the 17th of July, a large body of the French appeared upon the right of our line, where the Marquis of Granby had his headquarters, their irregulars advanced and fired on our piquets which were posted in a wood; the Kingsley and Hume Regiments, who covered the Marquis's quarters, immediately joined the piquets, and the enemy were repulsed. His Lordship removed his quarters to Saltsbach, and the two regiments joined the line.

ON the 18th, the Allies evacuated the town of Paderborn, and a party of French entered that place, but however did not think proper to keep possession of it. This day Honeywood's Cavalry Regiment from Ireland joined the Allied Army.

ON the 22d, the castle of Dillenburg was retaken by the Crown Prince, and the garrison made prisoners of war.

THE activity of our hussars and jägers rendered the arrival of the enemy's convoys to their camp very difficult and precarious. Captain Bülow, at the head of a detachment of Hanoverian jägers, near Giessen carried off and brought into camp a convoy belonging to the enemy of 300 wagons laden with provisions and ammunition, etc. which greatly distressed M. de Broglio's camp.

ON the 23d of July, M. de St. Germaine, who commanded the reserve of the French army that had been on the Lower Rhine, resigned, and returned to Paris, being succeeded in the command by the Chevalier de Muy.

THE hospital of the Allies, which was at Münden, was removed to Minden, and that at Kassel was removed to Münden.

ON the 24th of July, the French struck their tents, and set out in force - the Allied Army also struck theirs, and lay all day upon their arms, Monsieur de Broglio divided his army into three corps, one of which, consisting of about 15,000 men, he detached under the command of the Count of Lusatia towards Hersfeld and Fulda, by the left of the Allied Army, in order, if possible, to draw the attention of His Serene Highness on that side; he likewise detached towards our right another considerable body, under the command of his brother the Count de Broglio, and the Count de Vair, in order to endeavor to cut

91. Editor: Today Ebsdorf is part of Ebsdorfergrund.

off General Spörcken's corps from the main army under Prince Ferdinand, and prevent their junction: their main body, under his own command, marched forward that night a little to his left, to make a show as if he intended to direct his route towards Paderborn, whereas the real design of this movement was to seize, if possible, on the defiles and gorge of Münden, and cut off the Allied Army from the city of Kassel.

His Serene Highness Prince Ferdinand no sooner had notice of their different maneuvers than he immediately perceived the real intentions of the enemy, upon which he directly detached the Crown Prince to the assistance of General Spörcken, and to facilitate their junction, while he on the same night with the main body directed his march towards Kassel, having before sent off his baggage by Freienhagen; the French harassed his rear, and pressed him very closely, making several attempts to break in upon him, in which they were always repulsed with considerable losses on the enemy's side, that of ours was very inconsiderable in comparison. General Spörcken had a much more difficult task, having been harassed for two days successively by the corps under the command of the Count de Broglio, and particularly in passing a very troublesome narrow defile between Fischbach (where the army had rested all the night on their arms) and Wolfhagen, where he was obliged to order the cavalry to march around a hill at least two or three German miles, before they could join him on the other side; the infantry was no sooner out of this defile, than their rear, consisting of one battalion of Post, one battalion of Ersdorff, 400 piquets, etc. was attacked by a large body of the enemy, both horse and foot; nevertheless they continued their march, fighting all the way 'till they gained a rising ground, where they took post; here they maintained themselves, notwithstanding the great superiority of the enemy, for two hours and a half, at which time the cavalry came up under the, command of General Breidenbach, consisting of seven squadrons of Hanoverians, and two of Hessians, who immediately attacked the enemy in flank, and soon put them into confusion; the fury of the troops was so great, and so much were they exasperated, that they cut everything down before them.

THE enemy, by their own confession, lost above 1,000 men on this occasion, besides three general officers, viz. M. le Comte de Vair who was killed by a cannon ball, M. le Comte de Belsunce, and M. de Comoyras, who were wounded. The loss of the Allies did not exceed 200 men, neither had they one officer of note hurt.

THE Allied Army encamped the 25th near Wolfhagen; the 26th at Zierenberg, where the enemy ceased to follow us, and on the 27th by Kalle[92].

THE Chevalier de Muy, who commanded the reserve of the French army, passed the Diemel at Stadtberge, and extended his corps down the banks of that river, to cut off the communication of the Allied Army from Westphalia, while M. de Broglio, at the same time, advanced with their main body towards Prince Ferdinand's camp; Prince Xavier likewise was marching on our left towards Kassel.

His Serene Highness, therefore, determined to leave General Kielmannsegg with a body of troops at Kassel for the protection of that city, and with his army pass the Diemel between Liebenau and Trindelburg.

92. Editor: This may be Calden.

FOR this purpose, he ordered General Spörcken to march with his troops from the camp at Calden to Liebenau about 4 o'clock in the afternoon of the 29th; the Crown Prince followed the same evening with a body of troops, among which were the two English battalions of grenadiers, the two of Highlanders, and four squadrons of Mostyn's and Conway's.

THE Allied Army was under arms all day on the 30th, and about 11 o'clock at night it marched off in six columns to Liebenau. About 5 o'clock the next morning the whole assembled and formed on the heights near Körbecke on the other side of the Diemel.

THE Crown Prince reconnoitered the position of the Chevalier de Muy, who from the 30th in the morning was in possession of a very advantageous camp, situated with his right to Warburg, and his left near to the hill of Ossendorf. Fischer's Corps was posted in the town of Warburg. His Serene Highness immediately determined that the Crown Prince and M. von Spörcken should turn the enemy's left, while the main army under his own command advanced upon their front.

IN pursuance whereof the Crown Prince marched, on the 31st, in two columns to Donhelburg, leaving Lütgeneder on his left, and forming in two lines with his left towards Dössel and his right near Grimbeke. The enemy was attacked almost at the same instant in flank and rear by the Crown Prince and General Spörcken with great success; for after a very sharp dispute, they were obliged to give way, and by a continual fire were forced to fall back upon Warburg. The army was at this time marching with the utmost diligence to attack the enemy in front, but the infantry could not march fast enough to get up in time to second the attack. General Waldegerve at the head of the British infantry pressed their march as much as possible: no troops could show more eagerness to get up than they did; many men from the heat of the weather and overstraining themselves to get on through morasses and very difficult ground, suddenly dropped down on their march.

His Serene Highness then ordered the Marquis of Granby to advance with the cavalry of the right wing, who, with General Mostyn at the head of the British, advanced with so much expedition, bringing them up at a full trot, though the distance was nearly five miles, that they arrived in time enough to share the glory of the day: the French cavalry, though very numerous, retreated as soon as ours advanced, excepting only three squadrons, who were soon broken; General Mostyn then fell upon the enemy's infantry, which suffered extremely, particularly the Lockman Swiss Regiment.

CAPTAIN Phillips also brought up the English artillery on a gallop, and seconded the attack in a surprising manner, having, by a very severe cannonade, obliged those who had passed the Diemel, and were formed on the other side, to retire with the greatest precipitation.

His Serene Highness then ordered the town of Warburg to be attacked by the Legion Britannique. The enemy finding themselves thus attacked upon both their flanks in front and in rear, retired in the utmost confusion, with a considerable loss, as well from the fire of the artillery as the charge of the cavalry. Many, also, were drowned in the Diemel in attempting to ford it.

THE brigade formed of the English grenadiers and Scotch Highlanders greatly distinguished themselves, performing wonders. The brave Colonel Beckwith, who commanded them, was wounded in the head.

THE trophies taken were ten pieces of cannon, with some colors. The loss of the enemy was computed at about 1,500 left on the field of battle, besides about 2,000 made prisoners. The Brigades of Bourbonnois, la Couronne, Rochefort, and Planta, with the Auvergne Regiment, and Fischer's Corps, were the greatest sufferers. The chief loss of the Allies fell upon the British grenadiers and Highlanders, who had 415 men killed and wounded. The English lost in all 590 men: that of the other troops in the Allied Army was never made public, but we know it was very trifling.

THE evening after the battle the Chevalier de Muy retreated to the heights behind Volkmarsen, where the enemy lay all night on their arms. The Marquis of Granby, with ten British battalions and 12 squadrons, passed the Diemel the same evening, and encamped on the heights before Welda.

THE account of this action, as given by the French, is as follows.

"THE reserve of the left, commanded by the Chevalier de Muy, was encamped with its right at Warburg, and its left towards the heights opposite to the villages of Menne and Ossendorf. In consequence of the different accounts received from Marshal de Broglio of the enemy's march, M. de Muy, on the 31st of July at daybreak, detached the Marquis de Castries, lieutenant-general, with all the grenadier companies, and the jägers belonging to the foot, two regiments of dragoons, and Fischer's Corps, to observe the motions of the enemy. The Marquis de Castries could not perceive their march towards the camp at Warburg 'till a thick fog had dispersed, which was about half an hour after nine.

"As two columns of the enemy seemed to direct their march against the left flank, the Chevalier de Muy placed on the heights of Menne the four brigades of foot, of Bourbonnois, la Couronne, Jenner, and Planta, under the Major-Generals d'Amenzaga and de Travers. The brigades of la Tour du Pin, and Touraine, under the command of Lieutenant General de Maupeon and Major General de Roquepin, were disposed on the right on this side of Warburg. The Lieu-tenant Generals de Lutterberg and d' Auvet, with the Major-Generals de Lugear, de Soupire, and de Mangenon, with the cavalry, occupied the center opposite to a very extensive plain. The dragoons were placed between the right of the foot and the left of the horse and were commanded by the Duke de Fronsac. The brigade of Rouergue formed a reserve on a small eminence behind the left of the cavalry. The artillery was disposed in the front of the line, and Fischer's Corps occupied the town of Warburg.

"THE column of foot of the enemy's right wing having turned the heights behind our left by the village of Ossendorf the Chevalier de Muy caused the brigades of Bourbonnois, la Couronne, and Jenner, to advance to the tower which is on those heights, and at the same time brought up the brigades of Rouergue and Touraine to support them. The head of the enemy's first column got before us to the height behind our left, their second column at the same time advancing in a parallel line in the bottom.

"WHEREUPON the Chevalier de Muy caused the brigade of our left to form in two lines, and the engagement began. The brigades of Bourbonnois, la Couronne, and Rouergue, led by Messrs. de Castries, Segur, and Travers, charged the enemy five times with the greatest courage, and notwithstanding their superiority, forced them to give way several times. These brigades were well seconded by that of Jenner commanded by M. Amenzaga, which had the second column of the enemy to deal with. Meanwhile the enemy's horse came into the plain, and part of it advanced against the flank of our infantry, to protect which M. de Muy brought up the brigades of horse of Royal Piedmont and Bourbon.

"THE combat had continued on the left upwards of four hours, with equal advantage on both sides, notwithstanding the superiority of the enemy, when it was observed that some of the enemy were filing off towards our bridges on the Diemel. The danger was pressing; to prevent it the Chevalier de Muy marched thither with the brigade of Touraine under the Marquis de Roquepin. At the same time, he ordered thither M. de Maupeon with the brigade of la Tour du Pin and caused the cavalry and dragoons to re-cross the river. He then drew off the infantry of the left wing. The brigade of Planta covered their retreat with admirable order and bravery. M. de Lugear, who led the brigade of Bourbon, marched against the English horse just as they were going to fall on the foot, and put them in confusion. This vigorous and well-timed charge enabled us to pass the river in good order. The dragoons under the Duke de Fronsac covered the infantry as they came out.

ALL our troops afterwards drew up in order of battle on the heights before the wood on the right of the Diemel, where batteries were erected, which stopped the enemy.

"AFTER two hours we marched to Volkmarsen, where we encamped, without the enemy's daring to follow or harass us. This retreat, made in sight of an enemy so much superior in num-bers, shows the valor of the troops which fought that day. Not one pair of colors or standard was taken from us. We lost six pieces of cannon, which it was impossible to bring off, notwithstanding the pains of Major General Pelletier, by whom all our batteries were placed to the best advantage.

"WE have not as yet received the particulars of our loss; the enemy make it amount to 3,000 men killed and wounded: theirs must be more considerable.

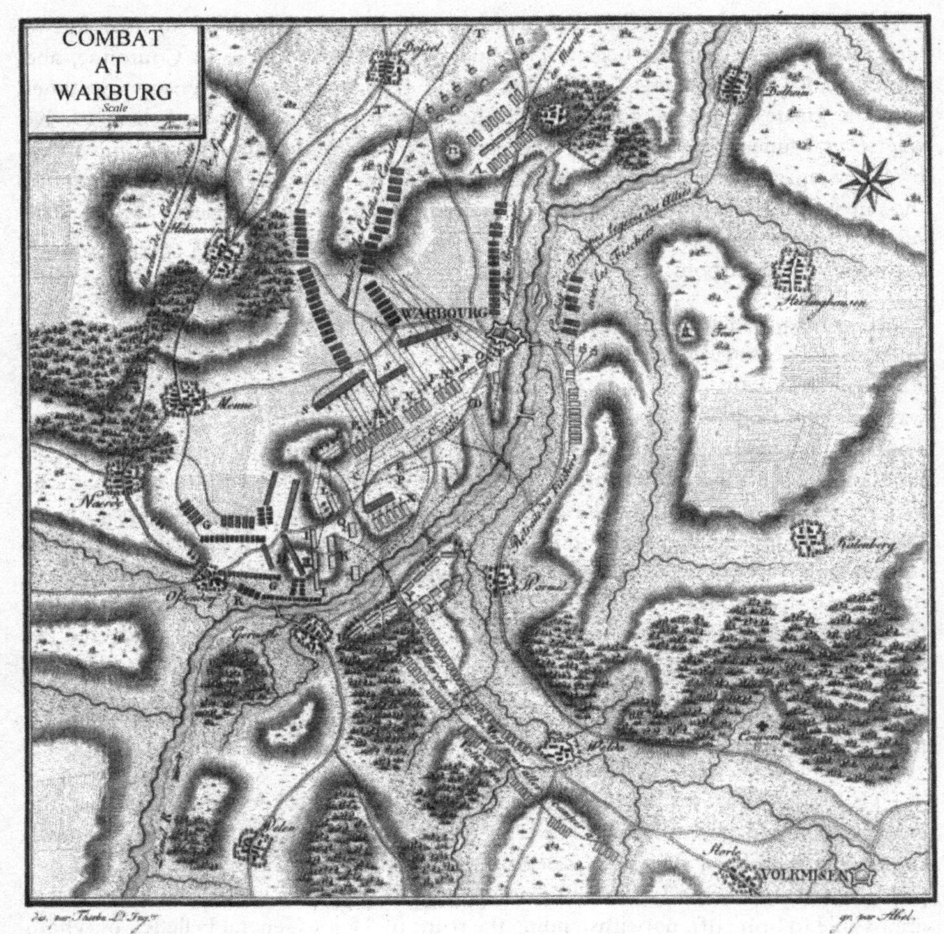

KEY TO MAP.

A French detachment, which had advanced from daybreak, to reconnoiter the Allied movements, when a heavy fog covered the ground. Having seen that their direction was on the left of the Warburg camp, Chevalier de Muy put his troops in battle formation, and gave them orders to be ready at day break, then put them in their first position.

B Infantry of the left.

C Dragoons and cavalry of the center.

D Infantry of the right.

E Reserve infantry.

F Cannon batteries.

G Two columns of Allied infantry, which having turned the left of the camp, move towards the heights

H   on the point of which there is a tower. Then Chevalier de Muy ordered his forces to a second position.

I   Infantry.

K   Cavalry.

L   Infantry.

M   Dragoons.

N   Cavalry.

O   Three battalions of the de la Tour du Pin Brigade, the fourth remaining near Warburg. Fischer's Corps holds this city and its vicinity.

P   Tourraine Brigade in march to move towards the tower.

Q   Batteries of cannon.

R   Allied troops move along the river to move towards the bridge thrown over the Dimel.

S   Allied cavalry, which began to debouch into the plain, vis-à-vis the French cavalry. The combat had already been long engaged.

T   Prince Ferdinand's army marches after the cavalry. The superiority of the Allies and the fear of being invested decided Chevalier de Muy, after a very stubborn battle, to take up a third position.

U   Tourraine Brigade and de la Tour du Pin Brigade, to protect the bridges, occupy the heights and woods, in order to faver the retreat. The dragoons, cavalry, and then the cavalry were immediately ordered to retreat.

X   The Bourbon Cavalry Brigade, which charged the English cavalry, and covered the retreat, then forms, with the Royal Piémont Brigade, the rearguard for the passage of the Dimel.

Y   Chevalier de Muy's corps in battle formation on the heights beyond the Dimel, where he established batteries, which prevented the Allies from crossing the river in force.

N.B. This combat began at 1:00 p.m., and ended at 4:30 p.m.

THE Marquis de Castries, Major General d' Amenzaga, and Brigadier de Montbarrey, have received severe contusions. Colonel Valance of the Bourbonnois Regiment, the Prince of Rochefort, and the Chevalier de la Tour du Pin, are wounded. The Chevalier de Muy gives the highest commendation to all the private men, as well as to the general officers and other officers who were engaged. He has likewise expressed his satisfaction with the field officers of the reserve, particularly M. de Valognie, who distinguished himself much in the action, and contributed greatly to the good order of the retreat by the openings he caused to be made. M. de Sauveur of the horse, and M. de la Tour du Pin, deserve high commendations: the latter was not wounded 'till the end of the action, after we had crossed the Diemel. M. Lochman was killed; and M. de la Roche, Colonel of the Aumont Regiment, died of his wounds.

ON the 1st of August, the Chevalier de Muy retired from the heights of Volchmiflen towards Wolfhagen, where he encamped.

THIS day the Count de Lusace at the head of the grenadiers and chasseurs made himself master of the town of Münden by a *coup de main*. The garrison, consisting of 350 men, were all made prisoners of war. He also took the town of Dransfeld, where there was a garrison of 300 men. He likewise took possession of Kassel, Göttingen, and Einbeck.

THE Marquis of Granby, having intelligence that the main army of the French were in full march towards him, struck his tents this evening, and the troops lay all night on their arms. On the morning of the 3d, he repassed the Diemel, and joined the lines by Warburg, the army being encamped on the heights near that place.

ON the 3d of August, M. de Combefort, who had been detached from the garrison of Wesel, made himself master of the town of Bentheim. There were only 48 men in that place.

ON the 5th, the Chevalier de Muy with the reserve marched from Volkmarsen towards Stadtberge where M. de Castries had before taken post with 6,000 men. The headquarters of the French army were at Oberustingen. It encamped upon the heights along the Diemel and was only separated by that river from the army of the Allies, which extended from Scherfeld on the right as far as Übelngönne on the left.

THE enemy made an attempt to take possession of one of the defiles near Stadtberge, but were prevented by the Crown Prince, who repulsed them with loss. The Allies were also masters of all the defiles along the Diemel. General Kielmannsegg was posted with a body of troops near Beverungen on the Weser; and Major-General Luckner was advanced on the other side of that river with some battalions and squadrons to make head against some detachments which were pushed forward in those parts by Prince Xavier.

THESE detachments were accordingly driven back from Einbeck and Northeim; but as there was only a small number of Luckner's Hussars left to garrison Northeim in order to observe the motions of the enemy, a detachment of the French, consisting of 500 horse and foot, appeared again on the 10th and attacked that town. Luckner's hussars were obliged to give way to superior force they, however, retired in good order: but being reinforced with some jägers, they soon after returned, forced one of the gates of the town, and fell upon the enemy sword in hand. The engagement was very sharp for some time, but it terminated to the disadvantage of the French, who had 150 men killed. Their commanding officer was dangerously wounded and made prisoner, together with ten other officers, 300 foot soldiers, and 30 dragoons, who were all conducted to Hameln.

AT the same time, Colonel Donop attacked a body of 2,000 of St. Vigor's Volontaires, who were detached by Marshal de Brogio into the wood of Sababurg, in order to preserve his communication with the corps under the command of Prince Xavier. The enemy, notwithstanding their advantageous position in a very thick wood, were utterly defeated and dislodged, having lost on this occasion 500 men killed, wounded, and made prisoners, together with three pieces of cannon, which were taken by the Prussian hussars. The remainder fled with precipitation to Münden.

IN consequence of these actions, and to keep open their communication, the reserve of the right wing of the French, under the Count de Lusace, removed from Esebeck to Melenhausen, and Prince Xavier removed to Münden. On their march there a party of 200 of their volontaires were almost all cut to pieces by some of Luckner's Hussars near Göttingen, which town the French evacuated.

ON the 11th of August, the castle of Ziegenhain surrendered to the French. The garrison, consisting of about 700 men, were all made prisoners of war.

ON the 20th, the two armies remained in the same position along the Diemel. Nothing material had passed 'till this day, when a large body of the French attempted to pass the Weser near Von dem Busschefelde to support Prince Xavier; but they were so well received by General Wangenheim, who was posted at Uslar, that they were obliged to retire with loss.

THIS day the French army made preparations for decamping. On the 21st, the Chevalier de Muy began by retiring with his reserve to Volkmarsen, leaving some troops to keep possession of Stadtberge. He also still maintained his posts opposite to Meerhof and Ossendorf. The French *volontaires* attacked Colonel Scheither's corps but were repulsed with loss. Our hussars carried off a post of the enemy near Rhoden, consisting of a captain and 30 men of the Royal Ecossois Regiment.

ON the night between the 21st and 22d, M. de Broglio broke up his camp, and marched by his right. The Crown Prince crossed the Diemel on the 22d with a body of 12,000 men, in order to gain the left flank of the enemy; and his advanced troops came up with their rear guard near Zierenberg, and the light troops engaged for some time with various success. The Crown Prince arrived in person with the Greys and Inniskilling dragoons, supported by the English grenadiers. The enemy were forced with considerable loss, and fled with precipitation to Zierenberg, into which place they entered, and shut the gates of the town.

M. de Broglio fixed his headquarters at Immenhausen, encamping with his right to Mariendorf, and his left to Hohenkirchen, with the Fulda in his rear, from whence he sent a considerable reinforcement to Prince Xavier.

THE castle of Bentheim surrendered, on the 22d, to Major de Wense. The French garrison, consisting of three officers and 85 men, were made prisoners of war.

THIS day two battalions of the Britannic Legion were sent to cover the city of Osnabrück.

ON the 25th of August, three battalions of the British Guards from England, under the command of General Caesar, joined the army near the village of Bühne, where His Serene Highness had his headquarters.

THE Crown Prince encamped at Breuna on the other side the Diemel with a considerable detachment both of regulars and irregulars. The latter scoured the country as fair as

Winterstasten near Kassel, which occasioned many skirmishes.

THE Crown Prince retired on the night between the 30th and 31st from Breuna and encamped behind Warburg. His light troops were still at Welda beyond the Diemel, extending towards their right, in order to observe the motions of the enemy on the side of Stadtberge.

ON the 29th, a detachment of the Allied Army marched to the left towards Borgholz, where the Marquis of Granby had his headquarters.

A French detachment entered the town of Göttingen on the 25th of July, and the Hanoverian garrison was obliged to retire before a force so superior. The whole reserve under the Count de Lusace marched in on the 26th and having demanded a contribution of 30,000 crowns proceeded to Efebec, where they encamped, leaving a strong garrison in that town.

THE heavy baggage of the French army filed off by Kassel, as did the artillery from Münden. The artillery that was at Kassel was sent to Ziegenhain, and their hospital was also removed from thence. Their bakers quitted the ovens at the orange gardens, making use of those of the town belonging to the city bakers, as they were before exposed to the incursions of the light troops of the Allies.

ON the 5th of September, His Serene Highness had still his headquarters at Bühne. The Crown Prince maintained his position between Warburg and Stadtberge. The body of reserve under the Marquis of Granby was at Borgholz and General Wangenheim with his corps was posted at Uslar.

MARSHAL de Broglio continued in his camp at Immenhausen, where he kept continually changing the position of the troops. Prince Xavier, with 42 battalions and as many squadrons, and a numerous corps of light troops, encamped still at Esebec.

THIS day a considerable body of the enemy, amounting to 20,000 men and upwards, attempted to made a general forage in the neighborhood of Hofgeismar; but Prince Ferdinand, having received previous intelligence of their design, crossed the Diemel early in the morning of that day, and went in person with a corps of troops to oppose them; and though His Serene Highness was much inferior in number to the French, yet he took his precautions so well by occupying some advantageous heights, and placing artillery there, that he rendered the enemy's attempt totally ineffectual, notwithstanding a large part of their army was in motion to cover the fo-ragers.

ON the morning of that day, likewise, the Crown Prince (upon intelligence that the voluntaires of Clermont and Dauphine, consisting each, when complete, of 600 horse and 600 foot, were cantoned at Zierenberg, and from the very small distance of the French camp at Dörnberg thought themselves in perfect security) went from his camp at Warburg to Malsburg[93], which is not much more than a league from Zierenberg, without seeing any of their posts, or meeting any of their patrols. This made His Serene Highness resolve on an attempt to surprise them; for which purpose, he ordered five battalions,

93. Malsburg is today a ruined castle within the town of Zierenberg.

a detachment of 150 Highlanders under the command of Captain M. Leon, and eight squadrons of dragoons, to be ready to march at eight at night. They left their tents standing, and passed the Diemel near Warburg, Maxwell's battalion of grenadiers, the detachment of Highlanders, and Kingsley's Regiment, forming, the head of the column. These were followed by two other battalions of grenadiers and by Block's Regiment. The eight squadrons of dragoons were Bock's, the Greys, and the Inniskillings. At the village of Witzen, about a league on the other side of the Diemel, they found all the light troops, which were under Major Bülow's command, and whose destination was to turn the town of Zierenberg, and to take post between it and Dörnberg, in order to intercept whoever should attempt passing to the enemy's camp. At the entrance of a large wood, near Malsburg, the Greys and Inniskillings were posted; at Malsburg, a battalion of grenadiers; the other battalion of grenadiers, the Block Regiment, and Boch's Dragoons, were posted at proper distances between Malsburg and Zierenberg to cover them in case they had been repulsed and pursued. At a mill about two English miles from the town, and within sight of the fires of the enemy's grand guards, Maxwell's Grenadiers took one road, Kingsley's Regiment and the detachment of Highlanders another. When they came within less than half a mile of the town, the vedettes of their grand guard challenged them, but did not push forward to reconnoiter them. The men marched in the most profound silence, and in a few minutes, they saw the fires of their piquets, which they had posted close to the town. The noise of their trampling over gardens gave them the alarm, and they began to fire; upon which the grenadiers, who had marched with unloaded firelocks (as had been agreed on), ran on towards the town, pushed the piquets, and having killed the guard at the gate, rushed into the town, and drove everything before them. Never was there a more complete surprise.

THE attack was so sudden that the enemy had not time to get together in any numbers but began to fire at them from the windows; upon which they rushed into the houses, and for some time made a severe use of their bayonets. They afterwards loaded and killed a great many of the enemy who had mounted their horses. It was about two in the morning when they got into the town, and about three the Prince ordered a retreat. The number of killed and wounded was very considerable, from an ill-judged resistance of those who were in the houses but, in justice to the men, it must be said, that they gave quarter to all who asked it; and there were several noble instances in the refusing to take money from the prisoners who offered them their purses.

"GENERAL Griffin, who went into the town with the Prince by another gate, at the head of Kingsley's Regiment, received a thrust in the breast with a bayonet (as is supposed) from one of his own people, upon hearing him talk French to a soldier whom he had seized, and who would not quit his firelock, but the wound proved a very slight one.

WHAT made this affair more satisfactory was, that it did not cost them ten men, which was wonderful in a night attack, where they might have expected to have lost more by their mistaking friends for foes.

THE behavior of the officers and bravery of the troops upon this occasion deserves the greatest commendation. Lord George Lenox was a volunteer in this expedition and had his horse wounded under him by a shot from a window. With the prisoners taken, they brought off two pieces of cannon; and, had they had time to search the houses, the number of their prisoners would have been doubled; but as day was coming on, and they might have been cut off from Warburg, they retired the same way they came, and arrived there at eight in the morning of the 6th without being at all molested.

M. de Norman, Brigadier, who commanded the Volontaires de Dauphiné, and M. de Comeiras, Colonel of those of Clermont, together with 34 other officers, were made prisoners of war, besides 231 private men of Dauphine, and 161 of Volontaires de Clermont, amounting in the whole to 428 men.

THE following is the French relation of the above *coup de main* made on Zierenberg, in which place the brigades of the Volontaires de Dauphiné and Prince Clermont were in garrison, amounting to 1,900 men, and is here inserted, as it mentions some particulars tending greatly to the honor of the troops concerned:

"A detachment of 9,000 or 10,000 men, under the command of the Crown Prince, set out from Warburg on the 5th at eight in the evening, and marched to Zierenberg in small divisions, conducted by some of the townsmen, and some deserters who joined them the night before; the latter made them avoid the patrols and the different guards, the former guided them to the different passages and breaches that led into the town. The enemy could not however avoid a main guard of dragoons, but those were soon overpowered sword in hand, and got to the gate of Zierenberg that leads to Warburg, at the same time with those dragoons that escaped.

"A captain of Volontaires de Dauphiné, who was upon guard there had, on the first alarm, assembled his men, and stood his ground 'till he received several stabs with bayonets, and was borne down by the two battalions of English grenadiers, who entered the town in columns by this gate, at the same time the two other gates were masked by some cavalry and two Hessian battalions, whilst six squadrons of hussars took post around the town; 150 Highlanders mounted the breaches, and were supported by some light infantry or jägers.

"THE columns of English grenadiers advanced in great order, with their bayonets fixed without firing a musket, by the two streets that lead to the churchyard, the only square or open place in the whole town, killing and seizing all who were running out of the houses, and had not time to reach the churchyard, the principal place of rendezvous in the whole town for the troops: these grenadiers advanced to the churchyard in the greatest order and the greatest silence, the night was so dark that they formed at the side of the French troops, who for some time imagined them to be their own piquets that had assembled; but at last discovering their mistake, a fierce encounter ensued with bayonets, and several were killed or wounded; the English being superior in number drove the infantry from the churchyard.

"MEANWHILE two regiments of dragoons made an attempt, sword in hand, to force through the gate that leads to Dörnberg; it was occupied by 400 grenadiers, who charged with their bayonets fixed: they went to another gate, where they met with the same resistance, being saluted with a sharp fire of small arms; they then took the resolution to leap breaches that were six feet high.

"THE Crown Prince in person was in the town, where the attack lasted about an hour and a half; the Prince seeing the obstinacy of the French troops, and being apprehensive lest we should receive a reinforcement from a camp, which was only a league distant, returned in the same order in which he advanced, carrying with him six officers of the brigade, and about 400 soldiers and dragoons, taken in defending the place, the greater part of whom were wounded with bayonets. There were found in the town about 100 men that were killed on both sides.

"As the enemy retired the French troops entered the town, and formed again in the church-yard, from whence a detachment of dragoons was sent to observe the retreat of the Crown Prince; two of the four pieces of cannon belonging to the brigade were retaken. M. de Vadreuil, Colonel of the Volontaires de Dauphiné, at the head of all that were not taken prisoners, by his resistance and activity prevented a greater loss, and restored order in the town, of which he retook possession as soon as the enemy quitted it; he had still above 1,000 men left, both dragoons and foot.

"THE Crown Prince, who is above all praise for the good order with which he conducted the attack, gave the vanquished on this occasion proofs of his usual magnanimity and greatness of sentiment. The humanity which all the English officers charged with the attack showed to the prisoners, both during the action, and after it, deserves likewise the highest commendation."

His Serene Highness having sent out a detachment towards the Upper Eder, in order to cut off the communication of the enemy on the side of Marburg, Major Bülow advanced to that town, where he made prisoners eight officers, and about 70 men, the rest having retired to the castle. He likewise destroyed the ovens which the French had there, took the uniforms of several of their regiments, and some hundreds of muskets. He then pushed forward Scheither's Dragoons to Butzbach, where they took two entire companies of the Rougrave Regiment, with two standards. They likewise destroyed at Grumburg and Langgöns between 200 and 300 wagons of flour, and for some time scoured that part of the country, intercepting the French convoys. On the 11th, Major Bülow marched to join Colonel Fersen at Frankenberg. For M. de Broglio, having advice of the success of M. de Bülow's expedition, he detached a considerable body of troops, under the com-mand of M. de Stainville, to open his communication with Marburg, and cut off the retreat of our detachment.

ON the 12th, M. de Bülow made a motion towards Frankenau, and M. de Stainville, who had arrived at Merdenhagen, marched to attack him, and came up with his rear near the village of Gemünden on the river Wohra. Col. Fersen, who covered the troops in the passage of that river, bravely charged the enemy, but had the misfortune to be made prisoner with some of his cavalry. Major Bülow, who had most difficult defiles to pass, was also obliged to abandon some pieces of cannon.

THIS affair was scarce over when the Crown Prince arrived with a reinforcement; but as it was then night, and his troops were greatly fatigued, having made a forced march of upwards of five German miles, His Highness thought it better to delay his attacking the enemy 'till early in the morning. But M. de Stainville did not think proper to wait for him but retired in the night towards Frankenberg. The whole then returned to join the army.

ON the night between the 12th and 13th of September, M. de Broglio broke up his camp near Immenhausen, and fell back upon Kassel, where he occupied a very strong camp, placing his right to that city, and his left to the village of Wessenstein. He at the same time recalled Prince Xavier from the neighborhood of Göttingen, who retreated to Münden and Witzenhausen. This camp they entrenched and fortified on all sides with redoubts, though it had been already remarkably strong by the nature of its position. The Gendarmerie were posted at Lichtenau[94] between the Fulda and the Werra.

ON the 14th, the corps de reserve under the command of the Marquis of Granby passed the Diemel and encamped near Hofgeismar. General Gilsa with his corps was advanced towards Sababurg and Rheinhartdswald, and General Wangenheim moved forward from Uslar, and took post at Löwenthagen[95]. Several smart skirmishes and cannonading daily passed between the advanced parties and light troops of both armies, while they remained in this position.

ON the 15th of September, General Wangenheim dislodged from the defiles of Scheden a party of the enemy belonging to Prince Xavier's corps, which had been detached with an intent, not only to cover his right, but also to secure that pass which led to Dransfeld, Göttingen, etc.

ON the 18th of September, Marshal de Brogio having formed a scheme to cut off General Wangenheim's corps, went in person with the Prince de Condé, the Prince de Beauvau, and his brother the Count de Broglio, to join Prince Xavier with a reinforcement of troops; and on the 19th, they advanced to Lowenthagen with 32 battalions and 18 squadrons; but Gen. Wangenheim, though he had only four battalions and six squadrons, made good his retreat, and, like an able general, conducted the whole with great judgment, not-withstanding the difficulty of the ground, and the vast superiority of the numbers, retiring to his former position at Uslar.

THIS affair in no measure answered the great preparations of the French. The loss of the Allies amounted in the whole only to 150 men killed, wounded, and made prisoners, besides four pieces of cannon, and some store-wagons, which he was obliged to leave behind for want of horses. The loss of the enemy was computed to be at least double that of the Allies in number of men.

PRINCE Xavier after this affair returned with the corps de reserve under his command to Friedland, and M. de Broglio repassed the Werra with those troops which he himself had led to reinforce Prince Xavier on this occasion.

ON the 22d, M. le Conte of Lippe-Bückeburg, was detached, with a large train of artillery, and a body of troops, towards the Lower Rhine.

On the 23d, M. de Luckner fell in with a detachment of the enemy's cavalry, belonging to Prince Xavier's corps, which had advanced towards Nörten[96], he immediately attacked

---

94. Editor: Today Hessische Lichtenau.
95. Editor: Today Löwenhagen is part of the community of Nieheimetal that is part of the joint community of Dransfeld
96. Editor: Today Nörten is called Nörten-Hardenberg.

and defeated them with considerable loss, making one lieutenant colonel, some subaltern officers, and 107 private men prisoners of war.

ON the 24th, The corps de reserve, under the command of the Marquis of Granby, quitted its camp near Hofgeismar, repassed the Diemel, and joined the main army near Warburg; General Gilsa also, who was posted at Rheinhartz-Wald, joined the army with his corps.

ON the 26th, the Crown Prince was detached with a body of troops to join the Count of Lippe Bückeburg.

ON the 27th, a party of the enemy's light troops attacked some of our advanced posts near Weldant though they were soon repulsed with loss.

ON the 1st of October, General Waldegerve marched towards the Lower Rhine, with a detachment consisting of two battalions of British grenadiers, the Highlanders, Kingsley's, Hume's, and one regiment of Hessian infantry, together with the English dragoons, Inniskillings, and one regiment of Hessian cavalry.

ON the 2d, General Howard also received orders to march to the Lower Rhine, at the head of the four following regiments of infantry, viz. Buckland, Welsh Fusiliers, Griffin, and Brundenell, together with Mordaunt's Cavalry Regiment.

A detachment of the troops under the command of the Crown Prince passed by Scherembeck, on the 30th in the morning, on their way to Wesel; another party crossed the Rhine at Ruhrort, on the 29th, and proceeding to Rheinberg, surprised some of Fischer's Corps who were posted in that place, and made them prisoners; they then continued their route to Wesel on the left bank of that river, while detached parties were sent to scour the country.

ANOTHER detachment on the 29th in the evening took possession of Rees and Emmerich, and on the 30th passed over the Rhine and marched towards Cleves, sending out flying parties to traverse that country; the commanding officer of the French troops in that town retired into the castle on the approach of the Allies; the reduction of that place was committed to the care of Colonel Ditfurth.

THE French troops, who had been posted in the redoubts along that river, abandoned them with so much precipitation that they left their artillery behind, and neglected to destroy the boats, by which means a sufficient number were found for the embarkation of the troops which had been destined for the passage of the Rhine.

ON the 3d of October, the castle of Cleves surrendered, and M. de Barral who commanded in that place, together with the garrison consisting of about 500 men, were all made prisoners of war.

THIS day the town of Wesel was invested. The heavy artillery arrived in the evening at the camp of the Crown Prince before that place, and His Highness used the greatest diligence in preparing everything necessary for opening the siege in form. The two Swiss regiments of Lochman and Planta, which had been sent in order to reinforce the garrison, were prevented from throwing themselves into the town.

THE 10th, the Allied Army on the Diemel received orders to build huts, both the cavalry and the infantry; and, on the 12th, a *feu de joie* was fired on receiving the news of the reduction of Canada.

ON the 16th, M. de Broglio, having ordered a large body of troops to assemble at Cologne under the command of M. de Castries, part of whom had been detached from the army in Hesse, and the other part sent from the Low Countries, had, by forced marches, advanced, on the 14th, to Rheinberg; and our light troops, who had been posted there, were obliged to abandon it; though His Highness the Crown Prince was there in person to support them, but he found it impracticable. His horse was shot in this short but brisk affair.

MAJOR General de Bock's corps, which His Highness had immediately ordered to join him, could not arrive 'till the next morning at 6 o'clock; Lieutenant General Waldegerve's corps passed the Rhine on a bridge about two miles below Wesel, and joined him likewise at 11 o'clock; and Lieutenant General Howard's division joined him about 8 o'clock in the evening. Four Hanoverian battalions of those who were destined for the siege, and were still on their march, could not complete their junction that night.

IT was necessary to engage at a sufficient distance from the Rhine, in order to run no risk in case of accident, especially as our principal bridge was so much impaired by the current of high water occasioned by a great storm, that it was with very great difficulty the troops and cannon had passed over it. The troops were posted in such a manner as to have Rheinberg in their front, and Ossenberg[97] in their rear.

THE enemy left no more than five battalions and some squadrons at Rheinberg and marching by their left came to encamp behind the Kamp Convent. According to our intelligence of their strength, they had not then been joined by their last troops, which were to arrive the next and following day; whereupon the Crown Prince thought it absolutely necessary to make use of his time that night to surprise M. de Castries in his camp, and by that means endeavor to gain an advantage over him, if possible.

His Highness had under his command 20 battalions and 20 squadrons; but, as has been said before, several battalions had not been able to come up in time, and four others with five squadrons were left under Major General de Bock in order to observe Rheinberg, and attack that post in case of success on the side of Campen. M. de Castries had with him 30 battalions, and 38 squadrons.

THE troops began their march, on the 15th at ten in the evening. In order to reach the enemy's camp, it was necessary to dislodge Fischer's Corps which occupied the Convent of Campen, at about half a league's distance from the front of their army. This could not be done without firing some musket shots, which gave the alarm to M. de Castries, and enabled him, at the same time, to put his troops hastily under arms. He was, however, attacked and driven back twice. There was a terrible and well supplied fire of musketry kept up from 5 o'clock in the morning 'till about nine at night without ceasing. His Highness had his horse killed under him, and received a slight hurt in his leg by the same ball.

97. Editor: Today Ossenberg is part of Rheinberg.

THE Crown Prince perceiving at length, that it would be to no purpose to persist in the attempt of driving the enemy out of the wood of which they had possessed themselves, and our infantry having expended all their ammunition, he found himself obliged to order a retreat, which was executed in good order, and the enemy were not very brisk in their pursuit. The troops drew up on a moor not far distant from the place of action, where they lay on their arms.

THE loss the Allies sustained on this occasion was ten officers, 16 non-commissioned officers, 221 rank and file, killed; 68 officers, 43 non-commissioned officers, and 812 rank and file, wounded; and seven officers, six non-commissioned officers, and 429 rank and file, made prisoners. Lieutenant Colonels Pitt and Lord Downe were wounded and made prisoners; Major Generals Elliot and Griffin, together with Lieutenant Colonels, Johnson and Harvey, were wounded; and Major Follock of Keith's Highlanders was killed. We also lost one piece of cannon which burst, and 14 ammunition wagons.

THE enemy owned the loss of 841 men killed, and 1795 wounded. Lieutenant General M. de Segur, and Brigadier General M. de Wangen, several officers, and about 4oo private men, were made prisoners. We also took two pieces of cannon, and one pair of colors.

THE Crown Prince marched by Ginderich, on the 17th in the morning. An attack was made on an advanced body of the Allied troops which was posted in a wood before Elverick, and ex-tended along the Rhine with its right at Geit, and some battalions beyond it to cover its flank. The firing both of cannon and small arms lasted 'till night. A column of the enemy's infantry marched through Wallach, taking up a position a quarter of a league distance in our front among the thickets: this was their vanguard commanded by M. de Chabot.

THE Rhine was so much swelled, and the banks thereof so much overflowed about the Kartäuser Insul, that the bridge which we had over that river was damaged to such a degree as made it necessary to repair and remove it lower down. It was 5 o'clock in the morning of the 18th before that work could be finished, and the bridge refitted. The enemy were only half a league off. The Allied troops, however, passed the Rhine the same day in their presence without the least molestation. The passage could not be conducted with more judgment.

ON the night between the 18th and 19th, the Crown Prince raised the blockade of Wesel; and, after he had sent away his artillery, ammunition, etc. marched to Brünen about a league from thence, where he encamped.

THE Count de Lusace advanced again with his reserve to the neighborhood of Göttingen, which place he took possession of, and sent advanced parties as far as Northeim; but they afterwards returned and joined the Count.

A considerable detachment of the reserve of the French army, under the command of M. Ferronnie entered the Duchy of Halberstadt on the 18th exacting a million and a half of French livres contribution, payable in 24 hours but, not having been able to obtain more than 28,000 crowns, they returned, carrying away hostages for the remainder.

OCTOBER 25, His Serene Highness reinforced General Wangenheim at Uslar, and M. de Broglio likewise reinforced the corps under Prince Xavier.

THE 27th, the corps commanded by Prince Xavier of Saxony decamped from Diegerode[98], in order to go into cantonments and the cavalry belonging to that corps, which had been quartered at Göttingen, likewise marched out to their cantonments. That town was garrisoned by all the grenadiers of the reserve, amounting in the whole to about 4,700 men; their advanced posts ex-tended to Weende[99], and those of the Allies in that quarter to Bovenden.

His Highness the Crown Prince quitted his camp at Brünen on the 26th, and marched to Scherembeck, and on the 27th to Lembeck, from whence he proceeded to Klein Reken, where he encamped.

THE 31st, M. de Castries sent off eight battalions to Hesse, to join M. de Broglio.

NOVEMBER 9. This day a *feu de joie* was fired in the camp of the Allied Army, on account of a complete victory gained over the Austrians near Torgau by His Majesty the King of Prussia.

THE 14th, the position of the two armies in Hesse continued nearly the same, no material alteration having been made.

THIS day the Allied Army was ordered to go into mourning for His Late Majesty: black crepe on the colors, drums, and banners; the officers to cover their swords, knots, and sashes, with black crepe, to wear crepe around their arms, and plain hats with crepe hat-bands.

ON the 15th, His Serene Highness set out from his headquarters at Daseburg to Uslar, and on the 16th he was followed by two battalions of Hanoverians, and two battalions of Brunswick, with a train of 12 pieces of cannon; the encampment of those troops was taken up by three regiments of Hanoverians and Hessians, who returned from the Lower Rhine.

ON the 20th in the morning, one regiment of Hanoverian infantry, two troops of Elliot's light dragoons, and one regiment of hussars, passed the Diemel.

ON the 25th, nothing material had passed on the Lower Rhine; the Crown Prince still remained at his headquarters at Klein Reckum, while M. de Castries encamped at Drevenack[100], within about two leagues of Wesel.

THAT part of the Allied Army about Warburg was cantoned in the neighborhood of that place, excepting some troops who remained in camp to defend some particular posts that guarded the passages of the Diemel, and those were to be relieved every eight days. All the troops were ordered to be ready to march by the first alarm, which was to be given by setting fire to a pitch barrel erected on the Desenberg, on which six cannon

98. Editor: This may be Deiderode, which is today part of Friedland.
99. Editor: Today part of Göttingen.
100. Editor: Today part of the community of Hönxe.

were to be fired from the British park, and those to be answered by six more from General Wanheim's corps, the regiments on this signal were all to assemble at their alarm posts, and from thence to advance directly to their former positions in camp.

NOTWITHSTANDING the excessive rains which had fallen for some time past, and rendered the roads almost impracticable, His Serene Highness advanced from Uslar to Hardegsen on the 23d, with a body of troops which he had assembled there; he also caused some detachments to advance towards Kassel and Münden. General Luckner was posted at Duderstadt, by which position he prevented the French from drawing any subsistence from Thuringia. On the 26th His Serene Highness moved forward to Esebeck, fixing his headquarters at Harste; and Count Kielmannsegg pushed forward with a corps of about 7,000 men to Sibolshausen.

THE French reserve under the Count de Lusace retired, on the approach of the Allies, from Begerode to Witzenhausen, leaving M. de Vaux to command in Göttingen with a numerous garrison of select troops.

ON the 29th, the main body of the troops under Prince Ferdinand were still encamped at Esebeck, and had taken possession of Boventen, Seimershausen, and Dransfeld a small body of Prussians, consisting of 1,500 men, that were detached from the garrison of Magdeburg, and had joined General Kielmannsegg, were posted behind Göttingen, so that town was entirely blocked up.

THE King of Prussia had also detached from his army a body of 8,000 men, consisting of infantry, cavalry, and hussars, under the command of Generals Saldern, Aschersleben, and Linden, to march through Thuringia towards Göttingen, in order to act in concert with His Serene Highness.

SEVERAL smart skirmishes passed between the troops in the neighborhood of Göttingen, particularly one on the 29th past at Heydemünden upon the Werra River, which post Major General Breidenbach, at the head of two regiments of Hanoverian and Brunswick Guards, with a detachment of Cavalry, attacked; and, having carried it took possession of the town, which was abandoned by the French detachment, part of which passed the river in boats, while the others threw themselves into an entrenchment which covered the passage, and which our troops made several attempts to force, but without success. At length, our people being much galled by the side of the enemy's redoubts on the other side of the river, General Breidenbach could not carry his point, and was obliged to fall back into the town, from whence he retired at midnight; but the enemy did not retake possession of it 'till 24 hours afterwards. Our loss on the occasion amounted to about 150 private men. Five of our officers were killed, and six wounded.

THE Crown Prince's headquarters remained still at Klein Reckum, and nothing material had passed in those parts, except that he made some detachments which had beat up and harassed the posts, which M. de Castries had established along the Lippe,

M. de Luckner, having in vain cannonaded and attacked Arnstein Castle, defended by M. Verduil, was obliged to abandon the enterprise, and retire towards Friedland.

DECEMBER 11. The inclemency of the weather and the badness of the roads having not only rendered it next to an impossibility for the troops to keep the field, but also made the conveyance of forage and provisions for the use of the troops utterly impracticable, His Serene Highness found himself reduced to the necessity of quitting his design against Göttingen, and changing the cantonments of the troops employed in the blockade of that town, in order to send them into winter quarters. He accordingly withdrew his forces from that neighborhood, retiring towards Eimbach and Uslar: in the latter of which places he fixed his headquarters. The troops, likewise, which had advanced on the left of the Diemel, and in the wood of Sababurg, repassed the Diemel, and the whole army went into their winter cantonments. The English Guards were at Paderborn, and the rest quartered in that country, and along the Diemel, Weser, etc. The Marquis of Granby had his headquarters at Corvey near Höxter.

THE troops under the command of the Crown Prince on the Lower Rhine went likewise into quarters, the greatest part of whom occupied the Bishopric of Münster; the remainder joined the army under His Serene Highness.

THE French under M. de Castries went also into their quarters, which extended from Cleves to Cologne. Marshal de Broglio likewise sent his army into their quarters. He fixed his headquarters at Kassel, and his troops extended towards the Upper Rhine.

THE detachments of Prussians which were on their march to join the Allied Army, stopped at Erfurt, where they took up their quarters.

ON the 23d of December, General Luckner, who was posted with a corps of 3,000 or 4,000 men at Heiligenstadt, was attacked by a body of 10,000 French under the command of Count Broglio. The town being nearly invested on all sides, General Luckner had no other method of retreat than by the road that leads to Witzenhausen, where he gained an advantageous eminence, from whence he cannonaded the French with such success, that he secured his retreat to Scharfenstein, without the loss of a single man, or a horse killed or taken, only of a few wounded in the affair; but an officer with 34 men belonging to the militia, who were left in the town, were taken. The loss of the French on this occasion was reckoned at above 300 men. On the 24th, General Luckner returned to Heiligenstadt, and finding the French had left it, retook possession of it.

THE CAMPAIGN OF THE YEAR 1761

ON the 1st of January, the Crown Prince was at Uslar, in order to concert measures with His Serene Highness relative to the future operations. Prince Ferdinand returned his thanks to the troops for their good behavior during the course of the last year, at the same time paying them the usual compliments on the New Year.

ON the 2d, the Count de Broglio and Lieutenant General M. de Stainville, at the head of a large body of French troops, attacked the town of Duderstadt, situated at the extremity on the left of the cantonments of the Allied Army. General Mansberg, who commanded there, found it necessary to abandon the town, not being able to defend it against so superior a force. The enemy entered that place, and he retired to the heights of Herbishagen[101], where he took post, and maintained himself 'till the arrival of the Generals Kielmannsegg and Luckner, who had immediately marched to support him. On the next day they attacked the French in Duderstadt, drove them from thence, and pursued them as far as Witzenhausen. The loss of the enemy, according to their own accounts, amounted to 600 men, among whom were three complete companies of French grenadiers. The loss on the side of the Allies was about 190 men.

ON the 8th of January, M. de Belsunce, having set out from Göttingen with a detachment consisting of 150 horse and two companies of grenadiers, surprised a party of the Allies who were posted in the neighborhood of Gieboldehausen, and dispersed them. The loss on the side of the Allies were four officers and 100 men.

ON the 13th, Marshal de Brogio sent to Göttingen a convoy of 6,000 horses and 80 wagons, all laden with provisions and ammunition, which had been collected at Müden, Witzenhausen, and the places adjacent. The whole got safely into that town. He used the precaution of sending so many horses instead of wagons, in order to elude the vigilance of the Allies.

ABOUT this time, the French sent off several detachments both of horse and foot towards Langensalza in Thuringia, to join Prince Xavier of Saxony. They also sent large detachments to the country of Eichsfeld, in order to cut off our communications with the Prussians. His Serene Highness, on the other hand, detached Major General Rheda-Wiedenbrücken, with four regiments of cavalry from Dorste[102], to Duderstadt; and four battalions of grenadiers who were at Moringen, and two regiments of fusiliers who were part of the garrison of Northeim, also took the same route.

101. Editor: This may be Hundeshagen.
102. Editor: This village may be part of the city of Osterode.

ON the 26th, Prince Xavier of Saxony made an attempt on the Prussian quarters at Sondershausen, on the left of the Allied Army, and carried off part of Wunsch's battalion from Ebeleben; but General Luckner coming up at the head of four battalions and 15 squadrons, the enemy retreated, and were pursued beyond Langenseltze. General Luckner seized on one of their magazines at Daiswitz, where he made two officers and 30 men prisoners of war.

ON the 27th, the enemy also attacked some of our posts which lay on the right of our cantonments. A detachment under the command of Monsieur de St. Victor advanced to the post of Stadtberge, where they surprised part of a battalion of the Britannic Legion. Major Delaune, who commanded there, was killed in his chamber, obstinately defending himself. Our loss was 180 men made prisoners. M. de St. Vigor's corps retreated without being pursued, as we had no cavalry in that neighborhood. M. de Maupeon, at the head of another party, at the same time attacked the post at Rhoden[103], but the enemy were repulsed with loss.

ON the 4th of February, General Howard's detachment, consisting of ten battalions and 12 squadrons, arrived in the neighborhood of Geseke.

ON the 9th, the army under the command of His Serene Highness, having been for some time in motion from all quarters, were all assembled at their points of rendezvous; viz. the main body on the Diemel; the detachments of the Generals Kielmannsegg and Wangenheim, under General Spörcken, on the Rhume; and the two corps under the command of the Crown Prince and General Breidenbach, in the Sauerland. Prince Ferdinand passed the Diemel, and went to Hofgeismar, where General Gilsa had marched with the detachment under his orders. The troops halted on the 10th, and the dispositions for the motion of the whole were communicated to the generals.

On the 11th, the army marched in four columns, and passed the Diemel. The first column, led by the Marquis of Granby, passed over the stone bridge at the lower town of Warburg; the second column, commanded by the Prince of Anhalt, crossed over at the stone bridge below it; the third column, under the orders of General Oheimb, marched by the bridge at Liebenau; and General Wutgenau, at the head of the 4th, passed over the bridge at Pillam. Each column was preceded by a vanguard of all the piquets, consisting of 50 men of each battalion and 20 of each squadron, which were formed into battalions and squadrons: these were to secure the head of the cantonments. The whole then advanced towards Kassel, on the side of West Usseln. The corps under General Gilsa advanced from Hofgeismar as far as Calden. The Marquis of Granby had his headquarters at Volkmarsen.

THE Crown Prince with the corps under his command marched by the way of Stadtberge [104]to Mengeringhausen[105]; and Lieutenant General Breidenbach advanced from Brilon to Sand, and on his march made 100 of the enemy prisoners in the village of Kustleburg.

103. Editor: Today this is part of the town of Diemelstadt.
104. Editor: The former name for Warburg.
105. Editor: Today part of Bad Arolsen.

ON the 12th, the army resumed its march in the same order as they had done the day before, arriving in the neighborhood of Zierenberg. Lieutenant General Gilsa with his corps marched to Dörnburg. The vanguards of the four columns were all united into one corps, and were joined by the grenadiers of the Guards, Elliot's Dragoons, Bauer's Hussars, and the brigade of chasseurs of Lindinch and Storkhoriens[106]. The Marquis of Granby was appointed to command this body; he took post at Ehlen[107], and sent forward detachments to the Cascade[108] and Weissenstein[109].

THE Crown Prince cantoned his troops about Züschen, and having received advice that the garrison of Fritzlar was not prepared for an attack, he went thither with a few battalions in hopes of being able to carry that place by a coup de main; the attack was accordingly made with great spirit, but Monsieur de Narbonne, who commanded there with a numerous garrison of choice troops, was prepared to receive him, and descended it so resolutely, taking all the advantages which the situation of the place afforded him, that the Crown Prince thought it most advisable to desist from the attempt, and to await the arrival of some cannon to reduce it. Lieutenant General Breidenbach marched to Münchausen[110].

ON the 13th, the army marched again and cantoned in the neighborhood of Niedenstein. The corps under the command of the Marquis of Granby marched to Kirchberg[111] and Metze; that under General Gilsa remained in their former cantonments at Dörnburg. The Crown Prince cantoned about Hademar, in the neighborhood of Fritzlar. Lieutenant General Breidenbach took possession of a magazine at Rosenthal, consisting of 40,000 rations, and advanced towards Marburg, which place he made an attempt to surprise, and vigorously attacked it; but the enemy were on their guard; and having a large garrison, who made a brave resistance, the enterprise failed. M. de Breidenbach was killed in this affair that excellent general fell greatly lamented. General Oheimb was appointed to the command of that corps.

ON the 14th, the army halted. The Crown Prince detached Major General Zastrow to Felsberg, ordering a part of the cavalry to pass the Eder. An attempt was made to intimidate the garrison of Fritzlar by firing some cannon shot, but to no purpose. In the mean while my Lord Granby made a movement towards Gudensberg, the garrison of which place, consisting of 200 men, retired into the old castle. In this village were found provisions and forage.

ON the 15th, the town of Fritzlar was bombarded, and M. de Narbonne offered to capitulate, if the most honorable terms were granted him; the Crown Prince returned for answer, that such should be granted him on account of his brave defense, upon condition however, that the garrison should not serve during the present campaign, and that the garrisons of Waldeck and Bad Wildungen should be included in the capitulation.

106. Editor: Storkhoriens may be a corruption of Stockhausen.
107. Editor: Today part of Habrichtswald.
108. Editor: Today this is the cascade in the park of Wilhelmshöhe Palace, in Kassel.
109. Editor: Weissenstein was once a monestary that was turned into the Wilhelmshöhe Palace.
110. Editor: Probably Münchhausen am Christberg.
111. Editor: Today part of Felsberg on the Eder River.

THE Commandant having refused to subscribe to that condition, a brisk cannonade was begun again, which continued for about half an hour, when the terms were agreed to, except those concerning the garrisons of Waldeck and Bad Wildungen, which were no longer insisted on, upon his declaring that the troops in those places were not under his command; he marched out of the town in the evening with his corps, consisting of seven piquets drawn from the Irish battalions, and 965 men of the Royal Grenadiers, besides 105 wounded or sick, agreeable to the capitulation.

ON the 16th, my Lord Granby sent word to the commandant of Guedemburg, that he was ready to grant the same conditions to him as M. de Narbonne had obtained, which proposal the commandant very readily accepted, as provisions, and particularly water, began to fail them.

ON the 17th, the army renewed its march, and advanced at far as Obervorschütz. The vanguard took possession of the pass of Feltsburg; Major General Zastrow of that at Niedermöllrich[112]; the Crown Prince posted himself in the neighborhood of Falkenberg[113], and was before-hand with, the enemy in taking possession of the post of Homberg[114] with a party of his hussars the reigning Count of Schaumburg-Lippe took the command of a great body of the army which remained in the neighborhood of Kassel, and were joined by the corps under General Gilsa.

THE same day, our troops entered Melsungen, which place Marshal de Brogio left the preceding evening in order to repair to Bad Hersfeld; the enemy had only time to destroy a part of the magazine there; and there was found remaining a quantity of meal and forage. Our troops seized another considerable magazine at Ober-Morschen. A courier who was dispatched by Messieurs de Stainville and de Solms, expecting to find the Marshal at Melsungen, was taken by our hussars.

ON the 18th, the army passed the Eder at Feltsburg, and at Nieder-Mellerich, and was cantoned between the Efzeand the Fulda, in the neighborhood of Homberg: the Crown Prince was a day's march before them towards Bad Hersfeld. Lord Granby marched to Frielendorf by the way of Ziegenhain.

THE enemy having re-assembled a body of troops under Oberweimar, and Niederweimar[115], not far from Marburg, Lieutenant General Oheimb determined at first to attack them, but altered his intentions upon receiving an account of the march of the Chevalier de Maupeon with a body of the enemy, who had come from Siegen with an appearance of making some attempt by Battenberg[116] and Barleburg[117] upon Frankenberg[118].

112. Editor: Today part of Warben.
113. Editor: Today part of Warben.
114. Editor: Today this town is called Hobmerg (Efze) so as to distinguish it from other Hombergs.
115. Editor: Today these two towns are part of Weimar, in Hessen.
116. Editor: Today this town is called Battenberg (Eder).
117. Editor: Today Barleburg.
118. Editor: Today called Frankenberg (Eder).

GENERAL Oheimb on the 16th left Wetter to go to Frankenberg, and he found the enemy posted near Röddenau[119] in order to defend the passage of the Eder, which was made difficult by the marshy ground there. The bridge of Frankenberg being broken by the swell of the water, M. von Oheimb was obliged to stop to repair it: the enemy taking advantage of these obstacles, withdrew themselves in the night towards Hallenberg, after having destroyed the bridge of Rodenau; M. von Oheimb was no sooner informed of that retreat, than he ordered a part of his cavalry to ford the river and to occupy the heights on the left bank of the Eder, and sent parties to Sachsenburg and Hallenburg to get intelligence of the enemy.

THE repair of the bridge of Frankenberg was finished. M. von Oheimb having learnt the 17th, that M. de Maupeon was with his corps at Sachsenberg[120], after having sufficiently provided for the security of the post of Frankenberg, and of the heavy artillery, put himself in motion on the 18th early in the morning to march towards the enemy, whose advanced guard he met with between Sachsenburg and Neukirchen[121]. It was that instant attacked and routed. M. de Maupeon, lieutenant-general, who was there in person, was taken, with a lieutenant-colonel, five officers, and 50 soldiers. The enemy having fallen back towards Hallenburg, M. von Oheimb returned to Frankenberg to give his troops some rest there, observing the movements that the enemy might make on the side of Marburg, towards which place several of their regiments had filed off. Major Scheither attacked the same day a detachment of the enemy near Padburg, dispersed it, and took 140 prisoners, among whom were four officers.

ON the 19th, the army arrived in the neighborhood of Schwartzenborn. The Crown Prince's corps posted itself at Ober-Geise, pushing detachments on to Gittersdorff. Lord Granby went to Neukirchen: the enemy's detachments at Ober and Nieder-Grentzbach, falling back upon Ziegenhain.

THE patrol of the Crown Prince reported in the night between the 19th and 20th, that they saw a fire at Bad Hersfeld, which gave reason to suppose the enemy had abandoned that place and had set fire to the magazine: this suspicion was confirmed the next morning, and our troops entered Bad Hersfeld, where there had been 15 French battalions, which marched away in the night towards Fulda. Great part of the magazine was saved, which had consisted of 80,000 sacks of meal, 50,000 sacks of oats, and a million of rations of hay.

ON the 21st of February, the army marched to Hausen; the Crown Prince was advanced to Niederaula.

THE following is an account of the motions of General Spörcken on the left since the 8th. to this day.

M. von Spörcken having divided the corps under him into two columns, one of which was commanded by Count Kielmannsegg, and the other by Lieutenant General Wangenheim, put Major General von Luckner at the head of a strong advanced guard, who marched, the 9th to Heiligenstadt.

119. Editor: Today part of Frankenberg.
120. Editor: Today part of Frankenberg.
121. Editor: Between Schwalmstadt and Bad Hersfeld

THE first column arrived at Büren, and the second at Worbis[122]. The troops halted on the 10th. M. de Luckner marched the next day to Küllstedt; Count Kielmannsegg to Helmsdorf[123]; and M. de Wangenheim to Beberstedt[124].

M. von Spörcken went to reconnoiter the enemy, several of whose regiments of infantry had passed the Werra at Eschwege. There were 5,000 French in the city of Mühlhausen: that of Langensaltze, and the villages in its neighborhood, were occupied by Saxons. M. von Spörcken found on the heights of Dome four battalions of Grenadiers of France ranged in order of battle, and the. infantry posted in a wood towards Eschwege, to protect the communication of the Werra with Mühlhausen and Langensalza. M. de Luckner had orders to attack them the next day in the morning with his corps, which was to be sustained by two battalions and six squadrons. The same day M. de Belsunce appeared, before Duderstadt with 3,000 men and some cannon of the garrison. of Göttingen. He summoned Lieutenant Colonel Rehbom, who commanded in that town, three times; and upon the negative answers received from him, he caused the gates to be battered for three hours; but his attempts were fruitless, and he returned the same night.

M. de Luckner, on the 12th, attacked the French and Swiss grenadiers who had passed the night under arms, in the wood of Dome, over against his advanced posts at Anrode and Bickenriede. He pushed them as far as the heights of Eigenrieden, where they gained a thick wood, which Count de Solms had fortified by felled trees. They cannonaded each other. The enemy received reinforcements from the quarters on the Werra and those of the Saxons.

THE night coming on, M. von Spörcken could not assemble his men so as to undertake anything against the enemy. He contented himself with making some changes in the dispositions of his troops, and pushed the enemy's skirmishers back. The skirmishes of this day cost him 40 men in killed and wounded. The loss of the enemy was more considerable, and four officers and 50 of their men were taken.

M. von Spörcken put his troops in order of battle on the 13th, at 7 o'clock in the morning, upon the height called Eisburg, but having found the enemy considerably reinforced, that they had occupied all the woods where the horse could not act, and that the troops of His Prussian Majesty were at the distance of three marches, he resolved to pass the Unstrut at Silberhausen and Horsmar, to draw near them by a forced march.

HE informed M. de Sieburg of his intentions; and the motion was executed in presence of the enemy without the least loss. The troops were cantoned between Kaiserhagen[125] and Marolterode[126].

THE corps of Prussians advanced the 14th to the heights of Langensalza, which were occupied by 3,000 Saxons. M. von Spörcken occupied the village on the left side of the Unstrut River with the troops, of his first line, and drew those of his second line as near as possible.

122. Editor: Today part of the town of Leinefelde-Worbis.
123. Editor: Today this town is called Helmsdorf (Eichsfeld).
124. Editor: Beberstedt, today part of the community of Dünwald.
125. Editor: Today part of Unstruttal.
126. Editor: Today part of Schlotheim.

HE agreed with M. de Sieburg, that the Prussian troops should pass the Unstrut at Merxleben, whilst he passed it at Thamsbrück and M. de Luckner at Bollstedt. In the night, the bridges which the enemy had broken were repaired.

ON the 15th at seven in the morning, all the troops came to the river side in order to pass it, but the thaw had increased the waters to such a degree in twice 24 hours, that there was an inundation from Mulhausen almost to Langensalza.

THE Prussian cavalry got through the passage of Merkleben while their cannon were battering the town of Langensalza. Eight squadrons of M. von Spörcken's first line passed at Thomasbrück, with a brigade of chasseurs, and a squadron of Luckner's, whose whole corps could not pass, the waters continuing out all day. In the meantime, the Prussian cavalry fell upon the enemy who were going out of Langensalza: and M. von Spörcken's corps did so likewise upon the troops which were coming down the hills to their assistance.

M. von Spörcken computed the enemy's loss that day at 5,000 men, at the same time that his own scarcely exceeded 100. Lieutenant General Hodenberg was wounded and taken prisoner.

THE Prussians took three battalions and seven pieces of cannon, and M. von Spörcken's troops took two battalions and six pieces of cannon.

DURING the action, the infantry of M. von Spörcken's first line passed the Unstrut at Thomasbrück, but the troops being greatly fatigued, M. de Sieburg cantoned his corps at Langensalza, and General Spörcken's corps re-entered its former quarters on the left of the Unstrut, except M. de Luckner's body, which remained at Mülverstedt[127] and Schönstedt[128].

ON the 16th, the first line under the command of General Spörcken passed the Unstrut again at Bolstedt, and advanced cantoning as far as Grossengottern[129] and Oppershausen[130]. The second line passed the Unstrut at the same place, and cantoned at Mulhausen, where still 53 of the enemy's sick were found, and made prisoners of war.

ON the 17th, Major General Luckner with his corps composed the vanguard, and marched to Eisenach, which he attacked, and forced the enemy, who were still there under the command of the Generals Stainville and Solms, to retire to Vacha. About 40 prisoners were taken there, and two Saxon officers. The army made a forced march in two columns, stationed in the neighborhood of Streck and Neukirchen; Luckner's Corps remained at Eisnach.

ON the 18th they halted. This day came in above 100 Swiss and Saxon deserters.

ON the 19th, Luckner's Corps, reinforced with four squadrons of Veltheim and Bremer, marched as far as Vacha (the bridge of which was barricaded), attacked and forced the

127. Editor: Today part of Unstrut-Hainich.
128. Ibid.
129. Ibid.
130. Editor: Today part of Vogtei.

enemy to abandon it about midnight, six of our men were killed, and about 30 of the enemy's wounded. General Luckner lodged the light troops Vacha, and cantoned the rest of his corps on the right of the Werra near Vacha; the first line marched to Oberellen[131] and Förtha, and the second to Eisenach.

ON the 20th, Luckner's Corps halted. The first line of Spörcken's corps marched to Heringen and Kieselbach, and the second to Fermbreitenbach and Frauensee[132]. The Prussian troops marched this day to Gotha to observe the army of the Circles, which was re-assembled at Arnstadt.

ON the 21st, Luckner's Corps marched to Mansbach[133], and passed the Werra at Vacha: the first line marched to Friedewald, Hamelhausen, and Lengers, passing the Werra at Vacha and Lengers; the second marched to Heringen and Vacha. Many deserters came in from Stainville's corps, which made its retreat by Mansbach to Fulda.

THIS day the brigade of British Guards joined the advanced corps under the command of the Marquis of Granby.

ON the 22d the Marquis of Granby marched to Treysa, where a large party of the enemy had been posted, who, on the approach of our troops, retired to Ziegenhayn, the blockade of which place was immediately formed; M. de Luckmantel commanded there a garrison of 700 men.

Lieutenant General Oheimb advanced to Kirchhain, and from this time was to receive his orders from Lord Granby.

FEBRUARY 23, the army marched to Grebenau, and the Crown Prince was advanced to Schlitz: eight battalions were detached from General Spörcken's corps, under the command of Major General Scheele, to reinforce the Count de of Lippe Bückeburg before Kassel, in which city the Count de Broglio commanded with a garrison of 17 battalions, beside the Volontaires de Saint Victor.

A detachment from the garrison of Gottingen pushed forward at far as Northeim, where they exacted 100,000 livres by way of contribution, and carried off hostages for the payment of that sum. Another large detachment from the same garrison marched out on the 23d, and advanced to Duderstadt, which place they took possession of: a party of 200 Hanoverians who were in garrison there were made prisoners of war.

ON the 24th, Major General Schlüter of the Russian artillery relieved the Marquis of Granby in the blockade of Ziegenhain; and His Lordship marched to Kirehain: the castle of Amöneburg, which is within cannon shot of that place, surrendered, and the garrison, consisting of two officers and 50 men belonging to the Irish Brigade, were made prisoners. Our hussars advanced as far as Homberg, where there was a detachment of the enemy, who immediately retired. The Crown Prince detached General Luckner from Schlitz to Fulda, who made upwards of 300 prisoners in that town and the neighboring

131. Editor: Today part of Gerstungen.
132. Editor: Today part of Tiefensee.
133. Editor: Today part of Hohenroda.

villages; the enemy had burnt their supply of hay, but had left behind a considerable depot of flour and oats untouched.

THE Army of the Empire, which was in the neighborhood of Gotha when General Spörcken attacked the enemy at Langensalza, retired precipitately, and took the route to Bamberg.

THE Prussian corps under General Sieburg, who acted in conjunction with General Spörcken, served to keep them in awe, and prevented them from advancing any farther.

THE French troops which were posted on the Lower Rhine were all in motion, and, by their different maneuvers, indicated a design against the town of Münster, but their views were frustrated by the prudent measures of General Hardenberg: that general was at this time assembling a considerable body on the Upper Lippe, to act as occasion required.

THIS, day in the evening, a detachment from the garrison of Waldeck, having been sent out to annoy our convoys, fell in with one of our parties near Freienhagen which was patrolling about that neighborhood to keep the castle of Waldeck in awe, and to protect our convoys: Captain Wittenius who commanded the party, had the misfortune to be dangerously wounded on the first onset by which means the advantage was on the side of the enemy, who took 30 horses; they failed however in their main design, the convoy arriving at its destination, except two wagons which fell into their hands.

ON the 26th, 27th, and 28th of February, the army arrived by several divisions, and cantoned between the Schwalm and Ohm Rivers, His Serene Highness fixing his headquarters at Schweinsberg. The Marquis of Granby, with Major General Oheimb under his command, took post, on the 26th, for some time on the heights near Kleinseelheim, but on their advancing, M. de Rougé, who had possessed himself of a very advantageous situation, retired towards Giessen; His Lordship then took post between the Lahn and the Ohm, cantoning his troops in Schröck, Heskem, etc. The French garrison in Marburg retired to the castle and abandoned the town, which was taken possession of by four Hessian battalions.

THE corps under the Crown Prince having been reinforced by a part of the troops belonging to the corps that was under General Spörcken, (who joined the army with the remainder), His Highness advanced on the 25th to Lauterbach.

LIEUTENANT Colonel Stockhausen fell in with a detachment of the enemy near Kaussungen, dispersed them and made 60 prisoners.

MARSHAL de Broglio, who was collecting all his forces together, had his headquarters on the 26th at Marienborn, on the 27th at Friedberg, and on the 28th at Vibel[134] and Bergen, where he was fortifying his camp with the greatest diligence. He received daily fresh reinforcements from the Lower Rhine.

---

134. Editor: Today Vibel is Bad Vibel.

THE Crown Prince advanced to Budingen, from whence he dislodged an advanced party of the enemy who were positioned there and took possession of that place. General Luckner also made himself master of Aschaffenburg.

ON the 2d, Major General Schluter, in order to strengthen the Fortress of Ziegenhain, formed the design of getting possession of the suburbs called Weickhaus: this enterprise had all the success desired. The suburbs were attacked and carried with great bravery: the enemy lost in the action 30 men killed and wounded, and two of their officers, with 56 private men, were made prisoners of war.; the loss of the Allies consisted in six men killed and 26 wounded. M. de Schluter proposed to M. de Luckner, who commanded, in Ziegenhain, to make a convention for the suburbs, but the proposition was rejected, contrary to the practice in such cases, and the commandant having fired from the fortress on the suburbs, M. de Schluter, to save the houses, drew off his, troops and placed them in their former quarters; his aide de camp was killed in this action.

MAJOR Scheither took the castle of Battenburg by assault and made prisoner one lieutenant colonel, one captain, four subaltern officers, and 250 Swiss, with ten hussars; he also took four pieces of cannon.

THE Count de Broglio made a sally out of Kassel with a considerable body of troops, but he was repulsed and oblige to retire in the utmost disorder with the loss of a great number of men.

GENERAL Hardenberg took post at Stadtberge with his corps from the country of Münster.

ON the 7th of March, the garrison of Kassel made a vigorous sally, and took possession of the trenches. They carried off four mortars, nailed up (spiked) one cannon, and destroyed the works of the ground battery; but the Count de of Lippe-Bückeburg, at the head of the Hessian guards, and Wangenheim's Grenadiers, drove them back into the town.

THIS day the trenches were opened against the fortress of Ziegenhain, and the batteries were constructed by the 9th, at which time a severe cannonade began.

ON the 8th, 9th, and 10th, the French troops from the Lower Rhine, under M. de Muy, arrived on the Main, and joined the army under Marshal de Brogio.

THE Count de of Lippe had finished his second parallel before the town of Kassel on the 10th, and on that night, he attacked and drove the French from their entrenchments which they had made on the front of the principal attack.

ON the 11th, the Marquis of Granby passed the River Lahn over a wooden bridge at the Neumühl, below Marburg, and cantoned his troops at Lohra, Damm, Rodgen, etc. He left at Marburg the four regiments that had taken possession of that town.

THE Crown Prince with his corps marched from Lauterbach to the neighborhood of Grünberg, having an advanced post at Laubach; General Luckner with his corps also fell back from Herbstein and joined the army.

MARSHAL de Broglio having assembled all his troops, and joined by all the reinforcements he expected from the Lower Rhine, quitted his camp at Vilben and moved forward, fixing his headquarters at Friedberg with his vanguard at Giessen, and the neighboring villages.

A smart skirmish passed between a detachment of the Allies and a body of the French, who were going from Wesel to Dülmen, in which the latter were defeated, and fled with precipitation to Wesel.

THE garrison of Göttlngen continued their incursions into the country of Hanover, laid the bailiwick of Westerhof under contribution, and placed a detachment of cavalry into quarters at Seesen.

ON the 14th of March, General Hardenberg, with the corps under his command, arrived at Kirchhain from Stadtberge.

ON the 17th, the French army marched to Giessen, where Marshal de Brogio fixed his headquarters; the same day the whole of his vanguard was advanced towards the Ohm.

THE Marquis of Granby with his corps repassed the Lahn at the Neumühl, and he immediately withdrew the four battalions from the town of Marburg, of which the French took possession of and shut the gates. At 9 o'clock in the morning, the whole drew up on the heights of Schröck, expecting to be attacked by the enemy's vanguard; however, nothing passed but some skirmishes between the light troops near Heskem. He cantoned the troops that night at Grossseelheim and Kleinseelheim; and on the 18th in the evening, His Lordship repassed the Ohm, and retreated to Kirchhain.

ON the 20th, the position of the Allied Army was as follows, viz. that of the main body upon the heights of Homberg, the headquarters of His Serene Highness were still at Schweinsberg; the Crown Prince with his corps was advanced towards Grünberg, the Marquis of Granby with his corps was posted at Kirchhain, and General Hardenberg behind Redecken[135], between Schweinsberg and Kirchhain; on the other hand, the enemy occupied all the country along the Lahn and Gladenbach, Allendorff, Lich, Hungen, and Laubach.

THE garrison of Kassel about this time made two very unsuccessful sallies, having lost a considerable number of men in each.

M. de Belsunce, who, with a detachment from the garrison of Göttingen, had been for some time in possession of Northeim, was driven from thence by some troops from Brunswick and Hanover, which were joined by a small party of Prussians.

ON the 21st of March, the corps under the command of the Crown Prince was attacked near Grünberg by a large detachment of the enemy, consisting of three columns of cavalry, and was obliged to fall back to the heights of Hainbach and Elpenrod; the enemy taking the advantage of the woods to conceal the march of their columns, particularly of that column which was to turn the Prince's right, were too near to suffer the retreat

135. Editor: Probably Rüdigheim. Today part of Amöneburg.

to be made without loss; they began the attack just as the troops were entering a defile, by which means part of our rear was cut off. We lost about 2,000 men made prisoners, belonging to the Brunswick Guards, the Roeder Regiment, and the battalions of Imhoff, some colors, and 13 or 14 pieces of cannon; we had very few killed or wounded. The Crown Prince, with the remainder of that corps, retired to the main army at Homberg. General Rheda-Wiedenbrücken, who commanded the Hanoverians, was killed. The enemy owned to the loss of no more than 100 killed and wounded, among the number of the latter was the Baron de Clausen, who commanded the whole.

THOUGH the position of the Allied Army on the Ohm was excellent with regard to military operations, yet it became daily more and more inconvenient with respect to subsistence, which unavoidably began to grow scarce, after so long a stay in a country where they had no magazines, insomuch that the scarcity of forage, etc. rendered it impossible for them to maintain their ground there any longer; His Serene Highness was therefore obliged to break up his camp and retire, which he did on the 24th to Neustadt, without any molestation from the enemy, excepting some trifling skirmishes with their light troops.

ON the 25th, Marshal de Brogio entered the town of Ziegenhain; the siege of that place having been raised. The garrison being joined by some cavalry, commanded by M. de Monchenu, pursued the rear of the besiegers in their retreat, and coming up with a party of them at the village of Leimsfeld, between Frielendorf and Niedergrenzebach[136], gained some advantage, making about 400 men prisoners, among whom were some officers of distinction; they also took two pieces of cannon.

THE Royal Legion likewise took possession of Arolsen, in which place they found about 300 sick men in the British hospital.

FISCHER'S CORPS having pushed forward to Korbach, in order to intercept the convoys of the Allied Army, detached the Chevalier d'Origny with a party of 3,000 men from thence towards Wolfhagen; he fell in with a battalion of the Britannic Legion, who were posted at Netze a little above Waldeck, and made the greater part of them prisoners.

ON the 27th of March, the Allied Army passed the Eder. The Crown Prince covered its passage, having attacked a party of the enemy near Kleineglis[137], repulsed them with considerable loss, and made 100 men prisoners on this occasion.

ON the same day, the Count von Lippe-Bückeburg made the proper dispositions for raising the siege of Kassel, and on the night between the 27th and 28th sent off his heavy artillery, etc. by the way of Hohenkirchen. Count Broglio sent out M. de la Borde with a battalion of foot, and some grenadiers to the right bank of the Fulda, with orders to get as near as possible to Sandershausen, and endeavor to cannonade the Allies as they filed off on the other side of the river. He also caused the grenadiers and jägers to take possession of the thirds parallel, which had been abandoned, but the Count von Bückeburg still maintained the first parallel with a considerable force 'till he should have removed all the stores and implements employed in the siege.

136. Editor: Today part of Schwalmstadt.
137. Editor: Today part of Borken.

ON the 29th, the Allied Army assembled on the heights near Züschen[138], and retreated towards Wolfhagen.

ON the 30th of March, it resumed its march, and encamped in the neighborhood of Volkmarsen.

THIS day Count de Broglio, who had marched out of Kassel with his garrison in order to harass the besiegers in their retreat, came up with their rearguard, and attacked them with some success, carrying off four pieces of cannon, some ammunition wagons, and several prisoners.

THE troops that were made prisoners in the affair near Grünberg were exchanged.

ON the 31st, Marshal de Brogio caused a *Te Deum* to be sung in his camp on account of the Allies having evacuated the county of Hesse; they also fired a *feu de joie* on the occasion.

THE whole of the Allied Army having repassed the Diemel by the 1st of April, His Serene Highness sent off a body of troops towards the Lippe, to observe the movements of the French on the Lower Rhine, and ordered the remainder to their former cantonments, leaving a chain of troops along the Diemel to secure the passages of that river.

MARSHAL DE BROGio also sent back those troops which had come from the Lower Rhine to join him, were destined to make a part of the French army which were to act in those parts. He also placed numerous garrisons in Gottingcn, Kassel, and Ziegenhain, and made large detachments to the country of Fulda; the rest of his troops returned to their cantonments; the Marshal fixing his headquarters at Frankfurt.

ON the 19th of April, the Marshal de Soubise, who was to command a separate army of the enemy this year on the Lower Rhine, arrived at Frankfurt, in order to concert measures with M. de Broglio, relative to their future operations, and on the 23d, he set out for Düsseldorf.

APRIL 20th seven Hanoverian regiments marched from the country of Paderborn towards Hamm, and that neighborhood.

The Crown Prince set out soon after for Münster, where he fixed his headquarters.

ON the 21st of April, a large magazine of hay, which the French had collected at Wesel, took fire. There were consumed 1,250,000 rations, which were computed to have been worth 2,000,000 of livres. Thirty-three soldiers of the Normandy Regiment perished in the flames. There were also above 60 boats burned and sunk.

APRIL 24, a detachment of the enemy, consisting of 300 men, advanced from Göttingen towards Uslar, and surprised one battalion of the Britannic Legion at the village of Feldhaven, in the neighborhood of that place, and made about 100 prisoners but General Luckner coming up with some grenadiers and hussars, they were dislodged, and forced to retire with precipitation, leaving behind 50 dragoons that were made prisoners.

138. Editor: Today part of the town of Fritzlar.

ON the 1st of May, another large party belonging to the garrison of Göttingen advanced towards Moringen, but they immediately retreated upon the approach of General Luckner, who pursued them as far as the Leine River, which river M. de Belsunce had only just time to get over, abandoning part of his baggage.

MAY the 5th, M. Luckner having received intelligence that a detachment of the garrison of Göttingen had marched upon an expedition towards the Hartz, with an intention to raise contribu-tions upon the country of Hanover, he immediately set out in search of that corps, with a body of 100 hussars under his command; and, coming up with, the enemy, who consisted of 300 horse, he had the good fortune to rout them entirely, making prisoners, one officer, 30 troopers, and 61 horses.

THE same day Captain Brinsky, who had been detached by M. Luckner, likewise attacked them, with 100 hussars and 50 of the Brunswick cavalry, with such success, that he drove them before him into Göttingen, and made prisoners, 2 captains, 1 lieutenant, 2 cornets, and 53 dragoons; their commander, M. de Belsunce, narrowly escaped being taken himself in the pursuit.

CAPTAIN Riedesel, at the head of 100 Brunswick hussars, attacked the village of Spielen, beyond the Fulda, in which was an officer with 50 of the enemy, took 30 of them, and killed the rest, with the loss of five hussars killed, and some few wounded.

ON the 14th, 15th, and 16th of May, the first division of infantry, as well as the dragoons of the army under M. de Soubise, marched forward, in order to form three camps; the first division encamped in the neighborhood of Rees, under the command of the Marquis de Voyer; the second division encamped near Düsseldorf, under the orders of M. de Chevert; and the third division, which was part of the main body of the French army on the Lower Rhine, pitched their tents between Büderich and Wesel, where M. de Soubise had fixed his headquarters.

THE Crown Prince also moved forward, with a large body of the Allies from Münster, towards the Rhine, to be near at hand to observe the motions of the enemy, fixing his headquarters at Nottuln. Some of the light troops, belonging to this corps, attacked and defeated some of the advanced posts of the two French camps at Rees and Wesel.

MAY the 17th, the heavy artillery which the French had at Frankfurt set out for Kassel and Hersfeld, and several of their regiments also filed off towards that neighborhood: they likewise reinforced the garrison of Göttingen with 3,000 men, and erected ovens in that town for the use of their troops.

MAY 29, Captain Lieutenant Nieheimeier being ordered by M. de Luckner to occupy the environs of Northeim with 100 horse of the Chevalerie Regiment, attacked and entirely dispersed a party of the garrison from Göttingen; he took on this occasion 1 lieutenant colonel, 34 dragoons, and 40 horse. M. de Belsunce, who commanded that party, very narrowly escaped by the goodness of his horse.

ANOTHER skirmish also happened about the same time in the neighborhood of Kassel, in which the hussars of the Allied Army made one lieutenant, and some hussars of the enemy prisoners.

MAY 30, General Spörcken took possession of the camp at Warburg, having under his command 13 regiments of German foot, and six regiments of German horse; and on the same day, the Crown Prince encamped at Nottuln and Shaapdetten[139]. A detachment of six battalions and four squadrons formed a separate camp at Appelhaülen[140]. His light troops were posted at Coesfeld, Dülmen, and Gescher.

ON the 16th of June, General Luckner took 84 oxen belonging to the enemy, under the walls of Göttingen, drove back a party of the garrison, killed and wounded 100 men, and made one captain and 14 private men prisoners.

JUNE 17, the French army on the Lower Rhine began to move forwards on the 12th in three divisions; that under the Marshal de Soubise from Wesel encamped on the 13th on Aolt, the 14th at Essen, and on the 16th he marched to Bockum, where he joined the division from Düsseldorf under M. de Chevert, who had arrived at that place, the day before, by the way of Steyl; the division under M. de Voyer, from Rees, having advanced by the way of Recklinghausen, encamped the same day at Grimberg on the Emser; Conflans's corps was at Gastrop, and all the volontaires of the army were at Dortmund, to which place their whole army came this day.

THIS day Major Schleiter crossed the Rhine at Bislich with 36 hussars, and burnt the French magazines at Xanten, which consisted of 36,000 rations of hay and straw, and 1,400 sacks of oats; from thence he went to Sonsbeck, and passed by Gueldren and Stralen in the way to Kakirchen and Ruhrmond; but learning that Ruhrmond was possessed by Austrian troops he went to Aersen, where he burnt a great magazine of hay and straw, which at a moderate computation consisted at least of a million and a half of rations, and two boats, having on board 4,000 sacks of oats which he cast into the Maas: near Gueldren he met 160 carts, which he caused to be unloaded and burnt. From Aersen he took the route of Gennep, and burnt the magazine there, consisting of 100; 1,000 rations of hay and straw, and some thousand rations of oats. In this tour he made 16 prisoners, whom he took along with him, besides a sergeant and 18 Austrians, and 40 French boatmen, whom not being able to take with him, he left to the magistrates of Stralen and Aersen 'till his return. He afterwards burnt four double boats of forage and crossed the Rhine again at Loberg.

AT Buderic there was a regiment of French cavalry with glandered horses. They detached 150 horsemen after him. Two hundred foot were sent after him, in three detachments, from Wesel, but he escaped them. At Bockholt a strong party waited for him in his return, but he made his retreat, and escaped them likewise, having performed all this in 93 hours' time.

ON the 19th of June, the Allied Army under His Serene Highness were all assembled, and encamped on the heights above Nehaus, and on the 21st they decamped and marched in six columns to Geseke. The Crown Prince was at this time encamped on the heights of Havel; and Lieutenant General Howard; was posted with his corps near Hamm.

---

139. Editor: Today part of Nottuln.
140. Ibid.

M. de Soubise, who was still at Dortmund, pushed forward a vanguard to Unna Kamen, and Lühnen, these gained some advantage over an advanced party of the Allies posted at Lünen, who were obliged to fall back, with the loss of 245 men made prisoners, besides two pieces of cannon.

ON the 23d of June, M. de Soubise marched to Unna, where he fixed his headquarters; the Prince de Condé was at Uelzen with the vanguard, and M. de Voyer at Kessebüren.

ON the 24th, the Prince de Condé marched to Fremerken, M. de Voyer to Oschbusen[141], and M. de Conflans was ordered to Arnsberg, in order to sustain M. Daufet, who was to take possession of the defile of Essen[142].

THE troops under the Crown Prince formed at that time three different camps, one at Hamm, another at Paradis, and a third at Soest.

THE army under His Serene Highness halted on the 22d at Geseke, and on the 23d by 3 o'clock in the morning, they decamped and marched to Alt-Geseke, within one league and a half of Lippstadt; from hence on the 24th, they proceeded to Soest, where they joined the corps under the command of General Howard, in this place the Marquis of Granby took the command of a separate corps, who encamped on the heights about a league from the front of the main army.

ON the 25th, a feu de joie was fired by the Allies, on account of the reduction of Belle-Isle.

THE army resumed its march on the 28th and encamped near Werl.

THE Crown Prince, having left General Kielmannsegg at Hamm, marched to Kirchdenhern; and from thence, on the 26th, to Sundern[143], where he encamped on the right wing of the grand army under Prince Ferdinand. The castle of Werl was attacked by the enemy, but without success, though they cannonaded it for some time: Major Raal commanded there with a garrison of 200 men.

ON the 29th of June, the whole army moved forward towards the enemy in nine columns, including the two under the command of the Crown Prince. Their reserve, commanded by the Prince de Condé, retired towards their grand army, and was harassed all the time of their retreat by the head of our columns. Part of the right wing of the Allies was ordered to fall back; and the whole army took an advantageous position between the Unna and the Ruhr. The firing on the van continued all this day and began also the next morning. The right wing encamped before the village of Lünern, where the headquarters were fixed, and the left reached behind the village of Kesebüren, which the French had burned as far as a fall of trees which covered their right; nothing but a ravine separated the right of the Allies from the left of the enemy, the front whereof they had fortified with redoubts.

---

141. Editor: This may be Ostbüren.
142. Editor: This is definitely not the Essen in the Ruhr. It is probably Niederense, today part of Ense.
143. Editor: This may be Sönnern.

THE corps under the command of General Kielmannsegg was posted at Kamen.

THIS day Marshal de Brogio advanced to the Diemel and passed that river; whereupon General Spörcken was obliged to abandon the town of Warburg, and retreat towards Paderborn. In his retreat he lost some pieces of cannon and a few men were made prisoners.

ON the 30th of June, M. de Chabot, who commanded the vanguard of that army, took possession of Dringelburg[144]; he likewise sent a detachment by Brakel to Steinheim[145] on the road to Hameln, and some of his troops took post at Höxter and Corvey: his main body marched to Dalhelm and Lichtenau. The light troops of the Allies kept possession of Holzminden.

ON the 1st of July at 11 o'clock at night, the army under the command of His Serene Highness decamped from Lünern, and turned the enemy's left flank with a design to attack them in the rear; but the weather being excessively rainy, and the country full of morasses, it was found impossible to bring up the cannon: Prince Ferdinand was therefore obliged to lay that attempt aside. The army continued its march along the enemy's rear; and, without any interruption or loss, took post on their other flank, the headquarters being fixed at Dortmund on the 3d, near which place the troops encamped, after a most fatiguing march of three days and two nights through roads that were scarcely practicable.

THE enemy had, on the 2d, attacked our piquets under General Wutgenau with a corps of 10,000 men - perceiving that four battalions of the corps under the command of Lord Granby were advancing to support them, they retired: they lost on this occasion M. de Pedemont, brigadier, who commanded the attack, besides one colonel and one major killed, and a lieutenant colonel wounded and taken. On the side of the Allies, the loss was, two Hessian officers and two or three private men.

ON the 4th of July, the whole army began its march by 1 o'clock, and by ten arrived at the rear of the enemy's strong camp, who immediately abandoned it, and retired behind Werl, placing the castle of that place (which continued in our possession) before their right flank; they then occupied the very same camp where we had been but a few days before, and the Allied army encamped on the heights of Hemmerde.

ON the 5th, the Allied Army placed their tents with the baggage assembled at Hemmerede, and the troops marched forward in six columns with an intent to attack the enemy, but their situation was found to be too advantageous, and the whole returned to their former camp.

ON the 6th in the evening, Marshal Soubise decamped and marched towards Soest, near which place the enemy pitched their tents.

ON the 7th, the Allied Army marched in the morning and encamped near Hilbeck, the little rivulet of Saltzbach parted the two armies.

---

144. Editor: "Dringelburg" may be Trendelburg.
145. Editor: This may be the present town of Stienheim am Main, part of Hanau.

MARSHAL de Broglio, having taken possession of Paderborn, marched to join M. de Soubise; and the two armies accordingly completed their junction in the neighborhood of Soest.

ON the other hand, General Spörcken, after his retreat Warburg, marched around by Blomberg, Detmold, Bielefeld, Rietberg, etc. with his corps, in order to join the main army under the command of His Serene Highness,

ON the 11th, His Serene Highness moved his headquarters, from Hilbeck to Haus-Hohenover and on the 12th, the main army marched to the left in order to draw nearer to that place.

ON the 13th, General Luckner marched early in the morning to Sarole, where the Count de Chabot was encamped with three regiments of dragoons, one regiment of hussars, the Volontaires de Flanders, and two regiments of foot, on this side the Lippe: this body he attacked so vigorously and successfully that M. de Chabot repassed the river in great confusion, having lost 150 men made prisoners, (among whom were two captains of horse) and above 200 horses. The Bauer Hussars, and those of Brunswick, which formed the attack, penetrated thrice into the du Roi Regiment, which they overthrew, and of which very few would have escaped but for the defiles, which stopped the hussars.

ON the 14th, Captains Kampen and Engel were detached towards Kassel with 200 cavalry, in order to destroy the French convoys of provisions; in which they succeeded; for whilst Captain Engel watched the causeway that leads to Kassel, and Captain Lieutenant Sandars that to the Diemel, Captain Kampen attacked and ruined the post and enclosure of Westuffeln, and Niedermeiser, where he lost one man; he afterwards destroyed 200 empty wagons, and hamstrung above 300 horses.

CAPTAIN Engel also broke to pieces all the carriages that were going to Kassel and hamstrung all the horses.

LIEUTENANT Muller being sent with a party of 20 cavalry to meet a column of carriages that was escorted by ten dragoons, two officers, and 50 soldiers, fell upon them so briskly that the two officers ran away directly, and the 50 soldiers were dispersed; he then pursued the dragoons to the very gates of Kassel, where they escaped him, his horses being spent with fatigue. Above 30 carriages, with bacon and other provisions, going, to the French headquarters were burnt for want of time to carry them off, in sight of the garrison of Kassel.

THEY took from the enemy in all 700 horses, and spoiled 2,000 more, by the enemy's own confession.

THIS stroke was very sensibly felt by the enemy, who were before in great want of provisions; having lost on this occasion a great quantity of bread, and also meal, part of which was carried off by the hussars, and the rest distributed to the peasants, who flocked in from all quarters.

UPON their return, this body of light troops took 250 recovered men of the enemy's troops.

ON the 15th and 16th of July, from the time the Allied Army occupied the camp of Haus-Hohenover, that of the enemy encamped at Soest, under the command of Prince Soubise, who was every day employed in reconnoitering the position of the Allies, this position was a very advantageous one, on account of the woods and defiles which it was necessary to pass before they could make any attack on it. There was not a day in which the advanced posts were not engaged.

His Serene Highness was informed, in the morning of the 13th, that Marshal Soubise's army had made a motion forwards, in consequence of which, he ordered the baggage away, and the army to hold itself in readiness to be put under arms on the first signal.

ON the 14th in the morning, the enemy's new camp was discovered, the right of which stretched toward the convent of Paradise and Soest, the left reaching to the heights of Ruhne; and all having appeared quiet there, the baggage was ordered back.

His Serene Highness, however, thought proper to make, a movement with his army, the intention of which was, to reinforce the right wing; the Crown Prince was at the extremity of it, which extended as far as the village of Burecke[146], which was guarded by a detachment. The body of the army occupied the heights of Wambeln; and the Prince of Anhalt the ground between Illengen and Hohenover. Lord Granby kept his position on the left, upon the heights of Kirchdinker; and Lieutenant General Wutgenau, who was encamped upon the heath of Uentrop, marched by his right to approach the village of Kirchdinker. The avenues and posts on the little Ahse River, and the Saltzbach, were guarded by the piquets of the army.

THIS was our position when His Scerene Highness was informed, on the 15th about six in the evening, that Soubise's army had struck its tents, and were marching on their right: almost at the same instant he heard, that the enemy had dislodged the advanced posts of Lord Granby at Haus Nehlen, and that they were advancing in a strong body towards his camp.

THESE informations determined him to make the following dispositions: he ordered Lord Granby to maintain his ground to the last extremity; he had under him ten battalions, six squadrons, and ten pieces of cannon, six-pounders.

LIEUTENANT General Wutgenau was ordered with his corps, consisting of seven battalions, and five squadrons, to march to the left to Bloch, upon the high road from Lippstadt to Hamm, (by which his retreat could alone have been made in case of necessity and which the French seemed chiefly to aim at) and to act in concert with Lord Granby, whose right was to be supported by the Prince of Anhalt, (with ten battalions and six squadrons under him, who joined it with his left, his own right reaching to the Ahse River, above Kirchdinker.

LIEUTENANT General Conway (with eight battalions, seven squadrons, some British artillery, and one battalion of Saxe-Gotha) replaced the Prince of Anhalt between Illingen and Hohenover. The Crown Prince ordered Lieutenant General Bose to march with part of his troops to occupy the heights of Wambeln, and left Count Kielmannsegg on the

146. Editor: This may be Budberg, today part of the town of Werl.

side of Bureck. The greatest part of the artillery was distributed by Count Schaumburg-Lippe on the front of the left.

M. von Spörcken, who was encamped at Herzfeld on the other side of the Lippe, was ordered to send six battalions, and six squadrons, over the Lippe, which were to support M. de Wutgenau; and he was to act with the rest in the manner he should think most proper.

THESE dispositions being made, His Serene Highness came to Lord Granby's camp, which was attacked very briefly; His Lordship had taken his measures so well, that he sustained the efforts of the enemy 'till the arrival of M. von Wutgenau, who coming upon his left, and having taken the enemy in flank, they could not withstand these united efforts, and were driven back into the woods, after a fire of artillery and small arms, which continued 'till late at night. M. von Wutgenau kept the ground he had just gained: he extended his right to Haus Vellinghausen[147], and turned his left towards the high road of Hamm, the defense of which place was his chief object.

His Serene Highness had learned from the prisoners that Marshal de Broglio had decamped at daybreak, and marched with his whole army from Erwitte, in order to give us battle, in con-junction with that of Prince Soubise. His Serene Highness judging that the principal efforts would be made on our left, ordered General Howard to bring up the brigade of foot commanded by Lord Frederick Cavendish, and that of cavalry by Major General Lord Pembroke; Colonel Grevendorff was sent with two battalions to Kirchdinker to barricade and fortify that village, who, in case of necessity, was to be supported by Lieutenant General Howard, with four battalions, seven squadrons, two brigades of Hanoverian artillery, and one battalion of Bückeburg. The enemy was in possession of some posts opposite to our piquets, and the patrols were skirmishing all night.

THE battle began afresh the next morning, being the 16th, at three; and the enemy redoubled their efforts against M. Wutgenau's corps, who sustained them with great firmness. The fire from the artillery and small arms continued five hours without the enemy's gaining one inch of ground.

IT was near nine when word was brought to His Serene Highness, that the enemy seemed to be planning to place some batteries upon an eminence opposite to Lord Granby's camp, which he had not been able to enclose within his lines: His Highness perceiving the necessity of preventing the enemy from seizing this eminence, from whence they might have very much galled the troops, and being informed of the arrival of the detachment under General Spörcken, resolved to take advantage of the irresolution which appeared in the motions of the enemy, and ordered the troops which were nearest at hand to advance upon them; viz. the battalions of Maxwell, Campbell, and Keith, British; two battalions of Imhoff, two battalions of Hanoverian Guards, and Boch's.

147. Editor: Today Burg Vellinghausen, a manor in Vellinghausen-Eilmsen, part of the community of Welver.

KEY TO MAP.

A The camp of Prince de Soubise's army, which was broken at noon, on the 15th, to march in four columns to point B.

B

C The camp of Broglie's army, which started movement in the morning of the 15th, in four columns.

D Vanguards of the two first columns moving towards D.

E and the Volontaires of St. Victor towards E.

F they attacked at 5:00 p.m., the posts of the Hanoverian army with a heavy cannonade The vanguard of the third column forces the post at Haus Hehle to assure communication with the bridges.

G Montagnars Battalions and light troops of Milord Granby, supported by the troops of theneral Wutgenau (who occupied the ground

H on the 14th) to oppose the French attack. The fire of the cannon did not stop until 10:00 p.m., and the two armies spend the night in bivouac. At sunrise of 16 July, the cannonade resumes and ws followed by heavy infantry fire. The reinforcement of General von Spörken, which encamped on the right bank of the Lippe, at Herzfeld, arrived by Haus-Haaren, at 9:00 a.m.,

I and immediately attacked. Towards 10:00 a.m., Prince Ferdinand seeing the French infantry advance

K immediately orders the troops

L to cross the Landwehr. These troops advance

M and force de Broglie's army to retire. The corps (at I) advances on it side.

N The Hanoverian troops pursue Broglie's army.

O During these movements on the right, Prince de Soubise moves to the left to force the passage over the Salzbach at O.

P Du Menil, who encamped at Ruhnen, moves with this coprs to P.

Q de Voyer, with another coprs, which was at Unna, must march to take the Allies in the back. The Column P, of the center, after 7 attacks, reaches the bridge and captures the vi llage of Scheidingen. But then the retreat of Marshal de Broglie begins, causing Prince de Soubise, aginst whom the entire Allied Army was advancing, to begin his retreat.

THIS movement was decisive and had all the success that could be desired. Having advanced with the greatest intrepidity these troops soon obliged the enemy to give way, and to retreat with precipitation, having abandoned their dead and wounded, and several pieces of cannon, some of which were 16 pounders. Maxwell's battalion of grenadiers took the Rougé Regiment, formerly Belsunce, consisting of four battalions, with its cannon and colors.

THE victorious troops followed the enemy as far as Haltrup; but, the nature of the ground not having allowed the cavalry to act, His Serene Highness was then obliged to content himself with detaching the light troops in pursuit of them.

A brisk cannonade was still continued on the side where the Crown Prince commanded. His Serene Highness Prince Ferdinand, perceiving the right wing of the enemy were entirely broken, flew to his assistance, bringing with him half of the British heavy artillery and Lord Cavendish's brigade; but, before this reinforcement arrived at its place of destination, everything was quiet on that side; for M de Soubise, upon the news of the defeat of their right wing, was very probably induced to give over his attacks in that quarter likewise.

HE had attacked in three different places our piquets, who defended the passages of the Saltzbach Rivulet. The attack on their right near the Ahse River was but faintly carried out, and without effect; that on the center made themselves masters of the bridge and village of Scheidingen[148]; but though they made seven different, vigorous attacks on a

148. Editor: Today part of Welver.

redoubt which commanded the debouche of that village, yet they were always repulsed. This redoubt was occupied by 200 men under the command of Major Limburg, who bravely defended it, and was supported by the piquets and seven battalions. The Irish Brigade attempted also the passage of that rivulet on the left of Scheidingen, but in vain: it was defended by some piquets supported by three battalions.

Crown Prince's Corps

Commander	Unit	Squadrons	Battalions
Lt. Gen. Oheimb	Von dem Busche Dragoons	4	
	Wolf		1
	Mirbach		1
	Balche		1
	Bülow		1
Lt. Gen. Kielmannsegg	Leib Dragoons	4	
Maj. Gen. Halberstadt	Bock Dragoons	4	
	1 Coy. Artillery		
	Schmiel		1
	Stirp		1
	Kielmannsegg		1
	Kraushaun		1
	1 Coy. Artillery		
	Manroy		1
	Halberstadt		1
	Prinz Carlos Bns.		2
	1 Coy Artillery		
	Prinz Carlos Bn.		1
Lt. Gen. von Bose	Block		1
Maj. Gen. Bartheld	Estorff		1
	2 Coys. Artillery		
	Meeding		1
	Scheele		1
	1st Bn, Leib Regiment		1
	2nd Bn. Leib Regiment		1
	1st Bn. Bartel		1
	2nd Bn. Bartel		1
	1st Bn. Erbprinz		1
	2nd Bn. Erbprinz		1
	Guards		1
Lt. Gen. Bockh	Regiment du Corps	2	
Maj. Gen.	Heise	2	
	Jung Bremer	2	
	Alt Bremer	2	
	Wolf	2	
	Gens d'arms	2	

Conway's Corps

Caesar	Guard Grenadiers		1
	1st British Guards		1
	2nd British Guards		1
	3rd British Guards		1
Townshend	Barrington		1
	Erskine		1
	Carr		1
	Kingsley		1
Douglas	Bland	3	
	Howard	2	
	Waldegerve	2	

Howard's Corps

Lord F. Cavendish	Bockland		1
	Griffin		1
	Brundenel		1
	Welsh Fusiliers		1
Earl of Pembroke	Blue Guards	3	
	Honeywood	2	
	Carabiniers	2	
	British Light Artillery		
	Saxe-Gotha		1
	2 Brig. Hanoverian Artillery		
	Bückeburg		1

Anhalt's Corps

Bischhausen	Mansbach		3
	Prince Anhalt		2
Harling	Imhoff		2
	Regiment du Corps		2
Scheele	Hanoverian Guards		2
Elliot	Conway	2	
	Mordaunt	2	
	Inniskilling	2	

Wutgenau's Corps

Gilsa	Wutgenau		2
Rosenberg	Gilsa		2
Bock	Bock		1
Bülow	Garde du Corps	1	
	Grenadiers à cheval	1	
	British Carabiniers	3	

	Marquis of Granby's Corps		
Beckwith	Walsing		1
	Maxwell		1
Waldegrave-Sandford	Hodgson		1
	Cornwallis		1
	Stuart		1
	Napier		1
Mannsburg	Hanoverian Artillery		1
	Mansburg		1
Becwith	Campbell		1
	Keith		1
Harvey	Greys	2	
	Ancram	2	
	Mostyn	2	
	Pentz		1
	Udam		1
	Elliot	3	
	Rusch	3	
	Mallachowsky	2	
	Corps de Wolff		
Ahlefeld	Zastrow		1
	Dreves		1
	Sance		1
	Alefeld		1
	Scheither		1
	Bischausen		2
Wolff	Erbprinz Hesse	4	
	Hessian Jägers	2	

A considerable body of Soubise's left, who were encamped on the heights of Ruhne, marched to the right of the Allied Army, and one column thereof, consisting of 16 battalions and 30 squadrons, under the command of the Marquis Dumesnil, took post near Bureke; another column, consisting of 12 battalions and 14 squadrons, marched to Unna; both these corps were destined to attack our right under the Crown Prince both in flank and rear, in case the attack under M. de Broglio on our left had succeeded. THE day ended with a general retreat of the French army.

THE LOSS of the Allies in this affair was, on the side of Vellinghausen, 290 killed, 927 wounded, and 183 made prisoners, besides three pieces of cannon; and that of the corps under the Crown Prince was, 21 killed, 84 wounded, and 9 made prisoners; amounting in the whole to 311 killed, 1,011wounded, and 192 made prisoners.

THE loss of the French was computed to be in killed, wounded, and prisoners, between 5,000 and 6000: they also had nine pieces of cannon and six colors taken. Their losses in officers, some of whom were of the first rank, was very considerable. The Duke of

Havre, and his son-in-law the Marquis de Cirrae, the Marquis de Rougé, lieutenant-general, and his son, the colonel, were killed, besides several other principal officers made prisoners.

The following account of the above affair was published by the French general:

"MARSHAL de Broglio having, early in the morning of the 15th, marched the body of forces which were encamped at Erwitte to Ostinghausen, went thither in person from Soest, and at four in the afternoon began his march with all the troops in three columns to take possession of the castle of Nateln and the village of Vellinghausen. The Marshal had concerted this movement with the Marshal de Soubise, who, on his part, was to encamp a part of his army the same day on the heath opposite to the passes that lead to Scheidingen, Neumühl, and Rommühl. It was supposed this reciprocal position would enable them to advance to the enemy with more safety, and with more knowledge of what they were about.

THE columns of the left, consisting of the vanguard under M. de Belsunce, and the corps of the Grenadiers of France, and; the Royal Grenadiers commanded by the Count de Stainville, were destined to proceed along the right side of the Ahse River, and seize the castle of Nateln, which he did accordingly. This castle was occupied, and an hundred prisoners taken, who made small resistance.

"THE columns of the right, of which Baron de Clausen led the van, were to march by Hultrop[149], advancing to Vellinghausen, and to make an attack upon that village; this was likewise executed with success: Baron de Clausen not only gained possession of the village, after an obstinate defense, but also drove the enemy's troops that were in it beyond the barricade before their camp, and took post in it, and at a redoubt which they had thrown up there. The whole body of troops which Lord Granby commanded made several attempts to dislodge us, but without effect: he would indeed in all probability have succeeded, if Marshal de Brogio had not considerably reinforced the six battalions of Nassau, and Royal Deux-Ponts, with the two battalions of grenadiers and the jägers, of Avergne and Poitou, and the Volontaires de St. Victor, who had made the first attack.

"THE Count de Guerchy, who commanded the division on the right, advanced very seasonably to support the Volontaires de St. Victor with the grenadiers and chasseurs of the Dauphiné Brigade; and this brigade, commanded by the Marquis de Maupeon and the Marquis de Rochechouart, as also the brigade of the King, commanded by M. de Meironnet, were sent or led by the Marshal to sustain M. de Clausen, by which means we remained masters of the village, of the barricades and redoubt, and of three pieces of cannon taken by St. Victor's volontaires and the Nassau . The fire of the small arms and cannon continued 'till after 10 o'clock at night,

"THE Marshal employed the rest of the night in relieving the six German battalions, the two battalions of grenadiers and jägers, and Volontaires de St. Victor, by fresh troops. The Duke de Havre led up the brigades of Rougé (late Belsunce) and Aquitaine; and the Duke de Duras and the Count de Vaux led up the brigades of Champagne, Avergne, and Poitou.

149. Editor: Today part of Lippetal.

"In this position (in which we contented ourselves with remaining upon the defensive, and of which the marshal sent notice to the Prince de Soubise at 11 o'clock at night), we waited to see what step the enemy would take next day.

"AT daybreak the cannonading began again, and continued with great vivacity 'till 5 o'clock, when it slackened considerably. The enemy appeared at that time to have no thoughts of attacking us; they seemed to be waiting the issue of what was doing on their right, to determine what part they should take. They did not remain long in suspense, for about seven we saw columns filing off, which came from the center and the right of their army, towards their left. The fire of the small arms which had been kept up all the morning on our right was now considerably augmented; the fire of the cannon was redoubled and soon after we perceived dispositions made, and columns marching, to attack us with a force much superior to ours.

"BUT the Marshal being informed of certain incidents, found that he had no other part to take than to return to the camp at Ostinghausen. He immediately ordered the troops to march out of the village of Vellinghausen. This movement, made in the presence of forces so much superior, was very critical, and was executed in the best order; only the Rougé Regiment, which was the most exposed, and had already suffered considerably, was overtaken, and partly intercepted by the enemy, who took many prisoners, and some of its colors; the horses which drew its cannon being killed, its four pieces of cannon were also lost. There were likewise left in the village, which is very much surrounded with hedges and marshy hollow ways, five pieces of cannon, of which the horses were killed, or which were dismounted in the moment of the retreat.

"THE Marshal himself formed the rear with the division of the Grenadiers of France, and the royal grenadiers, under the command of the Counts de Stainville and de Scey, and the Chevalier de Modena, who led them with all possible order and firmness. We retired in order of battle in several lines, and halted several times, keeping the enemy in so much awe, that they did not venture to advance beyond the hedges of Vellinghausen, only some of their light troops came as far as Ultrup.

WE brought away all our wounded, excepting about 50 private men, and five officers, who were not fit to be removed: we also brought away the three pieces of cannon, and about 200 prisoners that we took the day before. The army came to encamp at Ostinghausen, leaving the van under M. de Belsunce before us on the road leading to Ultrup, on the left of the Ahse.

"OUR LOSS, though considerable, was much less than there was room to expect from two such sharp and long engagements as those of the 15th and 16th. The returns of the killed, wounded, and prisoners, amount to 2,400 men, more or less. The loss of the enemy must be very great. The prisoners and deserters assure us, that the 15 English and Scotch regiments, whom we had to deal with in the morning of the 15th, suffered prodigiously. The officers of the enemy's light troops owned to ours that they had suffered much and had been obliged to send away to their rear the regiments that had fought on the evening of the 15th, and the next morning. As to the Brunswick and Hessian troops, who replaced the English on the morning of the 16th, we know not their loss.

"All our field officers behaved in the best manner and were of great use. In short, never did any army keep up more firmness and good order in two such long engagements, the last of which was very unequal, and on intersected ground."

THE troops of the Allied Army returned to their former camp, except some brigades of artillery, which remained on the left.

ON the 17th of July, General Spörcken with his corps returned to his former camp at Herzfeld[150].

MAJOR General Luckner took the town of Neuhaus, near Paderborn, by a coup de main; the action was very smart, as the enemy defended themselves bravely. He made on this occasion 150 men prisoners: he was afterwards obliged to abandon it, on the morning of the 19th, upon the approach of a large detachment of the enemy, which had been sent by Marshal de Brogio from his camp at Erwitte towards Paderborn.

JULY 18 to the 21st, Colonel Freytag, having marched on the 18th from Einbeck to Lagershausen, with three brigades of chasseurs, detached, on the 19th, Captains Engel and Hampen, with 100 chasseurs, towards Fulda, in order to harass the enemy in that quarter.

THIS detachment marched for that purpose at daybreak from Lagershausen; they arrived by noon at Allendorf, where they passed the Werra, and posted themselves in a wood at a league's distance from Rotenburg an der Fulda: here they took, on the 20th, three French commissaries, and burnt some boats laden with flour and oats.

CAPTAIN Engell set out with 80 chasseurs to destroy the enemy's magazines at Bad Hersfeldt; he met in his way 26 boats laden with flour, oats, balls, bombs, and 240 barrels of gun-powder, which he threw into the Fulda River, and set fire to the boats.

ACCORDING to the advices he had received, the garrison of Bad Hersfeld was supposed to consist only of 200 men, which induced Captain Engell to make his dispositions, after having cut his way through the outguard, for attacking the place.

SOME chasseurs appearing in the evening, the commandant had doubled the guard, and the piquet posted at the gates of the town; he had also ordered 60 dragoons from Melsungen, who arrived at Bad Hersfeld about three in the morning.

NOTWITHSTANDING, Captain Engell ordered the gate to be forced by a lieutenant, who, having dispersed the guard, penetrated into the city; but, finding the enemy's infantry very alert, and that they fired upon him from the houses, he was obliged to retreat. Captain Engell attacked at the same time the piquets, whose officer and 30 men threw themselves into a barracks thatched with straw. They were several times summoned to lay down their arms, but, on their obstinate refusal, the barracks was set on fire, and the whole piquet were cut to pieces except for four men, who had demanded quarters, and five, who perished in the flames.

150. Editor: Today part of Lippetal.

CAPTAIN Engell having got rid of the piquet, and meeting with no other obstacle, caused the hay, lodged along the Fulda, to be set on fire, and links of burning pitch to be fattened to the sacks of meal and oats. This fire communicated itself to many barrels of powder (of which there was a great quantity on the bank of the river), which blew up. If he had had a greater force he would have been able to have thrown many thousand bombs and cannon balls into the river.

THE whole loss attending this expedition consisted in one chasseur wounded in the hand by a bayonet, and one horse. Captain Engell rejoined Captain Kampen at Eimbach, bringing with him one lieutenant colonel, two lieutenants, and 14 private men, prisoners; from thence they set out for Eschwege, where they arrived on the 21st at eight in the morning, having marched 19 German miles in 48 hours.

COLONEL Freytag intercepted and destroyed a large convoy of provisions belonging to the enemy, on the road between Kassel and Warburg. The Brunswick hussars likewise ruined two French magazines on the Werra.

ON the 21st of July, His Serene Highness's headquarters were still at Hohenover, Marshal de Brogio was at Erwitte, and M. de Soubise at Haarstrang[151], with his right to Soest. Several smart skirmishes passed between the light troops and advanced parties, particularly this day, when the Black Hussars and Hanoverian jägers attacked a considerable body of the enemy posted near Ruhne. Prince Albert Henry of Brunswick, third son of the reigning duke, was dangerously wounded in the neck at this place.

ON the 26th, M. de Soubise (having sent 34 battalions, 200 men of the brigade of Pelletier, with 24 pieces of cannon, together with 44 squadrons, besides the hussars of Chamborant, to reinforce M. de Broglio) broke up his camp, and passed the Ruhr, directing his route towards Herding, Marshal de Brogio also decamped, and marched towards Paderborn.

ON the 27th, the Allied Army likewise decamped; the main body of His Serene Highness directing its march towards Paderborn, in order to observe the motions of M. de Broglio, en-camped near Borgelen[152], while the Crown Prince marched towards the Ruhr, to watch those of M. de Soubise.

ON the 28th, His Serene Highness resumed his march, and encamped near Ervitte.

THIS day, early in the morning, the Britannic Legion came up with and attacked a large body of the enemy, posted on the heights of Hölngen[153], whom they dislodged, but the Prince de Condé coming up with his corps obliged them to fall back on the chapel of Hoengen, where they maintained themselves 'till they were reinforced by some infantry and cavalry sent to the village of Bremen[154] for that purpose by His Serene Highness. The attack was again renewed, and the enemy was so briskly charged, that they abandoned the hill with great precipitation, and fled into the woods; but the Baron von

151. Editor: Haarstrang is not a town, but the name of a ridge of hills south of the Soest Plain.
152. Editor: This may be Borchen.
153. Editor: Part of Ense.
154. Editor: Today this is Ense-Bremen.

Würmser bringing up the Soubise Regiment, and the volontaires of the French army, the whole again advanced, and we were in our turn forced to retire to the chapel. The loss of the enemy on this occasion was very considerable, the Soubise Regiment, in particular suffered much. Prince Ferdinand of Brunswick received a small contusion his right arm on this occasion.

ON the 29th of July, His Serene Highness encamped near Geseke. The vanguard of the Allied Army had frequent skirmishes with the rear of M. de Broglio, who encamped between Paderborn and Driburg[155].

ON the 30th, the Allied Army continued its march in four columns and encamped near Büren. The Marquis of Granby with the vanguard was posted at Haaren. General Luckner attacked, near Lippspringe[156], the rearguard of the enemy with great success, and cut to pieces the whole Corps des Volontaires de Broglio.

THE French encamped near Lichtenau; and had pushed forward a body of troops to Hämelschenburg[157] on the Weser, nearly opposite to the town of Hameln; they were also employed in throwing up entrenchments at Höxter. M. de Belsunce likewise marched to Göttingen (where they were forming depots, and had fixed a bakery) with a corps of 6,000 men. This obliged Colonel Freytag, who had been so successful in his incursions into Hesse, to retire to Osterode in the Hartz Mountains, where he observed the motions of the enemy. Count de Lusace was ordered to observe the motions of General Luckner, who was at Blomberg: and Lieutenant General de Stainville, with a corps of 18 battalions, and as many squadrons, took post between Wrexen and Heddinghausen.

THE corps under General Spörcken and General Wangenheim joined the army under His Serene Highness; and the light troops of the Allies took possession of the town of Paderborn.

AUGUST 5, the corps under the command of the Marquis of Granby was reinforced on the afternoon of the 4th, by some battalions and squadrons who left their tents and baggage in the camp. His Serene Highness came also to Meerhof the same evening, where he stayed all night. The army and the corps under the Marquis of Granby, remained under arms 'till morning. At daybreak, General Spörcken's first line marched from Brenken[158] to Meerhof, leaving their baggage also behind them. These troops had just joined His Lordship's corps when the enemy, who advanced in great numbers from behind Stadtberge, began a brisk cannonade; soon after which the fire of the musketry began on both sides. At this time, General Wangenheim had quitted Büren with the corps under his command, and feigned a march towards Stadtberge; but instead of that, he suddenly turned to the right of that place, and took the enemy both in the rear and in the flank. This motion decided the whole affair. M. de Stainville, who commanded the enemy, was obliged to retire with considerable loss and in great disorder to Warburg. His Serene Highness pursued them above a league and a half beyond Welde, taking many prisoners, some cannon, tents, and baggage.

155. Editor: Today Bad Driburg.
156. Editor: Today Bad Lippspringe.
157. Editor: Hämelschenburg is a Renaissance palace.
158. Editor: Today part of the town of Büren.

ON the 6th of August, Colonel Freytag, with a detachment of jägers, intercepted a convoy belonging to the enemy, consisting of 250 wagons, which was going from Göttingen to Höxter. The meal and bread was dispersed and given to the country people, and the wagons and horses were sent back to their respective villages. This was the first convoy the French had attempted to send by that road.

ON the 7th, the Chevalier de Donceel, with a party of 30 men belonging to the light troops, surprised and dispersed an Austrian detachment that was posted there to guard 65 pontoons, the greatest part whereof were mounted on their carriages and ready to march. He burnt the pontoons, as also a small magazine belonging to the French.

ON the night between the 8th and 9th, Prince Albert Henry of Brunswick, died at Hamm (of the wound he received on the 21st of July in the affair of Ruhne), aged 19 years. He was attended by the best surgeons both of the Allied and French armies.

ON the 9th, Marshal de Soubise sent off another detachment to reinforce Marshal de Brogio, consisting of 14 battalions, viz. eight of the Royal Grenadiers, four of Tallern, one of the Queen's, and one of Forest, besides four squadrons of Thiange's Dragoons.

THE Crown Prince likewise marched with a detachment to join the grand army under His Serene Highness. He left General Kielmannsegg behind, with a corps of about 12,000 men, to observe the motions of Marshal de Soubise, who was encamped at Essen. General Kielmannsegg took post at Kamen.

ON the 10th, the Allied Army marched and encamped in the neighborhood of Delbrück.

ON the 11th, the Allied Army resumed its march, and encamped, near Stukenbrock, to the northward of Paderborn. General Luckner passed the Weser with his corps at Hameln, where he was joined by Colonel Freytag in order to observe the enemy on that side of the river and endeavor to dislodge them from the posts they were fortifying.

ON the other hand, Lieutenant General Stainville occupied his camp at Kleinenberg[159], with a flying one at Driburg. The different corps under the Count de Lusace, and Barons Clausen and Chabot, occupied three different camps at Merlsheim[160], Pomsen, and Nieheim. M. de Vaux commanded a corps at Höxter; and M. de Belsunce was in the Solling.

ON the 12th of August, His Serene Highness decamped and marched to Detmold, where the headquarters was fixed.

ON the 13th, the Allied Army resumed its march, and encamped near Blomberg, on the heights of Reelkirchen[161].

---

159. Editor: Today part of Lichtenau.
160. Editor: Today part of Bad Driburg.
161. Editor: Reelkirchen is a manor, castle or palace, which today is part of the town of Blomberg.

As the quartermasters were marking out the camp, the light troops appeared, and some smart skirmishes passed between them and our's. Marshal de Brogio had purposed to occupy the same camp, but the Allies were beforehand with him; so that he was obliged to encamp a good deal farther back, on the heights of Nieheim, opposite to His Serene Highness; who, by this means, had got into the front of the enemy, whereas he had been for some time in their rear. The Crown Prince took post at Hardehausen between Stadtberge and Warburg.

MARSHAL Soubise fixed his headquarters this day at Marl, between Dorsten and Haltern-am-See; and General Kielmannsegg, with his corps in the neighborhood of Münster.

On the 14th in the morning, the little town of Horn, into which Prince Ferdinand had thrown 300 men under the command of Lieutenant Colonel Diemar of the Hessian infantry, was attacked by a body of 8,000 French, with six cannon, in the presence of M. de Broglio. The enemy made diverse attacks, but were in everyone repulsed with loss, though M. Diemar had no cannon; and in the afternoon they retired. The garrison only lost 15 men killed and wounded in this engagement. M. Diemar, and all the detachment, received the thanks of His Serene Highness in a public manner, as also a handsome present.

GENERAL Luckner arrived this morning with his corps on the heights of Dassel; in the neighborhood of which place M. de Belsunce was posted with a detachment from the French army. M. de Luckner detached his regiment to the right of the enemy; and at the same time sent Colonel Freytag with all the light horse towards their left wing, in order to take them in flank, while he should attack them in front. M. de Belsunce, as soon as he perceived them, drew back all his troops from Dassel, and that neighborhood, towards the Solling Forest, and detached a large body of horse and foot to the high road that leads to Einbeck: this body was instantly attacked and totally routed by Luckner's Hussars; all that could not escape by flight were either taken prisoners or cut to pieces.

DURING this transaction, General Luckner, with the regular and light infantry, moved forward towards the enemy in front: a brisk cannonade began; but when they perceived our infantry continued to advance, they retired in tolerably good order towards the Solling Forest. In the meantime, Colonel Freytag was engaged with the light horse, and endeavored to take the enemy in the rear; but they did not think proper to wait for this attack but dispersed themselves with great rapidity into this forest.

ON the 15th of August, General Luckner's Corps rendezvoused at eight in the morning near Dassel. Captain Kampen was sent to observe Höxter. The Brunswick jägers set forward, and the whole marched to Uslar, where they arrived by four. As soon as the hussars and jägers showed themselves on the rising ground near Vahle, the enemy retreated by Allershausen[162] to the high mountain called Sonnenburg[163]: the heavy horse could not advance fast enough to overtake them in their retreat; however, upon the arrival of some cannon, the enemy were soon dislodged from this advantageous post, and were forced to retreat with so much precipitation, that the light horse were not able

162. Editor: Today part of Uslar

163. Editor: This may be Sömmerling Hill (252 meters).

to come up with them before they reached Solling. Lieutenant Colonel de Stockhausen had before entered the Solling by a detour and took the outpost there with his jägers and some artillery: he immediately attacked the enemy's infantry; and the Brunswick hussars (who had pursued them) coming up at the same time, they were utterly routed.

IN the different attacks of these two days, there were 44 officers, and 759 private men, made prisoners, among whom were M. Jenner, brigadier, one colonel, and two majors: three pair of colors, and 800 horses, were also taken. The second battalion of Jenner's Regiment of Swiss was entirely ruined.

ON the 18th of August, in the morning early, M. de Broglio decamped, and directed his route towards Höxter; and at noon the Allied Army also struck its tents and followed him, encamping at Holzhausen.

THIS day M. de Conflans, who was detached from Marshal Soubise's army, came up with the rearguard of a party of the Allies on their march from Münster to the Ems: they made some prisoners, and took the tents belonging to Scheither's cavalry, together with 30 baggage wagons.

THE French King's Household (Maison du roi), being sickly, encamped on the left bank of the Rhine, on the 17th, near Büderich, and this day they decamped in order to canton at Cleves and the neighborhood of that place.

ON the 19th, the French army resumed its march, and crossed the river Weser over some pontoon bridges which they had constructed near Höxter (in which place they left a strong detach-ment) and encamped near Fürstenberg. The Allied Army also decamped, and marched towards Höxter, pitching their tents in separate corps on the heights near that place; the two armies being in view of each other. Lord Granby with the vanguard greatly harassed the enemy's rear. Elliot's Dragoons, and the Black Hussars, took a considerable quantity of baggage.

PRINCE Ferdinand detached General Wutgenau with a body of troops to the other side of the Weser, who took a position at Halle, the road to Hameln. General Luckner, on the approach of the French army, was obliged to fall back towards Einbeck; and Colonel Freytag, with his chasseurs, was posted on the Werra, in order to intercept the enemy's communication in that quarter.

ON the 20th of August, M. de Soubise encamped at the village of Albachten, close to Münster, and detached M. de Voyer towards the Lower Ems. General Kielmannsegg had before thrown a numerous garrison into that city.

ON the 21st, the detachment of the French, who had been left in Höxter by the Marshal de Broglio, abandoned that place, and passed the Weser. A body of the Allies immediately took possession of it.

ON the 22d, the French army decamped, and marched towards Einbeck, fixing itsheadquarters at Sülbeck, between that town and Northeim. This day Marshal de Soubise invested the city of Münster.

As the French seemed to indicate a design on the city of Hanover, some regiments were sent from the Allied Army to reinforce the garrison of that place.

GENERAL Luckner and his corps was posted at Osterode; and Colonel Freytag at Gieboldehausen.

ON the 23d, part of Lord Granby's corps passed the Weser at Höxter, in order to harass Marshal de Brogio's rear, and clear the other side of the river. They returned to their camp the same night.

THIS day, early in the morning, a body of the French arrived before the town of Hamm; which they instantly bombarded, and continued so to do, 'till 12 o'clock at night, when they began to fire red-hot balls. The next day at noon they summoned the garrison to surrender; but as the commandant refused to comply, the firing was renewed with greater vigor, which lasted 'till four in the afternoon, when the French being informed that the Crown Prince, at the head of a large detachment, was in full march towards them, retired with great precipitation.

ON the 24th of August, His Serene Highness, at the head of Lord Granby's corps, and all the British troops, except the guards proceeded by forced marches towards the Diemel, forced all the enemy's posts in that quarter, particularly at Trendelburg, where he made upwards of 300 men prisoners, and then crossed that river; and, on the 26th, encamped at Hofgeismar, within six leagues of Kassel, pushing forward an advanced party to Winter-Kasten[164]. During this excursion, he left General Spörcken behind at Höxter with the remainder of the army, to secure that part of the Weser from Hameln to the Diemel.

ON the 30th, a body of the Allies surprised Dorsten, and made prisoners M. de Vierset, with the first battalion of his regiment, together with several piquets, after a vigorous resistance: next day the light troops took 300 wagons, a number of equipages, and the patrols of the French horse that were along the Lippe. This affair, and the Crown Prince's march, occasioned orders to be sent to the French King's Household (Maison du roi), who were quartered in Cleves, to assemble immediately at Büderich, in order to pass the Rhine, and keep open the communications.

THIS day the corps of the Marquis of Granby, with the rest of the troops, repassed the Diemel and encamped at Bühne and Körbecke[165].

ON the 31st, some detached corps of the French army passed the Hartz Mountains, and, by their great superiority, got possession of several considerable passes. Some corps of the Allies under General Luckner, Colonel Freytag, and Colonel Stockhausen, were obliged, after a brave resistance, to retire further back.

His Serene Highness ordered Lieutenant General Wutgenau, with his corps, to cross the Weser at Grohnde, in order to observe the motions of the enemy in that quarter.

ON the 3d of September, M. de Soubise detached M. de Vouge with a large body

164. Editor: This may be the Winterbüren Manor, part of Fuldatal.
165. Editor: Today Körbecke is part of Borgentreich.

towards Dorsten, in order to recover that post; he accordingly affected it and took 180 of the Allies prisoners and took one piece of cannon.

ON the 4th, Marshal Soubise raised the blockade of Münster, and marched that day to Holsterhausen and, on the 5th, he repassed the Lippe in three columns near Dorsten, encamping near Westerholt. The Crown Prince arrived this day at Dülmen, and the British Guards marched from the neighborhood of Höxter, by the way of Borgholz, towards Brogentreich, near which place they encamped, on the right of His Serene Highness.

ON the 7th, the Crown Prince had his headquarters at Bockeim near Hamm; and Marshal Soubise still kept on the other side the Lippe. His Serene Highness remained in his camp at Bühne; and the position of the troops under M. de Broglio was as follows: Prince Xavier of Saxony, with the reserve, encamped between Grene and Einbeck; the main army was at Sülbeck, with a large detachment before its right, and another before its left, on the side of Moringen; another corps was near Göttingen, with smaller ones between that place and Münden to keep open the communication and Lieutenant General Stainville with 36 battalions was at Grebenstein, fronting the Diemel.

ON the 16th, the British Guards joined the main body under His Serene Highness. The French had sent some strong detachments to Seesen and Gandersheim, from whence they pushed forward in advanced parties towards Hanover, Hildesheim, and Wolfenbüttel, who exacted large contributions; this occasioned some battalions to be sent to reinforce the garrison of Hanover.

ON the 17th, the Crown Prince, having drove back M. de Soubise to the Rhine, returned to Warburg; and at 11 o'clock this night, His Serene Highness, with the corps encamped on the Diemel, began their march in order to cross that river; the Crown Prince passed over at Warburg, the Marquis of Granby at Liebenau; and Prince Ferdinand, at the head of the main army, took the route of Sielen[166]. When the whole had got over, they halted 'till daybreak on the 18th, when they continued their march, and, passing by Hofgeismar, advanced towards Immenhausen, where Lieutenant General Stainville, with a large body of the enemy was posted, who, upon the approach of the Allies, retreated about four miles, where they drew up in a very advantageous position, but Count of Lippe bringing up some artillery, and the columns of the Allies advancing up briskly, they again retreated with precipitation, but not without losing a great many men, as they were closely pursued by Elliot's Dragoons and the hussars. The Crown Prince had at the same time advanced on their right to Wilhelmsthal, and also made a great many prisoners. The enemy retired to their strong entrenchments on the Kratzenburg near Kassel; and the Allies fixed their camp at Obervellmar[167].

AT the time that His Serene Highness passed the Diemel, General Luckner had also passed the Weser at Hameln, and Colonel Freytag took post at Halle.

AFTER the departure of the Crown Prince from the country, of Münster, Marshal Soubise again advanced, fixing his quarters, on the 18th, at Dülmen, and the Prince de Condé marched forwards towards Münster.

166. Editor: Today part of Trendelburg.
167. Editor: Obervellmar is part of the town of Vellmar.

ON the 20th of September, His Serene Highness, having an account that M. de Broglio was on his march with a large detachment in order to join General Stainville, removed somewhat to his right, encamping near Wilhelmsthal in a more advantageous situation.

ON the 22d, a body of 400 French attacked a party of 105 Highlanders that had been posted in Winter-Kasten, who, after a brave and obstinate defense, were obliged to surrender.

THIS day a *feu de joie* was fired in the camp of the Allied Army, on account of the coronation of their Majesties the King and Queen of Great Britain.

ON the 24th, the Crown Prince, who had been detached, by the way of Fritzlar, over the Eder, encamped at Holtzdorff, within four leagues of Marburg; his light troops pushed forward as far as Butzbach, and entirely cut off the French communications on that side, having surprised and intercepted many of their convoys.

A body of between 7,000 and 8,000 French, under the command of General Clausen, unexpectedly appeared in the morning before the city of Wolfenbüttel with a numerous artillery, summoned the garrison to surrender, and on their refusal, cannonaded and bombarded the town very briskly for four hours; but having information that General Luckner was in full march towards him, and at the same time perceiving that Gen. Stammer, with a garrison of about 2,000 men, was determined to defend the town to the last extremity, M. de Clausen thought proper to retreat the same day at three in the afternoon, by way of Hornburg.

M. de Soubise having detached the Marquis de Conflans, and M. de Campfort, with 3,000 irregulars into the country of East Friesland; they, on the 22d, took possession of Leer, Weener, and Jemgum, which places they immediately plundered, as well as all the adjacent farm houses; and this day they marched to Emden, the garrison whereof consisted only of 200 British invalids, who were obliged to surrender on capitulation, as the magistrates and burghers refused to join them in the defense of the town. The capitulation was, that all the burghers and inhabitants should enjoy their rights and privileges, as under the King of Prussia, without being molested or injured the garrison were to be accounted as prisoners of war but were to be at liberty. The barbarities the French exercised in this country were so great as to be hardly credible; this so enraged the peasants, that they had recourse to arms, and attacked a body of about 1,000 of the French, of whom they killed 150, and wounded M. Campfort their commanding officer: this obliged the first corps to retire, but they suddenly returned in greater numbers, and placed a garrison of 800 men in Emden.

THE city of Osnabrück was treated in the same manner by another party of them who had entered that place; they not only stripped the houses, but abused the inhabitants, and carried away to Wesel 112 wagons laden with clothes, linen, etc.

ON the 25th of September, the castle of Scharzfeld, situated in the Hartz, was obliged, for want of ammunition, to surrender to the French after a brave defense. The garrison, consisting of about 360 men, chiefly invalids were made prisoners of war. M. de Broglio ordered it to be dismantled and blown up.

ON the 1st of October, His Serene Highness sent off the heavy baggage of the army to Kalle, and the Crown Prince returned from his expedition on the Eder to Hof.

ON the 2d, the Allied Army decamped from Wilhelmsthal and marched to Breuna.

THE Crown Prince and General Hardenberg were detached with a considerable body of troops towards the Lower Rhine, in order to drive the French from the Bishopric of Münster and the country of East Friesland.

ON the 3d, they resumed their march, and encamped in the neighborhood of Volkmarsen.

THE Prince de Condé opened the trenches on the 1st of this month before Meppen, which place capitulated this day. The garrison, consisting of 500 men, was made prisoners of war.

M. de Soubise remained still in his camp at Coesfeld, and his irregulars overran the whole country of East Friesland even as far as Bremen. On the night between the 2d and 3d, a body of 500 or 600 French came in wagons to the gates of the new town of Bremen, with a design to surprise it. The garrison of the allies put themselves under arms at 1 o'clock in the morning. The French after skirmishing for some time retired, and a part of the garrison sallied out, but could not pursue them far, as the neighborhood swarmed with French trops.

PRINCE Xavier of Saxony and the Baron de Clausen were advanced to Seesen with a large body of troops, which obliged General Luckner to fall back to Hildesheim.

OCTOBER 10, Prince Xavier of Saxony having advanced from Seesen, invested Wolfenbüttel, which he both cannonaded and bombarded for some days very briskly. General Stammer, who defended that place with two battalions of militia, was obliged to capitulate on this day, to prevent the entire destruction of the town, part thereof having been already reduced to ashes.

ON the 11th, His Serene Highness decamped, and repassed the Rhine[168] a little above Warburg in four columns, and the army pitched its tents in the neighborhood of Borlinghausen. He ordered the bakery which was at Warburg to be transferred to Höxter.

ON the 12th, he proceeded to Brakel.

ON the 13th, he encamped near Marienmünster.

ON the 15th, he marched to Ottenstein on the Weser.

ON the 16th, he fixed his headquarters near the village of Ohr[169], about two leagues from Hameln, where he caused a bridge of pontoons to be thrown over the Weser. The Marquis of Granby with his corps was posted at Hilligsfeld[170], with an advanced guard near Halle[171]. The Crown Prince was at Hildesheim; for M. de Soubise on that Prince's

168. Editor: This cannot be the Rhine, as the only rivers there are the Diemel and the Twiste.
169. Editor: Today Ohr is part of Emmerthal.
170. Editor: Today Gross Hilligsfeld and Klein Hilligsfeld, part of Hameln.
171. Editor: Today Halle is part of Bodenwerder-Polle.

approach towards Münster, had recalled his parties from East Friesland, and retired towards Wesel; whereupon he only left a detachment 6ft the Lippe, and returned to join His Serene Highness on the Weser. Marshal de Brogio was at Stadtoldendorf[172].

THE sudden surrender of the town of Wolfenbüttel on the 10th, having prevented the succor sent to its relief from coming up in time, Prince Xavier of Saxony immediately proceeded to invest Brunswick, and open the trenches before it; a bombardment commenced with great fury: the garrison was very thin in proportion to the extent of the place, but they however were determined to make a vigorous defense. Prince Xavier, in order to cover the siege, had taken possession of Lehndorf[173], and the important pass of Olpen, which last place he had strongly entrenched.

GENERAL Luckner, and Prince Frederick of Brunswick, arrived by forced marches, on the 12th, in the neighborhood of Peine, having on their march met with, and defeated, the corps of Caraman and Chabot on the 8th, and drove them back on Dassel. The affair would admit of no delay, wherefore they, without waiting for the troops which General Mansburg was bringing up, proceeded on the 13th, directly towards Brunswick; but as all the avenues were blocked up, Prince Frederick determined to force the entrenchments at Olpen, which were defended by a body of 1,000 men, while General Luckner covered the attack. That post was accordingly attacked and carried. The French had 300 men made prisoners, among whom were General Daston and ten other officers; they also lost one cannon.

GENERAL Luckner, after the entrenchments were carried, returned with the cavalry to Peine, without meeting with the least disturbance from the enemy on their march.

ON the other hand, Prince Frederick proceeded without loss of time to Brunswick, which place he entered the same day with six battalions and was received with the greatest joy by the garrison and the inhabitants. Their arrival was notified to the besiegers by a general volley from the ramparts - whereupon the French abandoned the trenches with great precipitation, and retired to Fümmelse, about four leagues from Brunswick.

THE French likewise evacuated Wolfenbüttel, on the 15th, after levying exorbitant contributions, as they had done wherever they came, and retired to Gandersheim.

FROM this time nothing material happened during the remainder of the month of October. The armies on the Weser remained nearly in the same position; and the Prince de Soubise, on the Lower Rhine, contented himself with sending out small parties and patrols.

IN the beginning of November, whilst Prince Ferdinand had his headquarters at Ohr, upon the left of the Weser, Marshal de Brogio's position, upon the right of that river, was as follows. The Hartz was occupied by 2,000 men; Lieutenant General Stainville encamped at Seesen with 16 battalions; Prince Xavier of Saxony was at Gandersheim with 19 battalions; Marshal de Brogio with eight battalions was at Einbeck, which made the center; and General Chabot with 15 battalions at Eschershaulen: the rest of

172. Editor: Today part of Eschershausen-Stadoldendorf.
173. Editor: Today part of the city of Brunswick.

the infantry, with the cavalry, were cantoned in the villages behind the camp as above specified. To secure at the same time the communication with Hesse and Franconia, General Rochambeau was left at Kassel with eight battalions and the Irish Brigade upon the Eder.

PRINCE Ferdinand determined to march, if possible, directly to Einbeck, and to endeavor to prevent the French army so dispersed from collecting into a body: but that did not succeed in the manner that had been wished. The disposition made by His Serene Highness for that purpose was this: General Luckner was ordered to march with his detachment, joined by the garrison of Wolfenbüttel on the 3d and 4th, by Ringelheim[174] and Lutter[175], so as to be opposite M. Stainville's corps at Seesen on the 5th, and either to keep him in check, or to follow him if he marched. The Crown Prince was directed to march, on the 3d, by his right from Hildesheim, to cross the Leine at Koldingen, and to proceed the 4th to Alfeld, so as to be able to get possession of the Hube and Einbeck on the 5th. The Marquis of Granby was ordered to march on the 3d to Coppenbrügge; the 4th to Dufen[176], and to force the same day the post of Cappellenhagen, and to be on the 5th at Wickenfen, so as to block the defile which leads from Elcherhausen to Einbeck. His Lordship after a smart action forced the enemy at Cappellenhagen, and found means to be, at the hour appointed, on the 5th at Wickenfen. These several corps had been for some time upon the right of the Weser. Those upon the left crossed the river in the following manner. Prince Ferdinand, on the 4th, with the main body of the army, which encamped between Tündern[177] and Hastenbeck[178]; Lieutenant General Conway being advanced the same day to Borgel[179], and General Scheele to Bremke[180], who joined at Hall the 5th in the morning. The intention of His Serene Highness was to cut off General Chabot's corps, which lay at Elcherhausen, and he pursued this march for that purpose on the 5th. M. Chabot, finding himself likely to be attacked, left Eschershausen and marched towards Wickensen, in order to get to Einbeck and join Marshal de Brogio. Surprised to find a large body of troops in his way, which was that of the Marquis of Granby, he fell back upon the road to Eschershausen, 'till he could turn to the right towards Stadtoldendorf the only way left him to escape, and which, without an accident, he would have likewise found blocked up, and his retreat entirely cut off. Lieutenant General Hardenberg, who was to have passed the Weser at Bodenwerder on the 4th at night, so as to have been on the 5th in the morning at Amelungsborn[181], upon the road to Eschershausen was prevented by the pontoons overturning in a hollow way, which delayed his arrival at Bodenwerder 'till the 5th at seven in the morning; so that M. de Chabot had the good fortune to escape by Dassel to Einbeck, where he arrived about 12 o'clock at noon, and took post upon the Hube. The Crown Prince was disappointed by

174. Editor: Today part of Salzgitter
175. Editor: Today it is called Lutter am Barenberge.
176. Editor: This may be Duingen.
177. Editor: Today this is part of Hameln.
178. Ibid.
179. Editor: This may be part of Gross Berkel and Klein Berkel, today part of Aerzen and Hameln, respectively.
180. Editor: Today part of Halle.
181. Editor: A former Cistercian monastery kept on after the Reformation, and today belongs to the Lutheran Church of Niedersachsen.

this accident, likewise in his project upon Einbeck; for he arrived opposite the Hube at 2 o'clock and was joined by the Marquis of Granby and Lieutenant General Conway at four in the afternoon. A warm cannonading ensued 'till night while Marshal de Brogio collected so many troops, that the Crown Prince did not think it advisable to attempt to force the Hube under that change of circumstances.

PRINCE Ferdinand encamped at Eschershausen on the 5th at night, where General Hardenberg joined him.

THE 6th passed in skirmishes on all sides with different success.

His Serene Highness, on the 7th, ordered the Marquis of Granby to march from Wenzen to Vorwohle, and the Crown Prince to Ammensen. Marshal de Brogio taking this motion for a retreat pursued the Crown Prince, but without attempting to attack him. His brother, Count Broglio, who followed Lord Granby, attacked him just as he was beginning to encamp at Vorwohle, and drove in his outposts but his Lordship had the satisfaction, in the presence of Prince Ferdinand, to repulse the enemy, and to pursue them quite back to the Hube, with the greatest spirit and conduct.

IT not being found practicable to attack the enemy in their present position on that spot, Prince Ferdinand therefore resolved to attempt getting around their left flank, and to put them under a necessity of attacking him, or of abandoning Einbeck, and all that part of the country.

His Serene Highness, after having reconnoitered on all sides on the 7th and 8th, marched on the 9th, at three in the morning, to the height between Mackensen[182] and Lüthorst[183] the Crown Prince to replace Lord Granby at Vorwohle; and General Luckner to occupy the Crown Prince's camp at Ammensen. The Marquis of Granby was again attacked that morning upon his left, before he could march to follow the army, but His Lordship received the enemy with the same spirit as before, repuling them with a considerable loss. Major Fraser distinguished himself greatly on this occasion.

MARSHAL de Broglio finding, by his detachments which were driven off the heights of Lithorst, that Prince Ferdinand had gained his flank, and was partly in his rear, having it in his choice to risk an action or retire, chose the latter, and went off the 9th in the night; quitting Einbeck, and all the adjacent country.

AT the time His Serene Highness crossed the Weser, he sent General Bock with a detachment to give the enemy some uneasiness in the countries of Hesse and Waldec.

ON the 11th of November, the cantonments for the Allied Army were regulated; and, on the 12th; all the troops marched into them, except the following battalions, who (being the oldest in each brigade) were encamped under the command of Lieutenant General Conway, on the Hube, near Einbeck, viz. First Regiment of Guards, Hodgdon, Bockland, Barrington, Brunswick, Leib Regiment, one battalion of Imhoff, one of Hardenberg, and one of La Chevalerie, together with a train of 16 pieces of cannon,

182. Editor: Today part of Dassel.

183. Ibid.

and the Saxe-Gotha Regiment. The army received orders to assemble immediately on the firing of nine cannon and join this corps. Prince Ferdinand fixed his headquarters at Einbeck.

DURING the above important motions on the Weser and Leine Rivers, the army under the Prince de Soubise, which had been cantoned for some time in the neighborhood of Essen, had been employed in taking up its winter quarters, which were fixed on the other side of the Rhine. Strong garrisons were placed in Wesel, Düsseldorf, and Cologne. M. de Soubise's headquarters were at Düsseldorf.

ON the 13th of November, the Crown Prince came up in the evening, near Hatlenburg, with a large detachment of French cavalry commanded by M. de Clausen, whom he immediately at-tacked and routed with considerable loss on their side.

THIS day Marshal de Brogio arrived at Göttingen, and the main body of the French army encamped between that town and Münden.

ABOUT this time, M. de Scheither, having advanced as far as Lühnen, had the good fortune to surprize and carry off a whole troop of horse grenadiers, with their arms, and Major Wintzigerode took, in the neighborhood of Fritzlar, a French officer and 26 men, belonging to the corps under General d'Auvigny.

ON the 24th, a corps of some thousand French again advanced to the neighborhood of Northeim, with a design to keep in awe General Luckner, who was posted at Ahlshausen[184], and to prevent him from falling upon their heavy baggage which they were sending over the Werra towards their winter-quarters.

ON the 28th, the British Guards, and Highlanders, marched out of their cantonments in order to proceed to their winter quarters. The battalions which were encamped on the Hube likewise broke up their camp and joined their respective brigades this morning.

IN the beginning of December, Marshal de Brogio withdrew his troops from Nörten, and the whole of the French army marched to their winter quarters. The infantry were distributed in the neighborhood of Eisenach, Gotha, and Mulhausen; and the cavalry in the district of Fulda, and the towns and villages about Frankfurt. Marshal de Brogio fixed his headquarters at Kassel and placed numerous garrisons in that city and Göttingen.

ON the 4th of December, His Serene Highness fixed his headquarters at Hildesheim, and the whole army marched off successively to their winter quarters. The English cavalry quartered in East Friesland; the English infantry in the Bishopric of Osnabrück. The Crown Prince had his quarters at Munster; General Spörcken at Hameln and General Luckner at Einbeck.

---

184. Editor: Today part of the town of Einbeck.

THE CAMPAIGN OF THE YEAR 1762

ON the night between the 10th and 11th of March, a body of 3,000 French sallied forth from Göttingen, and fell upon the line of the Allies at daybreak; the attack was brisk and sudden, and made in several places. The principal one was at Gittel[185], where many were killed and wounded on both sides. The Brunswick rangers lost 30 men made prisoners. The French had one major dangerously wounded. At the attack on Kalefeld, the enemy were repulsed with the loss of one officer, and six men, made prisoners.

ON the 20th, a body of 3,000 of the Allied troops arrived in the neighborhood of Einbeck, in order to reinforce the line in that part, and keep the garrison of Göttingen in awe.

APRIL 6, General Luckner having detached 500 hussars to Heiligenstadt, the Marquis de Lortange marched out of Göttingen with 1,800 horse, and 2,000 foot, in order to intercept them; General Luckner, on information of their march, immediately put himself at the head of 1,600 horse; and, having come up with the enemy as they were retreating with great expedition towards Göttingen, he fell upon their rear, killed 30 men, and took 80 prisoners, besides 100 horses.

THE French about this time assembled a corps in the neighborhood of Mulhausen; and the Allies, on the other hand, were in motion about Einbeck; their light troops carefully observed what passed in the neighborhood of Eischfeld.

MAJOR Wintzengerode, who commanded the Hessian hussars, made one officer, with 50 private men belonging to the French hussars prisoners in the country of Eischfeld.

APRIL 19, the Crown Prince, having assembled a body of troops at Unna, proceeded to Arnsberg; and, by the 18th at 11 o'clock in the forenoon, some batteries were finished and mounted for the attack of the castle. The French commandant then offered to deliver up the place on the 21st, on condition of marching out with all the military honor, in case he was not relieved before that time; this delay could not be granted him, as the Prince knew the French troops were all in motion.

THE night between the 18th and 19th, everything was quiet on both sides, but, on the 19th at six in the morning, the batteries began to play. At nine, the Crown Prince made an offer to the commandant of permission to march out with all the military honors, and two pieces of cannon, which M. Muret rejected. The fire was again renewed with double fury, and about noon both the castle and town were all in flames; the garrison, consisting of nine officers and 231 private men, surrendered at discretion. There was found in the castle 26 pieces of cannon.

185. Editor Gittel may be Gittelde, which, today, is part of Bad Grund.

THIS excursion of the Crown Prince into the country of Berg greatly alarmed the French, for 400 men of each battalion, and 100 of each squadron from Cologne and Düsseldorf, passed the Rhine, and marched, on the 19th, to Rattenberg; on the 20th, cantoned at Langenberg and, on the 22d, proceeded to Hardenberg[186], in order to make room for M. d'Apchon, who had assembled a corps of 10,000 men at Hattingen; but, on information that the Prince had retired, they returned to their respective quarters.

THIS post was a place of great importance to the French, in order to preserve their communication between Wesel and Düsseldorf, and the reduction thereof enabled the Allies to raise contributions in the country of Burg,

ON the 20th of April, Marshal Soubise arrived at Kassel: he in conjunction with Marshal d'Etrees, was to command the French army on the Upper Rhine and Main.

ON the 24th, the Prince de Condé arrived at Düsseldorf, in order to take upon him the command of the French troops on the Lower Rhine.

MAY 9. the Crown Prince of Brunswick being determined to raise the contributions he had in his late expedition demanded of the country of Burg, suddenly marched with a large body of troops from Unna and appeared at Elberfeldt before the enemy had the least notice of his march. The corps under M. de Conflans, and the other French troops that were posted there, retired with the utmost precipitation, though not without loss. He thence proceeded to Solingen and having fulfilled the object he had in view; by taking hostages for the payment of the contributions, retired without any loss.

ON the first notice of this movement, the Prince de Condé assembled such troops as were nearest at hand and marched to Mettmann, but on advice that the Crown Prince had retired, he sent back the troops to the garrisons from which they had been drawn.

MAY 18, this day His Serene Highness, escorted by a battalion of Hanoverian guards, went from Hildesheim to Pyrmont, for which place the troops that were quartered in that neighborhood had filed off the day before. All the rest of the troops of the Allied Army on the Weser were likewise assembled in their respective cantonments. General Luckner took post on the Hube, and the pontoons were sent off from Hanover to the Weser. The Crown Prince had marched out of Münster and fixed his headquarters at Buldern.

THE French on the Upper Rhine had marked out several camps and were likewise in motion in order to assemble between the Fulda and the Werra. Those on the Lower Rhine were encamped in three corps at Düsseldorf, Wesel, and Rees, under Lieutenant Generals Monteynard, Levi, and St. Chamant.

MAY 24, General Luckner and Prince Frederick of Brunswick, having advanced on a reconnoitering party towards Göttingen, escorted by the hussars of Brunswick and Baur, forced the advanced guard, but M. de Lahr, lieutenant Colonel of the Volontaires of Austrasie, sallied out with a detachment of horse dragoons and hussars to sustain them, when he was attacked with so much impetuosity, that he was obliged to retire into

186. Editor: A castle.

the town in the greatest confusion; and those generals having made such observations as they purposed, returned to Einbeck, carrying off 80 prisoners and 100 horses. M. de Lahr was mortally wounded with the stroke of a saber.

JUNE 4, the English troops, which had been cantoned near Bielefeld, joined the corps under General Spörcken near Blomberg. All the infantry of the Allied Army were then assembled in the neighborhood of that place, and encamped on the heights of Belle[187]. General Kielmannsegg's corps was encamped near Brakel. The cavalry had not as yet taken the field,

ON the 18th, the cavalry having joined the Allied Army, the whole was this day assembled at the camp at Brakel.

ON the 19th, the corps under Lord Granby, which formed the vanguard, marched to Peckelsheim[188].

ON the 20th, the main army advanced from Brakel towards the Diemel, and encamped at Borgholz. Lord Granby's corps moved forward to Warburg, occupying the camp.

ON the 21st, the main army marched to Bühne, and occupied the camp between Körbcke and the Heights of Deisel[189].

THE same day, two battalions of British grenadiers, two battalions of Highlanders, the chasseurs of Lord Granby's corps, and Elliot's Dragoons crossed the Diemel and advanced to Volkmarsen, leaving their tents standing; the intent of their march was to gain intelligence of the enemy. This party returned to their camp on the next day.

THE chasseurs and hussars passed the Diemel, and attacked the castle of Sababurg[190], which surrendered; the garrison, consisting of one captain, and 50 men, were made prisoners of war; they afterwards proceeded to seize upon the Passes of the Diemel, taking up a post.

JUNE 22, the whole French army under Marshals d'Estrées and Soubise, advanced and encamped at Grebenstein and Meijenbracksen.

THE corps under M. de Castries encamped between Carlsdorf[191] and Grebenstein, on the right flank of their army, which was covered by Grebenstein, and several rivulets.

M. Stainville's corps encamped on the heights near Schachten in the front of their left wing, which was rendered inaccessible by several deep ravines.

ON the 24th, His Serene Highness Prince Ferdinand having determined to attack the enemy, and knowing of what importance the post of Sababurg was, for the march of his

---

187. Editor: Today Belle is part of Horn-Bad Meinberg.
188. Editor: Today part of Willebadessen.
189. Editor: Today part of Trendelburg.
190. Editor: Today part of Hofgeismar. It has also been known as Zappenburg and Zapfenburg.
191. Editor: Today part of Hofgeismar.

troops through the woods, caused a brigade of infantry to march towards Trendelburg and take post: he likewise ordered the troops which were posted on the other side the Diemel, to sustain that post in, case of necessity.

THE dispositions made for the attack were as follows, viz: Lieutenant General Luckner, who was posted at Sülbeck on the Leine, having Einbeck in his front, with six battalions of grenadiers, four squadrons of dragoons, and eight of hussars, to observe the motions of Prince Xavier, who lay encamped with his corps de reserve between the Werra and Göttingen, received orders, in the night between the 22d and 23d, to march to Gottsbüren in the Reinhardswald, with the grenadiers, four squadrons of horse, and his own regiment of hussars. The Hessian hussars were ordered to remain in the neighborhood of Moringen, in order to conceal his march and to observe Prince Xavier. General Luckner began his march accordingly from Hollenstedt[192] on the 23d at 6 o'clock in the morning, got to Uslar at noon, passed the Weser at Bodenfelde at 6 o'clock in the evening, and towards night reached Gotsbuhren, where he encamped. He had also orders to proceed, on the 24th at three in the morning, through the Sababurg Wood to Mariendorf, and to form between that place and Udenhausen, by seven in the morning.

THE Marquis of Granby passed the Diemel in three columns at Warburg, between two and three in the morning, with the corps de reserve under his command: this corps consisted of two battalions of British grenadiers, two battalions of Highlanders, the Blues, and Elliott's Dragoons; two regiments of Hanoverian cavalry, three regiments of Hanoverian infantry, some Hessian artillery, and Lieutenant Colonel Baur's Hussars. The first column marched by Breuna and Zierenberg, possessing themselves of the village of Dörnburg: the two others directed their march by Sieberhausen and Schreckenberg[193]; the whole was to join at the eminence opposite to Fürstenwald, where they were to form by seven in the morning, in order to fall on the left wing of the enemy.

THE Hessian and Brunswick chasseurs, who were destined to cover the left flank of General Luckner's Corps, marched by the great road, and formed by 7 o'clock, not far from Hohenchen[194].

THE main body of the army passed the Diemel at four in the morning in seven columns, between Liebenau and Sielen. The two columns on the left under the command of Gen. Spörcken, consisting of 12 battalions of Hanoverians, and part of the cavalry of the left wing, marched between Hümme[195] and Beberbeck, in order to form between Hombressen[196] and Udenhausen, on the right of the enemy. He had orders as soon as he had formed to attack the right flank of the corps under M. de Castries; while General Luckner should, at the same time, charge them in their rear, and if they succeeded, they were to continue their march in such a manner as to take the enemy's camp at Grebenstein both in flank and rear. Sixteen squadrons of cavalry, who followed the

192. Editor: Today part of the town of Northeim.
193. Editor: Schreckenberg is a hill north of Zierenberg.
194. Editor: Hohenchen may be Hohenkirchen, which today is part of Espenau.
195. Editor: Today part of Hofgeismar.
196. Editor: Today part of Hofgeismar.

march of the fifth column, stopped near Geismar, and drew up in order to attack the enemy in front at the same time that the attack on their right flank should take place.

His Serene Highness at the head of the other five columns, consisting of 12 battalions of the English, 11 battalions of the Brunswickers, and eight Hessian regiments, together with the English cavalry, and part of the German cavalry of the left wing, marched to Langenberg. The whole then drew up in the front of Kelze, opposite to the enemy. The piquets of the army formed the vanguard on the left, and the English light infantry, commanded by Lord Frederick Cavendish, with Freytag's Hanoverian jägers, that of the right. They were ordered to seize on the debouches of the Langenberg.

THIS whole plan was put into execution with such success, that the whole was in the presence of the enemy before they had the least apprehension of being attacked.

M. de Castries, seeing that his right was turned, formed his infantry to make headway against M. Spörcken; who began a severe cannonade, and drew up his cavalry, to oppose the corps under General Luckner. The body of cavalry, belonging to the Allies, advanced and entirely broke their infantry, and took two pieces of cannon. M. de Riedesel, also, totally overthrew the Fitzjames Regiment, took 300 of their horses, and their two standards. M. de Castries fell back with the greatest precipitation on the right of the enemy's army.

His Serene Highness at the head of the main body advanced on the enemy in front, while the Marquis of Granby advanced by Ehrsten and Fürstenwalde, in order to come around the left of French.

THE two Marshals seeing themselves attacked in front, flank, and rear, used the utmost expedition they could to gain the heights of Wilhelmsthal, marching by as many columns as the nature of the ground would admit of. They at the same time abandoned all their equipages at Grebenstein.

KEY TO MAP.

A French army.

B De Castries Division.

C De Stainville's division

D Hanoerian army, formed in battle formation. Prince Ferdinand, who encamped, on the 21st at Buhne, having resovled ot attack the French, had occupied all the debouches of the Dimel with jägers, and ordered General Luckner to move, on the 23rd, to Gotlsburen, to surprise de Castries, in marching all ngiht across the Rheinhardt, which he executed after capturing at Zappaburg, a guard of 50 men and an officer, he arrived in de Castries rear at E

E While Mylord Granby, who encamped at Warburg, had moved, by his right, around the Malzburger Woods and marched on Zierenberg at F.

F Granby then took de Stainville here in the flank. During these movements, Prince Ferdinand, who was before Buhne, crossed the Dimel, and moved in seven columns (D.) De Castries, who had opposed his cavalry at Luckner at G and Spörken at H.

G Luckner and his infantry.

H General Spörken. De Castries, unable to withstand the fire of the Hanoverians, withdrew to the right of the army, which then abandoned its baggage at Grevenstein, leaving the heights of that city, to retire on Wilhelmsthal at I.

I De Castries was followed by the Allied Army to I, but the corps of

K Mylord Granby had cut de Castres off from de Stainville

M De Stainville, who was in a wood to facilitate the retreat of the army

L to ease his infantry, which had suffered greatly. Finally, the French army, fearing it would be enveloped, retreated, which it did on Kassel

N from where it moved the next day to occup a camp at Langwehrhagen. Prince Ferdinand advanced to O.

O and was pursued until it was under Kassel's cannon.

NB. The action began at 4:00 a.m., and finished at 2:00 p.m.

M. Stainville, perceiving that the retreat of part of their army had been cut off by the maneuver of Lord Granby, particularly that of his own corps, immediately gained the wood of Meimbressen[197] with the Grenadiers of France, the Royal Grenadiers, the Aquitaine Regiment, and some other corps, being the flower of the French infantry, in order to favor the retreat of the main body, which would have been entirely routed but for this step, as they were closely pressed by His Serene Highness. But this resolution cost him dear; for he was immediately attacked by the Marquis of Granby's corps, and as our army advanced briskly to Wilhelmsthal its right gained a height, they thereby found themselves in his rear. The whole of his infantry were either killed, taken, or dispersed, after a gallant resistance, except two battalions who found means to escape. Some of these troops had before surrendered to Lord Granby's corps, but on the coming up of the army, the remainder, after one fire surrendered to General Hodgson's Regiment of Foot.

THE enemy placed some cannon on the height in the grand avenue of Wilhelmsthal, but it was soon silenced by a battery of ours: after which the enemy made no further resistance, but retired into their entrenched camp, under Kassel, being closely pursued 'till within reach of the cannon of that town.

His Serene Highness encamped the troops the same night on the heights between Holzhausen and Weimar.

THE French infantry consisted of 100 battalions, and the Allies had no more than 60.

197. Editor: Today part of Calden.

LORD Granby acquitted himself upon this occasion with his usual intrepidity and good conduct, and greatly contributed to the victory. All the troops in general behaved with uncommon spirit, but particularly the first battalion of grenadiers belonging to Colonel Beckwith's brigade, who distinguished themselves greatly.

THE LOSS of the enemy in killed and wounded was never particularly ascertained; they owned to the loss of 900 men, and, by the account of the Allies, it was above double that number; but the following is an authentic list of the French made prisoners.

Regiment		Prisoners
Grenadiers of France		635
Royal Grenadiers, Rochelambert		208
Royal Grenadiers, L'Espinasle		135
Royal Grenadiers, Le Camus		121
Narbonne		60
Aquitaine		432
Poitou		29
Royal Deux-Ponts		30
Waldner		108
D'Epring		55
Choiseul Dragoons		64
Royal Picardy Cavalry		30
Fitz-James's Cavalry		77
Chamborant		28
Monnet		112
Different corps		446
	Total	2,750
Officers belonging to different corps		162

THE trophies taken were, one standard, six pair of colors, and two pieces of cannon.

The following is the loss of the Allied Army as appeared from the returns:

	Killed	Wounded	Prisoners		Killed	Wounded	Prisoners
Grenadier Guards, British	8	25	27	Artillery	2	3	13
1st Bn, British Guards	7	28	30	Blue Horse Guards	1	5	
2nd Bn, British Guards		22	12	Elliott's Dragoons	2	3	
3rd Bn, British Guards	11	17	17	Hanoverian Infantry	6	14	8
Welsh Grenadiers	3	40	3	Schaumburg Lippe	6	2	
Maxwell's Grenadiers		1	55	Hanoverian Cavalry	2	4	7
Hodgson's Regiment		11	6	Brunswick Cavalry	3	1	
Keith's Highlanders	8	8	15	Hessian Cavalry	3	7	19
Campbell's Highlanders	5	10	12	Light Troops	27	49	81
Frasier's Chasseurs	1	11					

Two pieces of cannon and three ammunition wagons lost.

TOTAL, 4 officers, 10 non-commissioned officers, 194 rank and file, killed; 2 officers, 18 non-commissioned officers, 253 rank and file, wounded; and 4 officers, 5 non-commissoned officers, 306 rank and file, missing; the whole making 796 men.

THE only officer of any distinction killed was Colonel Henry Townshend, of the 1st Guards Regiment of Foot.

THE following account of this action was published in Paris by authority under the title of: *Journal of the French army under the Command of the Marshal d'Estrées and Soubise, from the 23d to the 27th of June.*

"ON the 23d of June, the enemy's whole army passed the Diemel and at night the English advancing on our left towards Zierenberg, from whence they might get to Kassel before us, the Marshals d'Estrées and Soubise thought proper to quit the camp of Grebenstein, in order to arrive at Kassel before the enemy. This march was performed in the greatest order.

"THE Marquis de Castries with the corps under his command, which had been detached before our right to observe the Allies, rejoined the army, after having successfully charged the enemy several times with his cavalry. The Alsace Regiment sustained with the greatest firmness the shock of the enemy's cavalry and killed many men. A considerable number of prisoners were also made in that part.

"ON our left the Count de Stainville, seeing the English advance to seize the heights of Wilhelmsthal, and being sensible of the importance of that post, attacked them, notwithstanding their great superiority, in the decisive moment for the safety of our army in its march. He succeeded in two most vigorous charges and took from them seven pieces of cannon. At the third charge, the Grenadiers of France being too far back in the wood, several companies of that corps, and part of the Aquitaine Regiment, were surrounded by the enemy's whole right wing, and taken prisoners. This was the only disaster that happened during our march.

"ON the 24th at night, the army encamped near Kassel, and the corps under the Marquis de Castries was placed before the right wing.

"ON the 25th, we pitched our camp at Landwerhagen, in the territory of Hanover, our right wing extending towards Münden. The Count de Stainville remained in the entrenched camp under Kassel. The corps under the Count de Lusace took post on the other side of the Werra.

"ON the 26th, the Allies sent us back the prisoners they took on the 26th: their number amounted to 1,600, most of them belonging to the Grenadiers of France, the Royal Grenadiers, and the Aquitaine Regiment. There were also among them some private men of the Poitou Regiment. This regiment and that of Aquitaine formed the brigade which distinguished itself so much in Count Stainville's attacks.

"FROM the returns of the regiments that were engaged, it appears that our loss in killed and wounded does not amount to 900 men. The Chevalier de Narbonne, colonel of the Grenadiers of France, was the only officer of distinction that was killed. The Marquis de Peyre, and the Marquis de la Rochelambert, colonels of grenadiers, and the Duke of Picquigny, were slightly wounded.

"THE prisoners we made amounted to 300, and the killed and wounded of the enemy to many more. Of the seven pieces of cannon taken by M. Stainville in his repeated attacks five were retaken at the third charge; the two others, which were heavy cannon, were sent to Kassel."

ON the 25th of June, the two French marshals passed the Fulda with their army, encamping near Landwerhagen; their right extending towards Münden. Lieutenant General Stainville was left behind with his corps at the Kratzenberg Hill. The corps under Prince Xavier of Saxony, which was encamped near Dransfeld, retired from thence, and crossed the Fulda in order to join the main army; but during their retreat they lost their baggage, moving hospital, and medicines, which, together with their escort were all taken near Volkmarshausen[198], by M. de Speth, major of the corps of Brunswick jägers.

THIS day the Allies fired a *feu de joie*, on account of the victory gained on the day before over the French.

M. de Conflans, with all the cavalry belonging to his corps, marched to Recklinghausen, where he surprised a body of 400 horse belonging to the Allies, who were obliged to retire, with the loss of some men killed and made prisoners.

ON the 28th, the British Guards changed their position, and encamped at Winter-Kasten; but the Marquis of Granby still had his quarters at Dörnburg, and Prince Ferdinand remained atWilhelmstathal.

JULY 1, Prince Ferdinand having received advice, that M. de Rochambeau had assembled some brigades of infantry and cavalry near Homberg, with a view to cover the communications of the enemy's army with Frankfurt, took the resolution of dislodging him from the post which he had taken possession of. For which purpose His Serene Highness ordered Lord Frederick Cavendish to advance with the light infantry of the army's infantry, Freytag's jägers, and Bauer's and Riedesel's Hussars, from Lohn to Felsberg; and Lord Granby, with the brigade of the British grenadiers, Elliot's, the Blues, and the four Hanoverian squadrons, from Hoof to Fritzlar. The former were to march towards Homberg, in such a direction, as to cut off the enemy's corps from Melsungen and Fulda; the other, to cut off their retreat to Ziegenhain: which orders were executed in the following manner: The hour of rendezvous on both sides of Homberg, for the attack of M. de Rochambeau's corps, was agreed on. The discharge of three pieces of cannon from Lord Frederick Cavendish's troops was to be the signal of his arrival. Elliot's being arrived at a quarter of a league's distance from Homberg, attacked the advanced posts, and drove them from the heights, and took post there. The rest of Lord Granby's corps were in the rear of Elliot's, behind the declivity of the height, and the enemy's tents continued standing. At the same time Lord Frederick Cavendish's hussars began to exchange some shot with the enemy, when their tents were immediately struck, and

198. Editor: Today part of the town of Hannoverisch Münden.

they got under arms at the foot of the mountain and in the hedges near the town: their cavalry formed on the plain. The three discharges of cannon were made; whereupon the enemy's infantry defiled on their left, their cavalry covering their march. Lord Granby perceiving they intended to retreat marched all his corps as fast as possible to the right, when the enemy's cavalry, who put on a good countenance, began to move on at a quick rate. Upon this His Lordship ordered the cavalry to advance, following close with the infantry, which began an attack on the enemy's rear with the greatest ardor and success, making two onsets in an instant; but the enemy's cavalry facing about immediately, and falling sword in hand upon Elliot's Dragoons, that regiment would have suffered greatly, had not Colonel Hervey at the head of the Blues, seeing the danger, passed the village on full gallop; and notwithstanding he could oppose only eight or ten men in front to formed squadrons, he overthrew all that came in his way, and saved Elliot's Dragoon Regiment.

THE situation of the two regiments was at this time very critical; but the mutual support which they gave each other, Elliot's Dragoons by continual skirmishing with the enemy, and the Blues by their maneuvers in squadrons, and by their steady countenance, kept the enemy at bay 'till the infantry could come up. They then began their retreat in the utmost hurry, the grenadiers and Highlanders following them with their usual ardor. If their infantry had not posted themselves in a hollow way, to sustain their squadrons which the Blues and Elliot's were charging, the whole would have been routed. During their retreat, Lord Cavendish's corps, which could not advance sooner, followed them close, and pushed them vigorously.

COLONELS Hervey and Erskine, and Majors Forbes and Ainsley distinguished themselves greatly.

THE LOSS of the Allies in killed, wounded, and taken, was computed at about 80 men. That of the enemy was very considerable, as the number of prisoners taken amounted to upwards of 250 men, exclusive of the killed and wounded.

THE troops returned to Melsungen, having first sent off the two regiments of hussars of Bauer and Riedesel to Rotenburg an der Fulda, in order to destroy the enemy's magazines. Colonel Riedesel accordingly burned 150,000 rations of hay, 40,060 rations of oats, and carried off from thence 70 oxen belonging to the French.

M. de Chevert with his corps replaced the corps of Prince Xavier near Dransfeld.

M. de Grandmaison having penetrated through Langensaltz and Mulhausen, at the head of 500 light horse, suddenly advanced to Halberstadt and Quedlinburg, where he demanded a 75,000 rixdollars contribution; but the inhabitants not being able to raise more than 5,000, he took with him four hostages, and hastily retired.

JULY 3, a detachment from the French army on the Lower Rhine fell in with M. de Scheither, who, with about 120 of his party, were made prisoners in the neighborhood of Coesfeldt.

JULY 6, the position of the two armies in the neighborhood of Kassel was nearly the same; Prince Ferdinand remaining encamped between Holzhausen and Weimar, having a considerable detachment on the Eder, and another at Uslar in the Solling[199]: the Guards' Brigade, with Eland's and Waldegerve's Dragoons, were posted near Hof. The French main body was on the heights between Kassel and Münden, having a detachment of 8,000 men near Dransfeld, and another of 15,000 between Melsungen and Homberg.

GENERAL Luckner took prisoner the French partisan Monet, with his whole corps, at Schaffhoff[200], within 200 paces of Kassel.

THE Prince de Condé detached a body of troops towards the Lower Ems and Hase Rivers amd they destroyed in East Friesland, and its neighborhood, several considerable magazines, and exacted large contributions from the country of Lingen, and that of Tecklenburg; they likewise intended to have made an attempt on Osnabrück, and some magazines that were there, but were prevented by a party of the Hanoverians posted near the village of Lengerich. They afterwards returned to Dillenburg.

ON the 10th, part of the bakery belonging to the Allies at Warburg was destroyed by the Marquis de Chamborant, who carried off one commissary, and 80 other persons, besides some horses.

M. de Riedesel made the Brigadier de Norman prisoner, in the neighborhood of Marburg, and brought off 80 horses.

ON the 11th, the Castle of Waldeck, in the neighborhood of Fritzlar, surrendered to the Allies, having been bombarded by General Conway for two days; the French garrison, consisting of four officers, and 160 men, surrendered by capitulation, on the condition of not serving against the Allies for the space of one year.

THE Prince de Condé detached a corps of ten battalions and six squadrons, together with all the grenadiers and chasseurs of his army, under Lieutenant General d'Auvet, with an attempt to surprise the city of Münster, but, having intelligence on their march, that the garrison was on their guard, they returned again to join their main body.

JULY 13, the corps under General Caesar, that was posted at Hof, marched to Guedensburg, where the whole corps under the Marquis of Granby were again assembled; his Lordship's headquarters were fixed at Niedervorschütz.

---

199. Editor: Solling is a range of wooded hills. The "Wild Hunt" is a European folk myth involving a ghostly or supernatural group of huntsmen passing in a hunt. In the Solling, but also in the Hartz Mountains, the chief huntsman is supposed to be the ghost of Hanns von Hackelberg or Hackelnberg (1521-1581), chief forester of Brunswick. According to the tale, he dreamed that he would be wounded by a wild boar the next day. His friends tried to dissuade him from the planned hunt, but he insisted, and met a wild boar. He slew the boar. In the evening at a feast, though, he lifted the boar's head with his hand, and mocked the boar, as he had not hurt him, after all. Suddenly, the head fell out of his hand, and one of the sharp tusks penetrated his foot. A few days later Hackelberg died.
200. Editor: This is probably properly spelled Schafhof and may be part of the city of Kassel, but today there is no such district in Kassel.

GENERAL Luckner, at the head of Elliot's Dragoons, one regiment of Hanoverian dragoons, the chasseurs, and some hussars, marched from Bad Wildungen, in order to attack a party of the French posted in the neighborhood of Felsberg, but the enemy were so much superior in numbers, that they halted near Homberg.

ON the 14th, the corps under the command of Lord Granby marched by daybreak to Felsberg, where they drew up on the Eder River, took possession of a bridge, and cannonaded the enemy: in the evening, they encamped there. General Luckner had at the same time advanced from Homberg towards Falkenburg but retired again the same evening.

ON the 15th, His Serene Highness Prince Ferdinand marched; from Wilhelmsthal to Hoof and on the same day all the enemy's posts along the Fulda, as far as Melsungen, were attacked in particular, the corps under the Marquis of Granby advanced to the Eder leaving their tents standing. The British grenadiers, Highlanders, and Bland's, forded that river between Nieder-Möllrich and Felsberg, while General Freytag, with the hussars and jägers, passed over the bridge at Felsberg, these drew up in the front of the enemy, while General Luckner, who had been before on that side the Eder, advanced on their flank; but the enemy having considerably reinforced that post the night before, and their situation being also too strong to be forced, His Lordship returned that night to his camp, and General Luckner retired to above Otterhaus.

THE French, uncertain what might be the intention of the Allied Army, struck their tents, and Lieutenant General Chevert was recalled from his post at Dransfeld to join the main army. The garrison of Göttingen, having likewise taken the alarm, abandoned that town in the afternoon, but they returned again the next morning.

THE French marshals after that quitted their camp at Landwerhagen, encamping along the Fulda at Melsungen and that neighborhood, leaving a strong detachment at Luttemberg, and another on the Kratzenburg, in the entrenched camp before Kassel.

JULY 16, this morning the corps under the command of the Marquis of Granby returned to Gundersburg, and encamped in the neighborhood of that place.

ON the 22d, the corps de reserve, under Lord Granby, marched from Gundersburg, and, crossing the Eder on the stone bridge at Fritzlar, encamped near Kraetzenhausen.

His Serene Highness also removed from Hoof to Gundersburg, fixing his headquarters at Nieder-Worschutz.

ON the 23d, Lord Granby marched to Singlis, where he encamped at about a league's distance from Homberg in front, near which place the enemy had a strong detachment posted on the heights.

His Serene Highness having determined to dislodge the corps under Prince Xavier from the post of Luttemberg (which was composed of all the Saxon troops, and 13 squadrons of French) made the following dispositions for the attack.

GENERAL Gilsa was ordered to pass the Fulda at Spele with eight battalions; General Block was to cross it with eight squadrons at Spiegehnuhl; and General Zastrow at Willemshausen, General Waldhausen posted Colonel Plesse at Bonnafort, in order to cover the left of the attack, and curb the garrison of Münden, while he, in conjunction with Colonel Schleiben, who had been towards Göttingen, and was on this occasion to pass the Werra at Heidemunden, should endeavor to take the enemy in the rear.

ALL this was executed with the greatest bravery and success. The attack began by 4 o'clock in the morning. The grenadiers on the left began it, by passing the river in the presence of the enemy, amidst a severe fire of cannon and musketry, which they sustained with surprising intrepidity; the rest of the infantry followed their example, though the water was above their waists.

GENERAL Gilsa immediately caused a wood to be occupied that was on the enemy's right, which obliged them to change their position a little in order to cover their flank, and at the same time divided their attention.

THE affair was sharply disputed for some time, but the enemy were at length driven out of four palisaded redoubts one after another, as also from all their entrenchments. During this action, and at the juncture the enemy was giving way, Major General Waldhausen, with M. de Schlieben's corps, gained the rear of the enemy's right flank, and charged it with such vigor, that they overthrew the French squadrons.

THE Saxons, apprehensive of having their retreat cut off, retired with the utmost precipitation by the road that leads to Kassel: in their retreat, they lost one regiment of cavalry, and two regiments of grenadiers, made prisoners; that of cavalry had suffered greatly before they were taken.

DURING the time of this attack, Prince Frederick of Brunswick had marched towards the enemy's entrenched camp on the Kratzenburg and cannonaded their lines. General Stainville, who was posted there with a corps of 10,000 men, having an account of the defeat of the Saxons quitted the entrenchments, and marched to cover the retreat of Prince Xavier. That strong camp was immediately taken possession of by Prince Frederick, who caused all the works, redoubts, etc. to be destroyed.

THE loss of the enemy, killed and wounded in this action, was very considerable: the number of prisoners taken amounted to 1,100 men, among whom were Lieutenant General Prince d'Isenburg, and several officers; besides 12 pieces of cannon, and two standards; whereas the Loss of the Allies did not in the whole exceed 200 men.

ON the 24th of July, the Marquis of Granby ordered out the 1st British Guard Regiment, one battalion of Hanoverians, and 100 men from each of the other regiments, who advanced to the heights of Homberg, from whence they dislodged a party of the enemy, and occupied that post all night.

THE Prince de Condé, leaving only some light troops under M. Cambefortin the country of Münster, decamped the 16th from Coesfeldt, and arrived the same day between Haus-Dülmen and Siten. A violent rain, which continued all day, had so greatly damaged the roads, that the light troops of the Allies, who pressed them very closely, took a quantity of baggage, horses, etc. besides many prisoners.

ON the 17th, they marched by St. Annen and Bossendorf towards the Lippe, which they passed near Haltern-am-See.

ON the 18th, they continued their route to Wefterboit, where they halted.

ON the 21st, they proceeded to Bockum, from whence they arrived at Düsseldorf this day.

THE Crown Prince having driven all the French detachments from the neighborhood of Osnabrück and being informed of the march of the Prince de Condé, decamped, on the 18th, from Wolbeck, and was this day encamped at Mark, near Hamm, in order to observe his motions.

JULY 25, His Serene Highness crossed the Eder this night, with three brigades of infantry, and eight squadrons of horse, and joined the corps under the Marquis of Granby, who had also marched, at one clock in the morning, from Singlis through Homberg, and were drawn up on the heights of Falckenburg: the enemy, who occupied those heights, having retreated on His Lordship's approach. The intention was, if practicable, to attack the left flank of the main body of the French army, posted between Hilgenburg and Melsungen, whilst General Spörcken should engage their front, and Prince Frederick of Brunswick their right. General Spörcken was to pass the Eder at Felsberg, and Prince Frederick at Brunclar.

His Serene Highness found, upon reconnoitering so close to the enemy as to be exposed to the fire of three batteries, that their position was too strong, and too well provided with troops, to risk an attack. Whilst Prince Ferdinand was doing this he left his army formed in columns, presenting the heads of the columns only to their view; but observing them to be embarrassed, he formed, at 8 o'clock in the evening, within cannon-shot, and General Spörcken began to cannonade them. At 10 o'clock at night His Highness withdrew the troops to the heights of Falkenberg, leaving the piquets advanced to keep the fires burning to deceive the enemy. At 2 o'clock in the morning, he marched to repass the Schwalm at Harte, and the Eder at Nieder-Möllrich[201]; suspecting however that the French would decamp in the night, he left Lord Granby upon the Falkenburg, with orders to stay 'till daylight, and, in case the enemy had retired, to take possession immediately of the high grounds of Melsungen. His Lordship found that the French had repassed the Fulda in the night and executed the orders he had received; so that Prince Ferdinand had succeeded in obliging the enemy to abandon a post they gave out was not to be forced without risking a double action, and which could not fail to cost a great many lives. The French then returned back again towards Kassel and Lutterberg, abandoning entirely their communica-tions to the discretion of Prince Ferdinand, having only left a body of about 10,000 men under Lieutenant General de Guerchy opposite Melsungen.

201. Editor: Today part of Wabern.

THE same day General Stainville, marching along the right of the Fulda towards Rotenburg an der Fulda, with four regiments of dragoons, fell into an ambush at Morschen, where General Freytag commanded, by whom M. de Stainville was very roughly handled, his dragoons were routed and dispersed with great loss. General Freytag's troops got a great deal of booty.

JULY 26, General Luckner, who had been encamped on the 23d near Neukirchen, received orders to march to Bad Hersfeldt, where he arrived about nine in the evening, and made an attempt to take it by surprise, but the garrison being too strong, and on their guard, he was obliged to desist, with the loss of two men killed and 30 wounded. He then marched by Schlitz to Fulda, which place he took this day without any loss; the garrison, consisting of 400 men, were made prisoners of war. They also took a considerable quantity of baggage, a large convoy of wine, and 300 fat oxen that were going to the French army, besides a contribution of 70,000 florins. By the taking of this town the communications of the French army with Frankfurt was entirely cut off.

JULY 28, General Stainville, at the head of a considerable body of French troops, being detached to open the enemy's communications, by the way of Fulda, advanced this day to Vacha, near which place he fell in with a party of 400 of the light troops belonging to the Allies, whom he defeated: from thence he advanced to Mansbach[202] and Hunefeld on his way to Fulda. General Luckner was obliged to quit that city on his approach, which he did, on the 31st, taking post at Grossenlüder.

AUGUST 1, the two armies on the Fulda having formed a chain of piquets along that river, were with great diligence fortifying their posts on each side, and erecting batteries: frequent skirmishes passed between the out parties, with various successes.

M. de Rochechouart, and M. de Lostanges, came up with a detachment of the Allies near Uslar, whom they entirely dispersed, taking near 200 prisoners. They afterwards divided their forces, the one taking the route of Carlshafen[203], and the other that of Beverungenn; they took or destroyed at those places, one magazine, and 29 boats laden with provisions. About the same time, M. de Vertueil destroyed another magazine at Brakel, and made 60 men prisoners.

THE Baron de Blaisel marched from Giessen to Amöneburg, and surprised 400 of the Allies, whom he made prisoners of war.

THE Prince de Condé having received repeated orders to join the two marshals with his corps, they filed off from Düsseldorf in four divisions by the route to Opladen, Siegburg, and Hachenburg, at which last place the whole was assembled this day.

AUGUST 2, General Freytag, who was posted at Neumorschen on the Fulda, was attacked by a large party of the French, but they were repulsed with loss.

THE private men of the Allies and French, as the troops were so near each other, used to pass the sentinels, and come into the same fields promiscuously, in order to gather

202. Editor: Today part of Hohenroda.

203. Editor: Today Bad Karlshafen.

roots, in which they amicably assisted each other, and conversed friendily together; this occasioned positive orders to be isued, that no one should presume to go beyond the sentinels, or have any conversation with the enemy. I mention this, though immaterial, as an extraordinary instance.

AUGUST 4. The enemy under the Prince de Condé marched, on the 2d, from Hachenburg to Hain; they proceeded from thence, on the 3d, to Roth; they passed the Dill River this day at Herborn and encamped at Hohensolms[204]. He then detached four regiments to Gladenbach and pushed some detachments between Marburg and Giessen. The Crown Prince was arrived at Wetter.

ON the 7th, the Count de Stainville, at the head of 800 men, appeared before the town of Friedewaldee, which surrendered after a severe cannonade the garrison, consisting of 50 men, were made prisoners of war. They plundered the villages, and stripped the inhabitants.

PRINCE Frederick of Brunswick marched with great rapidity to the rear of the French army, and took possession of Eschwege, Wanfried, and Mulhausen, by which the communications of the enemy were effectually cut off on all sides.

LIEUT. General Julius Caesar died this morning at his quarters in Elfershausen[205]; his death was occasioned by a fall from his horse.

ON the 8th of August, Lord Granby's corps de reserve marched towards the Fulda, when a brisk cannonade ensued. Prince Ferdinand with the main army moved forward in several columns. The river, by a sudden rain, had swelled to such a height, as rendered the fording thereof too dangerous for the troops to venture across, as had been intended: a body of the infantry of the right wing however patted over, and, driving the enemy from one of the passes, took post opposite the center of their camp. The French made several attempts to dislodge them, but they were constantly repulsed with loss: these attacks were made not far from Melsungen: Lieutenant Colonel M'Dowal was ordered with a detachment from the 2d and 3d British Guard Regiments to attack that town they accordingly cut down the chevaux de frise, and endeavored to force one of the gates, but it was gorged with dung, which rendered the attempt impracticable. The army lay out on the nights of the 8th and 9th; and, on the 10th in the morning, they returned to their former encampment.

COLONEL DE Würmser was ordered by the Prince de Condé, who was posted at Grünberg, to advance with his regiment of light troops to reconnoiter the castle of Ulrichstein, which was occupied by the Allies. The Prince, in consequence of his report, detached the same night a body of horse and foot, under the command of Lieutenant General d'Affry, with four pieces of cannon, and two howitzers, to reduce it.

HE, at the same time, sent orders to M. de Levis to make a false attack with his advanced guard upon the front of the Crown Prince's camp, who was posted on the heights of Homberg; this was done with a view of covering M. d'Affry's march. M. do Levis accordingly began his attack by eight the next morning and retired about noon.

204. Editor: Today Hohensolms is part of Hohenar.
205. Editor: Today part of Malsfeld.

M. d'Affry arrived in the morning before the castle of Ulrichstein, which he immediately invested and cannonaded: the garrison, consisting of 60 foot and 50 chasseurs, surrendered at discretion by noon.

M. de Conflans, who commanded a detachment belonging to the army under the Prince de Condé, sent a party of 200 men to seize the town of Pattenberg (or Padberg), together with a redoubt, which, by its situation, commanded the town. The French accordingly made themselves masters of that post; the garrison, consisting of 72 men, were made prisoners of war, after a vigorous defense.

THE French made an attempt to force the left of the Crown Prince's corps at Romrod, where General Hardenberg commanded, but they were repulsed with loss.

ON the 16th of August, the French evacuated the city of Göttingen, having first destroyed part of the ramparts, but not the outworks; they also set fire to the powder magazine, by the explosion whereof 60 Saxons perished, and the town was much damaged. They retreated by the way of Witzenhausen, leaving behind them three pieces of brass cannon, and a great quantity of ammunition of all sorts.

PRINCE Frederick of Brunswick was with his corps at that time in the neighborhood of Einbeck, having just returned from the expedition he had made on the Werra, he immediately marched to take possession of that city.

ON the 17th, the two marshals broke up their camp and abandoned the banks of the Fulda, marching away by their right to occupy the space between Spangenberg and Lichtenau[206]; they also withdrew the garrison from the town of Münden, which Prince Frederick directly entered.

ON the 18th of August, His Serene Highness marched and encamped in the neighborhood of Homberg; the corps de reserve being at Burnshashusen[207].

COLONEL Riedesel dislodged M. Conflans from the town of Pattenburg, with the loss of one captain, and 70 private men, beside a number of horses.

PRINCE Frederick invested the city of Kassel and summoned the commandant. The French left a garrison in that city of 11 battalions, and 2 regiments of cavalry, under the command of M. de Dielbach.

ON the 19th, the Allied Army encamped near Osterode.

ON the 20th, they marched and encamped near Neuenstein.

ON the 21st, they halted. General Luckner, who was encamped at Eimbach, this day dislodged a party of the enemy from the neighborhood of Reibertenrod. The light troops made one captain, one lieutenant, and 120 men, prisoners on this occasion; they also took one piece of cannon, and several horses.

---

206. Editor: Today Hessisch Lichtenau.
207. Editor: This may be Berndshausen, part of Knüllwald.

THE two French marshals were encamped near Bad Hersfeldt and were covered by the Fulda. The Prince de Condé was at Grünberg. The Crown Prince observed his motions and directed his route so as to prevent his junction with the grand army.

ON the 22d, the two marshals decamped from Bad Hersfeldt, and fixed their headquarters at Mohr[208]. The Allied Army marched this day to Trillingen.

THE Crown Prince attacked this day the vanguard of the Prince de Condé, under the command of M. de Levis, who was obliged to fall back to the main body; the French lost about 150 men in this affair. The two armies then drew up in order of battle and continued in sight of each other 'till night.

ON the 23d of August, the two marshals marched to the Fulda; and His Serene Highness encamped near Nieder-Jossa. General Luckner this day joined the Crown Prince.

ON the 24th, the Crown Prince marched from Lich, in order to surprise the Prince de Condé in his camp at Grunengen, but as it was dark before he could come up, the French had time to retreat to the heights near that town.

ON the 25th, the corps under the Crown Prince, and that under the Prince de Condé, cannonaded each other; but as the latter were too advantageously posted to be attacked, the Allies returned to Münzenberg, having lost five officers and 50 men, besides three field pieces.

THE Marquis d'Auvet, who commanded the French on, the Lower Rhine, appeared, on the 20th, before the town of Hamm, which he immediately invested, and the same night began a furious cannonade, firing red-hot balls, which set fire to, and consumed several houses. The siege continued 'till the 25th, when M. d'Auyet thought proper to break it up and retire to the Rhine, upon receiving intelligence that a detachment of 4,000 men from the Allied Army were in full march to its relief.

ON the 30th, His Serene Highness Prince Ferdinand encamped this day in the neighborhood of Nidda, having marched from Nieder-Jossa by the route to Mahr, Sickendorf[209], Herbstein, Brungelhausen[210], and Schotten; the French army under the two marshals having fallen back by the Fulda towards Friedberg.

THE Prince de Condé having retired successively as far as Friedberg, in order to make a junction with Marshals Soubise and d'Estrées, abandoned even the heights near that town, and marched to Rodheim[211] on the 29th; on which day, the Crown Prince arrived at Wölfersheim. His Highness thought it necessary to push General Luckner forward, on the 30th, to the other side of the Wetter, to occupy those heights with eight battalions and seven squadrons, whilst he marched forward with his main body to Assenheim. On his march he was informed that a large body of the French were returning towards Friedberg and being desirous to keep possession of the above high grounds, he altered

208. Editor: This may be Maar, part of Lauterbach.
209. Editor: Today part of Lauterbach.
210. Editor: This may be Breungeshain, today part of Schotten.
211. Editor: Today Rodheim vor der Höhe, part of the town of Rosbach vor der Höhe.

his plan; and, instead of continuing his march to Assenheim, determined to support General Luckner.

THE Prince had at that time no reason to imagine that the Prince de Condé had been reinforced, though it afterwards appeared that he had been joined by the Count de Stainville's corps, and that the grand army of the French was at hand to support them. The Crown Prince's infantry attacked them with the greatest bravery between Bad Nauheim and Friedberg, and in a short time drove the enemy into the plain from the steep mountains called Johannesberg, where they had been posted; but receiving considerable reinforcements from Marshals Soubise and d'Estrées, they, in their turn, attacked the Allies with advantage, and obliged them, to repass the Wetter.

PRINCE Ferdinand, upon the first intelligence of the Crown Prince being engaged and being better informed than the Crown Prince of the real situation of the French army, immediately marched with a considerable part of the Allied Army from his camp at Nidda, in order to support him, and arrived time enough to prevent the enemy from pursuing their advantage.

THE LOSS of the Allies on this occasion was 2 commissioned officers, 6 non-commissioned officers, and 60 rank and file, killed; 19 commissioned officers, 16 non-commissioned officers, and 331 rank and file, wounded; 34 commissioned officers, 46 non-commissioned officers, and 880 rank and file, made prisoners, or missing; the whole, amounting to 1,398 men. They also lost 10 small pieces of cannon. The French owned to the loss of 500 men killed and wounded, though it was generally imagined to be much more considerable. The brigade of Boisgelin suffered extremely, and M. de Guiche, lieutenant general, who commanded it, was made a prisoner.

THERE were no other British troops in this action than Major General Elliot's Dragoons, and the chasseurs under Lord Frederick Cavendish.

THE Crown Prince was wounded by a musket shot as he was rallying the troops in the time of the retreat; the ball entered on the right side a little above the hip-bone, which it grazed, and came out on the back part of his body about four inches below. Colonel Clinton, of the First Guards Regiment, who acted as aide-de-camp to the Prince, received also a wound nearly in the same place; he remained two hours with His Highness after he received this wound, without mentioning it to him; nor did the Prince know anything of it 'till on giving him orders to carry the account of the action to Prince Ferdinand, the colonel was obliged to declare himself incapable of executing his commands.

THE remainder of the Allied Army came up the next day, and encamped behind the Wetter, opposite to the French army: Prince Ferdinand's headquarters being fixed at Bingenheim on the Horloff River, the Marquis of Granby at Giess-Nidda, and the Crown Prince's corps at Butzbach.

ON the 3d of September, His Serene Highness advanced on the enemy, marching to Staden, where he fixed his headquarters, being the center of the army; the right extending towards Giessen, and the left towards Hanau. Lord Granby's corps was pushed forward near the villages of Steinheim. The position of the main body of the French army was between Assenheim and Friedberg; the Prince de Condé between Butzbach and Ostheim[212]; the Count de Lusace between Bergen and Vilbel, and M. de Castries joined him on the side of Kraben.

GENERAL Luckner's Corps, which was posted at Butzbach, was driven from thence, and removed to Gambach[213].

"ON the 6th, the French army encamped at Ober Wesel[214]; and, on the 7th, they made a movement by their left towards Giessen, and encamped near Langgöns.

ON the 8th, the Allied Army decamped from Staden[215], and marched to Grünberg. The Marquis of Granby took post at Staden with his corps de reserve, from whence he removed at noon to Ulsse.

ON the 9th of September, the French continued their route by their left, and established their headquarters at Burkhardsfelden[216]. The Prince de Condé, with the vanguard, was posted at Buseck. On the contrary, the Allied Army marched to Homberg and Lord Granby was posted at Ober-Scheffertenrode[217]. The two marshals had an intention to make themselves masters of the heights of Homberg, by which means they would have had it in their power to relieve Kassel; but His Serene Highness by this march was beforehand with them and prevented their parting the Ohm.

M. de Castries, who commanded the rearguard of the French army, attacked the escort of the baggage of one of the columns of the Allied Army, which he dispersed, took some pontoons, part of the baggage, and made several prisoners.

ON the 10th, His Serene Highness marched to Schweinsberg[218]; and Lord Granby, with the corps de reserve, was posted at Maulbach[219]. The French army directed their march towards Marburg. This night and the next morning several smart skirmishes pased between the enemy's advanced guards and Lord Granby's corps de reserve, in which the former were driven back with considerable losses.

ON the 13th, the French army, having parted the Lahn River, encamped in the neighborhood of Marburg and Niederweimar: their corps de reserve, under the Prince de Condé, was posted at Grossfeln[220]; and M. de Levis, with the advanced guard, and light troops, occupied the town of Wetter, and the height behind it.

---

212. Editor: Today part of Butzbach.
213. Editor: Today part of Münzenberg.
214. Editor: probably Hochweisel, today part of Butzbach ("Ober-" means "upper" and "Hoch-" "high"; this village lies on the beginning of the Taunus Mountains in contrast to Niederweisel, which lies "lower" in the eastern plain of the Wetterau).
215. Editor: Today part of Florstadt.
216. Editor: Today part of Reiskirchen.
217. Editor: This may be Ober-Seibertenrod, today part of the Ulrichstein.
218. Editor; today part of the Stadtallendorf. The castle is still owned since almost 800 years by the Schenck/Schenk [cup-bearer] von Schweinsberg family; they were the hereditary cup-bearers of Hesse.
219. Editor: Today part of Homberg (Ohm).
220. Editor: This may be Grossseelheim, part of Kirchhain.

ON the other hand, His Serene Highness marched to Kirchhain; and Lord Granby encamped near Schweinsberg, with his right to Amöneburg; he was here joined by Hardenberg's and Bock's corps, with the troops of the left wing.

ON the 14th, the main body of the Allies encamped at Schwartzenberg[221], and Lord Granby's corps at Schönstadt. Generals Luckner and Conway took post at Wollmar, between Wetter and Frankenberg, in order to observe M. de Levis, and cut off his communication with the last of these places.

THE design of the French appeared to be to get around the right of the Allied Army, through the country of Waldeck, for which purpose the Prince de Condé had been employed to open march routes towards Frankenberg; which afterwards served for the march of the Allied Army.

ON the 15th of September, His Serene Highness being determined to dislodge the enemy from Wetter, where they had considerably reinforced M. de Levis with a large body under the command of M. de Conflans, who were supported by the whole corps under the Prince de Condé on this side of the Lahn, with the main body of their army on the other side close to the banks, made the following dispositions for that purpose. The main body was to occupy the heights of Oberrosphe, Unterrosphe, and Mellnau[222], in the front of the enemy; Lord Granby's corps de reserve, which was at Schönstadt, had orders to keep itself in readiness to march, either to support the main body or to move to its left in case the French should attempt to pass the Ohm River anywhere between Kirchhain and Burgemunden; General Conway had orders to march by the right on the night of the 14th, with a large detachment, all Germans, except Monpesson's brigade, and to cross the Wetschaft about three leagues above Wetter, and from thence march towards the enemy's left, and begin the attack as soon as he perceived the main body appear on the plain in their front; General Luckner, who was posted at Wollmar[223], was to make a circle and get into the rear of their left, with the chasseurs of the army, six battalions of grenadiers, two regiments of cavalry, besides Elliot's Dragoons, and his own hussars.

THE whole was conducted with the utmost precision, and all the columns were at their several destinations to a moment of the time appointed. General Luckner, who had arrived at Warzenbach[224], began with a brisk cannonade on the back of the hill above the town, from whence the enemy very soon retired. The town was then cannonaded for some time, which they immediately quitted as soon as General Conway came up, retiring with a good deal of confusion up the hill, from whence they also soon after retreated with great precipitation and repassed the Lahn, their rear being all the while severely cannonaded. The army afterwards encamped where it had formed in order of battle, their posts extending from Wartzbach on the Lahn to Homberg on the Ohm.

ON the 16th of September, on the movement which the army had made to its right towards Wetter, the enemy passed the Ohm with a large body of light troops under

221. Editor: This may be Schwarzenborn, part of Cölbe.
222. Editor: Today Oberrosphe, Unterrosphe and Mellnau are part of Wetter (Hessen).
223. Editor: Today part of Münchhausen (am Christenberg).
224. Editor: Today part of Wetter (Hessen).

M. de St. Victor, and pushed forwards towards Alsfeld with an intent to destroy the bakery of the Allied Army, which was then removing from that place. General Freytag was immediately ordered in quest of M. de St. Victor, and came up with him between Alsfeld and Neustadt[225] very opportunely to save the bread wagon train. The enemy were dispersed and repassed the Ohm with the greatest precipitation.

UPON General Freytag's quitting Homberg, another body of the enemy, mostly cavalry, passed the Ohm at Nieder-Ofleiden[226], between Schweinsberg and Homberg, and pushed forward as far as Niederklein[227]. Lord Granby was ordered with part of the reserve to march in pursuit of them. They made a show of maintaining themselves at Schweinsberg; but on some cannonading they soon abandoned it, and repassed the Ohm,

GENERAL Hardenberg was left with six battalions and eight squadrons on the heights of Rodeker, and the rest of the reserve marched to Stautsebach[228], where it encamped.

ON the 17th in the morning, the enemy carried off one of Hardenberg's out parties posted in a fleche beyond the Ohm.

ON the 18th, General Wangenheim was detached to Dannenrod[229] with three battalions and four squadrons, to supply General Freytag's place, who was still in quest of the enemy's light troops.

ON the 19th, the enemy had considerably reinforced their right by marching their reserve to Deckenback and posting the greatest part of their army between Holzhausen and Bauerbach[230]. General Wangenheim's corps was reinforced. Lord Granby's reserve marched to the heights behind Kirchhain, where it arrived by daybreak on the morning of the 21st. General Wessenbach replaced Lord Granby at Stautsebach, with ten Hessian battalions, and eight squadrons. Beckwith's brigade, those of English Guards, and of Malsburg, occupied the heights of Langenstein.

AT this time Amöneburg was occupied by a battalion of the Britannic Legion, and a detachment of 200 men from the corps of the reserve. Kirchhain had a garrison of 400 men; and the bridge over the Ohm at the Brücker Mühle[231] was guarded by a detachment of 200 men from Hardenberg's corps, the greatest part of which were posted in a small work on this side of the bridge.

IN the night between the 20th and 21st, the enemy having resolved to get possession of Amöneburg, raised several batteries for that intent, and seized on the Brucker Mühl, where they threw up a small breastwork, and a kind of trench to secure the entrance.

225. Editor: Today this town is called Neustadt (Hessen). "(Hessen)" has been added to address the issue that there are many towns in Germany named "Neustadt."
226. Editor: Today part of Homberg (Ohm).
227. Editor: Today part of Stadtallendorf.
228. Editor: Today part of Kirchhain.
229. Editor: Today part of Homberg (Ohm).
230. Editor: Today part of Marburg.
231. Editor: Today part of Amöneburg (a water mill first mentioned in 1248, and a stone bridge of the 13th Century.)

ABOUT SIX in the morning of the 21st, the weather being extremely foggy, the French attacked the redoubt on the other side of the bridge, which was bravely defended by the Hanoverians; they planted at the same time some cannon at the foot of the hill of Amöneburg, to bear on the redoubt.

ON the fog's clearing up, it was perceived they had both cavalry and infantry formed on the height beyond the bridge; their cavalry was cannonaded and dispersed, their infantry likewise gave way but were soon supported by fresh troops: the cannonade and fire of small arms continued very severely on both sides. In the meantime the British Guards Brigade was ordered to march to the left to sustain the battery and flanks on the river, both above and below the Mühle; this succor came just in the proper time, as the Hanoverian troops had already suffered very much, and their ammunition of every kind was almost expended: the Guard Grenadiers were ordered to enter the battery and relieve the Hanoverians, which was done with the greatest bravery, though they were obliged to march nearly 400 paces exposed to a most severe fire of small arms, and cannon laden with grapeshot.

ABOUT this time some heavy 12-pounders were brought up and played with great success. The enemy on their part still kept bringing up more cannon; and the Allies did the same. The 1st Guards Regiment relieved the grenadiers, and so on alternately through the brigade. Four Hessian battalions were then ordered to relieve the English. The fire both of cannon and small arms was kept up on both sides with the utmost severity, and most determined resolution, 'till dark night at last put an end to it. There was no attempt made on either side to pass the bridge, but the troops were relieved in the redoubt as soon as their ammunition of 60 rounds was expended.

THE whole affair lasted 14 hours without a moment's intermission, and though there were nearly 50 pieces of cannon employed, their execution was confined to the space of about 400 paces. History can scarce furnish an instance of so obstinate a dispute.

THE LOSS of the Allies was computed at about 800 men. The French acknowledged the loss of 300 killed, and 800 wounded; among the number of the latter were M. de Castries, and the Chevalier de Sarzfield.

WE maintained the redoubt, and the enemy the Mühl, during the attack of the bridge; the enemy played likewise some batteries upon the town of Amöneburg, which they also kept up all night, and, having made a breach, assaulted it; but without success.

THE following is the French account of this affair:

"THE castle of Amöneburg being in the center of the King's army, and about a league from the front of the camp, the two marshals determined to seize it, and to entrust the command of this expedition to the Marquis de Castries.

"THE 18th and 19th of September, the avenues of the place were reconnoitered, and other dispositions made, and the troops destined for this expedition prepared a sufficient quantity of gabions and fascines.

"ON the 20th at dusk, they were ordered to be ready to march; the Volontaires de Hainault, the battalions of grenadiers and chasseurs of the brigades of Vaubécourt, Alsace, and Epting, began the march, with their laborers, followed by the brigade of Vaubecourt, which consisted of the Vaubecourt and Lorraine Guard Regiment. The grenadiers stopped within cannon shot of the castle, to support the *volontaires* in the attack of the redoubt at the village of Kirken on this side the Ohm, and at the right of which was a stone bridge. The Allies had only a small post there, which made no resistance. The laborers were afterwards carried to the face of the castle, in that part a little obliquely, in order to establish a *boyau de tranchée*[232]. They could not have been covered by daybreak, had they not been favored by a thick fog. This being done, we mounted cannon to batter in and breach the opposite faces of the castle, which was speedily executed.

ON the 21st in the morning, the batteries began to play. The Allies almost at the same time appeared at the head of the bridge and began a very brisk fire of small arms on the Hainault Volontaires, who were supported by the grenadiers and chasseurs. The enemy being reinforced, our people were so likewise, and the fire became no less obstinate than smart. Two pieces of cannon were mounted in battery, which played upon the enemy at the entrance of the bridge. During this cannonade, the fire of the small arms, instead of slackening, increased. The Marquis de Castries, who kept with the grenadiers, received a shot in his left arm, which touched the bone. The Vaubecourt and Lorraine Guard Regiments came up with a most military countenance; they began a smart fire of small arms, which was well kept up 'till the barrels of their guns became so hot that they could load them no longer; however, the fire of the enemy's cannon was removed further off; and slackened, by the manner in which our cannon was served, and by our small arms.

"At five in the evening, the brigade of Vaubecourt was relieved by that of Poitou; and the firing did not end 'till night, excepting that before the castle, the siege of which continued 'till the 22d, when it surrendered: the garrison, consisting of 600 men, were made prisoners of war."

ON the 22d of September, in the morning everything was quiet, and at daylight it was perceived that the enemy had worked hard in repairing their redoubt and had likewise added considerably to their trench of communication. The Allies had wrought hard all night to put their redoubt in a state of defense, and to make an entrenchment about 100 paces in the rear of it. The French drew off their cannon in the night, and left only three pieces behind, to which the Allies had opposed an equal number on both sides continued the works they had begun, without the least molestation. The Allies also traced out a large redoubt upon a hill, within the reach of grapeshot of the bridge, as the enemy did a battery on their side. The advanced sentinels were not ten yards distant from each other.

As everything appeared quiet on the side of Amöneburg, His Serene Highness returned to his quarters, which were removed to Kirchhain. The avenue to this town on the side of the enemy was by a causeway leading through a morass. A little rivulet which runs close by the town, falls into the Ohm at a small distance from it. A battery was made

232. Editor: A "boyau de tranchée" is a communication trench.

on this causeway to keep the enemy at a distance, and some heavy cannon were placed in the churchyard, which is the highest part of the town; but all the carriages were ordered to remain without the town, as the place might be bom-barded. The enemy were perceived marching from Kirchhain in the road leading to the town of Amöneburg, and no opposition made from within; soon after which their sentinels appeared on the walls.

ON the taking of this town, the grand army of the enemy made a movement to the right, posting a considerable body between Amöneburg and Kleinseelheim[233].

GENERAL Conway was ordered to quit the heights of Wetter and to fall back to those of Mellnau[234]. The grand army likewise made a movement, and encamped with the right at Schönstadt, and the left at Stausebach. Lord Granby's reserve occupied the ground before Niederklein, to be at hand to defend the passage of the Brücker Mühle: His Lordship's headquarters was fixed at Niederklein. General Wangenheim remained on the heights by Dannenrod to face the Saxons; and General Luckner occupied the gorge of Niederasphe[235], on the right of General Conway.

ON the 23d of September, Captain Kruse, who had commanded at Amöneburg, was sent back with his garrison as prisoners of war and he gave such reasons for capitulating as satisfied His Serene Highness: a large breach had been made in the wall of the castle where he was posted, (the detachment from the enemy being charged with the defense of the town) by which an officer and 50 men of the enemy had got into the courtyard of the castle, on the night of the 21st, and others were following them; but they met with such a reception, that those who had entered were either all killed or made prisoners, and the rest were repulsed. The morning of the 22d they made a show of storming again, with many batteries, but first summoned the place: the commandant, on such a formidable apparatus, having no provisions, and very little ammunition, capitulated.

ON the 24th, the enemy made a *feu de joie* for the taking of Almeida in Portugal.

A party of the French surprised a post on the right of General Luckner's Corps but were soon repulsed by the cavalry. The Allies had one officer and 30 private men belonging to the infantry made prisoners.

ON the 25th, the enemy made a regular communication on the other side of their redoubt, by which they could come into it by the hill of Amöneburg under cover.

THE large redoubt of the Allies by the gallows was almost finished, and others to the right and left begun. As the Ohm was at this time fordable in many places, the Allies collected all the harrows they could find in the adjacent villages, and placed them in the most practicable fords.

ON the 26th of September, His Serene Highness having intelligence that the enemy had detached a corps towards Alsfeld, ordered Lord Granby to march in the evening with 17 squadrons, a brigade of infantry, and some heavy cannon, to attack them. General

233. Editor: Today part of Kirchhain.
234. Editor: Today part of Wetter (Hessen).
235. Editor: Today part of Münchhausen (am Christenberg).

Wangenheim, whose corps was part of the troops that were under Lord Granby's orders, on this occasion marched with them. Beckwith's brigade replaced Wangenheim's infantry on the heights of Dannenrod. Some other movements were made on the right of the Allies, but of no consequence, one brigade only taking up the ground which another was ordered to leave, for preserving the communications.

On the 27th, Prince Ferdinand, having had intelligence that the Prince de Condé's corps was to march to Siegen this day, ordered General Conway to occupy the heights of Wetter, and General Gilsa to replace him on those of Melnau. Luckner's Corps was at the same time to march to Watzenbach, to prevent the enemy's coming by the gorge of Kombach[236] into General Conway's rear. The enemy's main army continued in the same position they had been in for some time past. Their grand guards were posted on the hills above Wetter but fell back upon the approach of our troops. Three battalions marched this day to reinforce Lord Granby.

SEPTEMBER 28. Deserters, who came in on the night of the 27th, affirmed, that the enemy intended to attack the left of the Allies this morning; and the story was so probable, that His Serene Highness ordered three battalions from his right to reinforce his left, and went himself at daybreak to Nieder-Ussleiden; but finding everything quiet, he returned to Kirchhain, and ordered the three battalions, which were met on their march, and who had left their tents standing, to return to their former positions.

ON the 29th, Lord Granby returned to his former position, as did the other troops. His Lordship arrived at Romrod the 26th at midnight; the 27th he had an account that the enemy had pushed on towards Ziegenhain, and that they had fallen back to Eifa [237] in the evening, upon which he marched to Alsfeld. They retired in the night, and he had orders to return.

THEY had pushed a considerable detachment of cavalry to escort wagons to Ziegenhain and thought themselves strong enough to force Major General Freytag; but he attacked and pursued them to Alsfeld, killing, wounding, and taking 400 men. It was imagined their intention was to have laden their wagons with meal, of which they had great quantities at Ziegenhain, and to endeavor to supply the garrison of Kassel, which was at that time said to be in great distress for want of provisions. M. de Poyanne commanded this corps.

ON the 30th of September, there being intelligence that part of the corps was still in the neighborhood of Ulrichstein, Major General Alfelt was detached at two this morning, with two battalions and eight squadrons, and some pieces of cannon, from General Wangenheim's corps, to attack them.

THE enemy having likewise occupied Burgemunden, Major General Freytag, whose corps was at Mulbach since his pursuit of the 27th, was ordered to attack that post this evening.

His Serene Highness went to the heights of Homberg about noon.

236. Editor: Today part of Biedenkopf.
237. Editor: Today part of Alsfeld.

THE enemy were dislodged from both these places, but a large party of them took post at Nieder-Ohmen[238].

OCTOBER 9, the position of the two armies continued nearly the same, the enemy contenting themselves with making detachments on the right and left of the Allied Army, in order to open a communication with Kassel, and the whole of the operations terminated in some skirmishes between the light troops.

GENERAL Luckner, with the two squadrons of Elliot's Regiment, and a detachment of infantry, marched to Berberburg, where he attacked some light troops of the enemy, and drove them from thence.

BOTH armies were employed in making redoubts and batteries in the front of their camps, on either side of the Ohm and Lahn, from Meelan as far as Caldern[239].

OCTOBER 10, two thirds of the cavalry of the Allied Army went into cantonments, the remainder continued in camp at the same time the whole army began to construct huts.

ON the 12th, the Allied Army fired a *feu de joie*, on account of the reduction of the Havannah by the British forces.

ON the 15th, they also fired another *feu de joie* on account of the surrender of Schweidnitz to his Prussian Majesty.

As forage was very scarce, one half of the baggage of the Allied Army, with all the spare horses of the cavalry, were ordered to be sent to the environs of Hameln.

ON the 16th, the trenches were opened before the city of Kassel, which had been closely blocked up for some time before by Prince Frederick of Brunswick, the loss of the Allies on this occasion was about 20 men killed and several wounded. The garrison made a sally, but without success, being quickly repulsed.

ON the 22d, General Diesbach, the commandant of Kassel, made a sally with the whole garrison, and obliged the ordinary guard to retire, but Prince Frederick, at the head of four battalions, immediately came up to their support, and drove the enemy back into the city with great loss, before they had time to destroy any of the works.

ON the 30th and 31st of October, the French partisan Cambefort took and plundered the city of Osnabrück which had no garrison to defend it.

NOVEMBER I, the city of Kassel surrendered to the Allies upon the following articles of capitulation:

ARTICLE I. The garrison shall go out with the honors of war, their arms and baggage, drums beating, and lighted match, to be conducted by the nearest road to the King's Army - *Granted, Thursday morning.*

---

238. Editor: Today part of Mücke.
239. Editor: Today part of Lahntal.

ART. II. The sick from the hospitals, with the effects thereto belonging, shall have free liberty to depart, and carriages or boats shall be furnished them *gratis* for this evacuation, as soon as the sick and wounded shall be in a condition to be transported to the King's Army. - *The hospitals may have free liberty to go out with their effects but the carriages shall not be furnished gratis.*

ART. III. The artillery, and all the royal effects, shall be transported to the King's army by boats or carriages of the country gratis. - *No. In favor of the gallant defense, 1 grant two pieces of cannon, 12-pounders, and one 4-pounder, for Baron Diesbach, commandant of Kassel.*

ART. IV. Covered carriages and boats shall be furnished to transport the equipages, and agents, which shall not be visited. *Granted.*

ART. V. The treasurer of the troops the agent-victuallers, and others, shall go out with their effects and papers without any impediment. - *Granted.*

ART. VI. The garrison shall be furnished with bread, provisions, and forage, everyone gratis, according to his rank, 'till their arrival at the King's army. - *the garrison shall provide themselves with bread and forage but shall pay for it on their march.*

ARTICLE VII. All the effects belonging to the King's officers and troops may be freely carried off with them, or sent after them. - *Granted.*

ART. VIII. When the capitulation shall be signed, leave shall be given to send an officer to the marshals to acquaint them with it. - *Granted.*

ART. IX. The garrison shall be escorted by a proper detachment. - *Granted.*

ART. X. The boatmen too, victuallers, and other subjects of the King, shall have free liberty of going out with their effects, on paying the debts they may have contracted in the city. - *Granted.*

At the headquarters at Ihringshausen, November, 1762.

FREDERICK AUGUSTUS, R. B. von Diesbach.
Duke of Brunswick and Lüneburg.

CAPITULATION for the HOSPITALS.

ARTICLE I. There shall be reserved out of the King's provisions remaining at Kassel, 300 sacks of flour, each weighing 200 pounds, 20 oxen, and 100 sheep, for the consumption of the said hospitals. - *Granted.*

ART. II. The necessary quantity of wood shall be continued unto them at the stated price. - *Granted.*

ART. III. Every kind of assistance that shall be wanted by his most Christian Majesty's commission, who has the government of the hospital, shall be furnished to them. - *Granted.*

ART. IV. The effects, provisions, and medicines, shall be left for the King's profit. - *Granted.*

ART. V. The carriages necessary for conveying the sick and their effects to the King's army, by the shortest road shall be furnished. - *Granted.*

A RT. VI. No damage shall be done to the agents, commissaries, and surgeons, who will remain to take care of the sick after the garrison shall have evacuated the place. - *Granted.*

At the headquarters at Iringshaussen, November 1, 1762.

FREDERICK AUGUSTUS, R. B. von Diesbach.
Duke of Brunswick and Lüneburg.

THE effects belonging to the French King, which were found at Kassel, were computed to amount to the value of above one million of German crowns.

NOVEMBER 4, the Allied Army fired a *feu de joie*, on account of the reduction of the city of Kassel.

ON the 5th, they also fired another *feu de joie*, on account of a signal victory gained over the combined army of Austrians and Imperialists near Freiberg, by Prince Henry of Prussia.

ON the 8th, His Serene Highness acquainted the generals, that he, the night before, had received from the two French marshals the preliminaries of peace between England, France, and Spain, as also proposals for a suspension of hostilities; but though he had nothing more at heart than to prevent the effusion of blood unnecessarily, yet he must wait for His Majesty's instructions.

NOVEMBER 9, The orders given out by Prince Ferdinand this day to the army were in the following terms:

"His Serene Highness acquainted the generals yesterday of the conditions he had proposed to Marshals d'Estrées and Soubise, to agree upon a suspension of hostilities, viz. The evacuation of Ziegenhain, and though he has not as yet received the least account from His Majesty of the conclusion of the peace, he would nevertheless show his readiness in agreeing to so salutary a work, and put a stop to hostilities, reconciling this sentiment of humanity to that which honor dictates to him; but as they, as yet, hesitate to agree to the condition, His Serene Highness has thought proper to inform the generals of the state of the negotiation, from whence it follows, that the same vigilance and exactness are to be observed by the troops as before."

IN consequence of these orders the siege of Ziegenhain was resolved upon, as the Prince could not in honor suspend the operations whilst the French kept possession of a garrison in the rear of the Allied Army, which prevented his going into winter quarters.

GENERAL Luckner was this day detached towards Münster, in order to repel a body of

French light troops, who continued their incursions into that bishopric, but they retired to Wesel on his approach.

ON the 14th, His Serene Highness Prince Ferdinand received by a messenger from His Britannic Majesty, confirmation of the preliminaries of peace being signed, on the 3d of this month, at Fontainbleau, together with a full power to treat of a cessation of arms with the French marshals 'till the ratification of the peace.

NOVEMBER 15, Prince Ferdinand issued out orders that all hostilities must cease from this day.

ON the 16th, the army was informed of the following convention, which was concluded and signed the day before, being the 15th of November, between His Serene Highness Prince Ferdinand Duke of Brunswick and Lüneburg on one part, and the Marshals Count d'Estrées and the Prince of Soubise on the other part. This contained three articles, viz.

I. THAT a suspension of arms between the troops of the two armies shall take place from the day of the signature and ratification of this convention, by the generals on each side, and as soon as possible with the troops at a distance.

II. THERE SHALL be a line of boundary to separate the two armies, specified as follows: For the center, the course of the Lahn, from its source to its junction with the Ohm River, and from thence up this river as far as Merlau[240]. For the left of His Britannic Majesty's army, and the right of the French army, passing by Lauterbach, from thence directly to the Fulda, along the Altefeld River, having Schlitz in front; then passing the Fulda by Hünfeld and Hudingen[241], and the river that passes it, and falls into the Salle. For the right of His Britannic Majesty's army, and the left of the French army, from the source of the Lahn to that of the Lenne, then the course of this last river through the Duchy of Westphalia, from thence this line will extend to Neheim[242] on the Ruhr, by Unna, Dortmund, Haltern-am-See, and Coesfeld, ending on the frontiers of Holland.

III. THE French garrison at Ziegenhain shall remain quiet and pay henceforward ready money for what it wants 'till it shall evacuate the town. A place shall be assigned it to cut wood necessary for its use, which shall be furnished for money at the price established and known in the country.

ON the 19th of November, the two armies began to file off towards their respective quarters; the English troops had theirs in the Bishopric of Münster; and His Serene Highness established his headquarters at Neuhaus. I shall not trouble, the reader with a detail of this march, as it contains no particular maneuver of the army, but only the most commodious and most expeditious route for the conveniency of the troops.

DECEMBER 24. Immediately after the convention His Serene Highness Prince Ferdinand wrote to His Britannic Majesty to congratulate him on the peace, and at the

240. Editor: Today Merlau is part of Mücke.
241. Editor: This may be Hundsbach, today part of Tann.
242. Editor: Today merged with with Hüsten as Neheim-Hüsten part of Arnsberg.

same time to ask his permission to quit his army, where his presence was no longer necessary, and His Majesty was pleased to give him a very favorable answer by a letter, a copy of which is annexed.

"COUSIN,

"I thank you for the obliging congratulations in your letter of the 23d past, on the happy conclusion of the peace, to which your good conduct, at the head of my army, hath so greatly contributed. I readily consent to your demand, and am very glad that after so much fatigue, you will enjoy in the bosom of peace, that glory which you have so justly acquired being, moreover, convinced how much I owe to your great merit: you may be assured of my persevering in those sentiments, being, with much esteem and devotion,

Your devoted Cousin,
ST. JAMES
December 3, 1762

IN consequence of this permission, His Serene Highness resigned this day the command of the army to General Spörcken; and at the same time desired that general to return his thanks to the whole army, in his name for their behavior.

DECEMBER 30. The following declarations of Prince Ferdinand to the army having been received by General Conway, he this day communicated them to the British troops.

"His Serene Highness declares to the army, that he shall always preserve the most flattering remembrance of having fought successfully at the head of those brave troops, who, composed of different nations, exerted themselves so vigorously for the public liberty, and for the honor of their own and his country; that this remembrance will not cease but with his life, and will never fail to recall to him the obligations which he has to the generals and other officers, who, by their valor and experience, have assisted and enabled him, at the same time, to serve his country, and to make a suitable return for the confidence which His Britannic Majesty has been pleased to honor him with; he, therefore, returns them his thanks for the same, and to the army in general for their obedience which they have constantly shown during the time he has commanded them."

JANUARY 13, 1763. General Conway communicated to the British troops, that the Hon. the House of Commons had ordered their thanks to be returned to them for the meritorious and eminent services which they had done for their King and country during the course of the war.

HE likewise communicated to them the following letter, which was addressed to them by his Excellency the Marquis of Granby; a general who truly merited the appellation of father of the army, not only animating the troops on all occasions by his presence and example, but at the same time, with the greatest humanity, and unbounded generosity, supplying their immediate wants with necessaries and provisions at his own private expense, whereby they were enabled to support the incredible fatigues of forced marches, made through bad roads in the severest seasons: his Lordship's own expressons will best describe how sensibly he was affected at the grateful return made by the soldiers, in embracing every opportunity to manifest, by their gallant behavior, the ardency with which they desired to merit his esteem and protection:

"LORD Granby had hoped to have it in his power to have seen and taken his leave of the troops before their embarkation for England, but a severe illness having detained him at Warburg, and his present state of health obliging him to take another route, he could not leave this country without this public testimony of his entire approbation of their conduct since he has had the honor to command them.

"THESE sentiments naturally call for his utmost acknowledgments; he, therefore, returns his warmest thanks to the generals, officers, and private men, composing the whole British corps, for the bravery, zeal, discipline, and good conduct, he has constantly experienced from every individual, and his most particular and personal thanks are due to them upon their ready obedience upon all occasions to such orders as his station obliged him to give.

"His best endeavors have always been directed to their good by every means in his power, and he has some satisfaction to think he has some reason to flatter himself of their being convinced, if not of the efficacy, at least of the sincerity of his intentions, if he may judge by the noble return their behavior has made him; a behavior, that while it fills him with gratitude, has endeared them to their King and country, and has covered them with glory and honor.

"HIGHLY sensible of their merit, he shall continue, while he lives, to look upon it as much his duty, as it will forever be his inclination to give them every possible proof of his affection and esteem, which he should be happy to make as apparent as their valor has been, and will be, conspicuous, and exemplary to after ages."

JANUARY 25, the first part of the first division of the British troops began their march through Holland; their route was through the province of Guelderland, Nijmegen, and Breda, to Wilhelmstad[243] where transports were ready to receive and convey them to England.

FINIS.

243. Editor: Today part of the Dutch town of Moerdijk.

DUKE FERDINAND'S STAFF

By Dirk Rottgardt

Prior to August 1758, the Allied Army consisted of Hanoverians, as well as of Hessian, Brunswick and Bückeburg troops in British pay. In August, British national troops were sent to reinforce that army. The army was originally commanded by the Duke of Cumberland, a son of King George II. Cumberland was not successful and concluded the convention of Kloster Zeven with the victorious French. It stipulated that the Hanoverian Army was to be disbanded and Hanover to be neutralised. This pleased the Hanoverian government, but not the British govenrment. Eventually the King of England did not ratify the convention. Cumberland was recalled in disgrace and was replaced as commander-in-chief in November/December 1757 by Duke Ferdinand of Brunswick.

When he entered the service of King George II, Duke Ferdinand was a close confidant of King Frederick II, the Great. As Frederick's brother-in-law, he was family, even if Frederick did not much care for his wife, after his ascension to the Prussian throne. As a Prussian general, Ferdinand was thoroughly trained in the Prussian doctrines of modern warfare and knew all the tricks of the business. Ferdinand seldom spoke to his generals and after the Battle of Krefeld refrained from holding a council of war. He preferred to communicate with them in writing. Usually, he was quite tactful. He also attempted to introduce mission-type tactics or mission command. However, in this, he sometimes failed, as many old-fashioned subordinates expected to be told exactly what to do, like the senior Hanoverian General von Spörcken, and would do nothing more. So, he chose his assistants carefully and purely by merit. Noble birth was not required. This was, however, a deviation from Frederick's ways.

Ferdinand was very secretively minded, lest his plans might fall into the hands of the French – perhaps because less security-conscious members on his staff or generals of his army might talk about them and be overheard by French spies. Some of the generals had apparently no thought that the enemy might listen ("Feind hört mit!"– as this was expressed much later).

Ferdinand despised the customary jog trot in the Hanoverian officer corps and their often-unmerited pride as privileged Hanoverian noblemen. He also disliked the conditions in the British Army, with quasi-amateur officers buying their commission, and leaving the training of their soldiers to the non-commissioned officers. This contrasted greatly to the professionalism of his Brunswick, Hessian and his few Prussian troops. However, he had to accept these situations, because he needed the Hanoverian and British troops.

In principle, only Ferdinand's private secretary Westphalen and later also his quartermaster Bauer were informed from the beginning – or they might even have helped to formulate the original plans. For all others, including his Hanoverian Adjutant General von Reden there was on a strict need-to-know basis, and they were informed only when they needed to know.

On the other hand, he kept his own network of spies. In this, he was helped by his brother Ludwig, commander-in-chief of the Dutch Army, who conveyed to him all information obtained by Dutch sources, even though the Netherlands were neutral. In addition, intelligence and entertaining spies became, according to the Prussian custom was prescribed by the secret Prussian Reglements, the regulation books for the different arms. Intelilgence was a task of the hussar regiments' commanders, first of all of Lieutenant General Luckner (originally a commoner). When Luckner's hussars were to be reformed, in 1763, he resigned from the Hanoverian Army, and entered French service. The light infantry and jäger commanders, like Freytag, also gathered information.

Spies, however, were very important and sometimes paid even better than Hanoverian generals for specific tasks (up to 200 *Taler*). In other cases, they would receive a regular salary between 5 and 40 *Taler* per month (for a comparison, the following was paid per month in the Prussian infantry: a sergeant received 4 *Taler*, a *Premierlieutenant* 13 *Taler*, 18 *Groschen* (24 *Groschen* per *Taler*), and a captain 45 *Taler*, 15 *Groschen*, 2 *Heller*.

The French set up a similar spy network. Sometimes they were informed by members of the Hanoverian administration. In spite of their prince elector, who was also the King of England, many preferred to keep the convention of Kloster Zeven, by which Hanover would have dropped out of the war.

Ferdinand set up a network of supervisory post stations. Letters would be clandestinely opened, read, evaluated and then sent on if their content was not directly dangerous. For instance, King Frederick II had, in this manner, learned of the Austrian, Russian and French plans to attack him in 1757, and struck one year early, before his enemies' preparations were ready. Westphalen, Ferdinand's secretary, was the son of a post master and might have provided information on post routes and which of the postmasters could be bought. For this process, Ferdinand also employed individuals who could read German, English, French, Italian and even Russian – the Russian ambassador at neutral Hamburg, e. g., was convinced that nobody but he and his correspondents could read Russian. This was also used to identify enemy spies, or to determine if the Allied Army's officers blabbered too much or to the wrong people.

Regarding this system, Ferdinand did not cooperate with a similar bureau of the Hanoverian ministers, who also employed code breakers, etc., or with the British secret service.

Ferdinand kept a larger headquarters, of which a small circle formed the small headquarters. Ferdinand used men from this small headquarters to convey orders on the battlefield and also to accompany detached corps and council their commanders on the missions to perform in accordance with Ferdinand's ideas. Frequently they would temporarily be given a number of troops to perform a specific objective. Ferdinand occassinoaly appointed them as permanent commanders of troops, usually of the new and expanding light troops. All this was Prussian custom. Several of Ferdinand's staffers rose to generals, after the war.

Only this smaller staff would be liable to know more or even everything – if not in advance then at least later by talking among each other, after such knowledge was not anymore pernicious for the Allied Army's operations.

In 1758 and 1759, including the Battle of Minden, the small headquarters consisted of the following officers:

1. Special Individuals:

a. **Christian Heinrich Philipp Westphalen** (* 27 March, 1723; + 21 September, 1792; no military service at all): The relationship between Duke Ferdinand and Westphalen was quite uncommon in their time. Westphalen was the son of a Brunswick postmaster. He studied law at Helmstedt and Halle. From 1749 onwards, he accompanied a Mr. von Spiegel on a cavalier tour through France, Italy, and Southern Germany. In 1751, he became Ferdinand's secretary. Ferdinand trusted him completely. In fact, they seem to have become close friends in spite of the difference of their rank. Ferdinand was a member of the European high aristocracy, and, in fact, as a Guelph, a member of one of its oldest families, dating back to the 8th century A. D., and related to the Carolingian emperors, while Westphalen was just a commoner. They stayed friends until they died. After the war Westphalen was ennobled by the Emperor as Edler von Westphalen on request of the reigning Duke of Brunswick and his brother Ferdinand. During the Seven Years War, Westphalen performed his peacetime tasks as a private or later secret secretary and de facto chamberlain of Ferdinand's household. However, more and more he took on military tasks, even if he was not a soldier. King George II appointed him aide-de-camp general, but he never used that title. He effectively functioned as Ferdinand's chief of the general staff, though, counselling him in all military and private matters. He also bolstered him up if Ferdinand had doubts about what to do. Both kept this completely secret, so that Ferdinand appeared to others as an extremely cool general in every situation. Employing Prussian standards and methods, Westphalen prepared plans for the supply in victuals, ammunition, clothing, recruits, necessary transport, etc., and sent appropriate requests to the commissariat. Together with Bauer, he planned operations and entire campaigns. Ferdinand would often carry them out as planned, without any change. He was also responsible for Ferdinand's secret correspondence with Kings Frederick II and George II, with the reigning Duke of Brunswick, Ferdinand's elder brother, with the Landgrave of Hessen-Kassel, with the British Prime Minister, the Duke of Newcastle, with the British secretaries of state, with the Hanoverian and Hessian ministries, with the Hanoverian chancery of war, with the Dutch, and with the generals of the army or with the commanders of its different or detached corps. He drafted these letters for Ferdinand or would even write in his place if Ferdinand was not available. King Frederick II later used the letters received for his history of the war, published after peace was made. The Hereditary Prince of Brunswick once dubbed Westphalen "Ferdinand's foreign minister", but he would also be his minister of the interior and minister of war. If Ferdinand was absent and time was pressing, he would even give orders to the generals of the Allied Army. This was most unusual. The gentlemen would grumble and needed some time to become accustomed to it.

Westphalen spoke and wrote French. His correspondence with Ferdinand and many others was in French, as all of civilized Europe spoke French. Practically nobody but the British spoke English. So, French was the lingua franca in the Allied Army. Only the correspondence to the Hanoverian government or to him was on order of King George II in German. Only after the correspondence with George went via the British secretary of state, was it translated into French. Westphalen might also have spoken English, at least later. In 1765 he married a Scotswoman, Jeanie Wisheart.

Westphalen wrote a book on Ferdinand's campaigns that was to be published in German and French. However, this did not materialize during his lifetime. A grandson published the inherited manuscripts in the 1850s. After the war, Westphalen bought a manor in Brunswick and later in Mecklenburg, but usually spent his winters in Brunswick. As an odd note, one of his granddaughters married Karl Marx, in 1843.

b. **Friedrich Wilhelm Bauer** (* 4 January, 1731; + 15 February, 1783; Hessian, later Prussian service): Bauer was an exception in Ferdinand's staff like Westphalen. Son of a Hessian forester, he was gifted in mathematics. He was taken into the service of Landgrave Wilhelm VIII von Hessen-Kassel and was trained as a surveyor. As an artificer of the artillery, in 1755, he accompanied the Hessian forces to England. In 1756, he was commissioned as a Stückjunker, ranking about as an ensign, and then promoted lieutenant. In 1757/1758, he caught Ferdinand's eye as a promising young man, and was groomed by him. He served as an engineer as well as an aide-de-camp, becoming the second most important staff officer after Westphalen. From 1759 onwards, he served as 2nd Quartermaster General effectively handling all matters of this branch with the exception of fortresses, replacing von Borchmann and von Gohr. Bauer had proposed his tasks himself in a memoir. He also increasingly planned operations and campaigns and was rapidly promoted to captain and lieutenant colonel. In 1758, he organised a small corps of guides and a pioneer and sapper corps, as well as, in 1759, a hussar regiment. This was a free corps, raised from volunteers for the duration of the war. In 1761, Bauer changed from Hessian into Prussian service. In 1762, he was promoted colonel, and after Britain and France made peace, his hussars became a Prussian regiment.

When peace was signed between Prussia and her remaining enemies, in 1763, his hussars were disbanded for economic reasons, and he was dismissed. King Frederick would not tolerate non-noble officers in his peacetime army. An exception would have been made in the hussars or the artillery, but Frederick had to provide for too many officers from wartime formations of his own campaigns. Subsequently, Bauer bought a manor. Even then, it was speculated, how he had earned the necessary money. Perhaps, his share in the booty of his hussars taken from the French was large enough. He drafted maps for Westphalen's planned history of Ferdinand's campaigns. When this project did not materialize, he published them separately. In 1769, however, Catherine II of Russia engaged Bauer for the current war (1768 to 1774) in Moldavia against the Turks as a major general and quartermaster general for the army of Count Pyotr Alexandrovich

Rumyantsev-Zadunaisky (he was dubbed Zadunaisky [Trans-Danubian], after he had won that war, having crossed the Danube River). Bauer's first action was to procure decent maps of the operational area. Having been wounded, he improved, during the winter of 1770, the Novgorod salt works. In 1771, he returned to the army. In 1772, he was made its Quartermaster General en Chef. He then became commander of the Russian pioneer corps, which he had created, and was made Director General of all Russian salt works. In 1773, he was promoted lieutenant general and became the engineer general. After the war, he improved many fortifications in Russia by providing drafts and building plans. He also built or improved harbours and shipyards at St. Petersburg, Kronstadt and Riga, canals, water conduits and sewers, roads, or civilian buildings including the Bolshoi Theatre at St. Petersburg. Shortly before his death, he also became director of the German Theatre in that city.

2. Lieutenant colonels, colonels or generals:

a. **Johann Wilhelm von Reden** (* 7 March, 1717; + 8 January, 1801; Hanoverian service): Ferdinand inherited Lieutenant Colonel von Reden from Cumberland. He belonged to a noble Hanoverian family, first mentioned in 1180, he was a son of the Hanoverian Oberhofmarschall [literally, chief court marshal; great chamberlain or chief steward] von Reden. He was soon promoted to colonel, in 1759 to major general, and in 1762 to lieutenant general. As the Hanoverian adjutant general, his principal task was to turn Ferdinand's short notes or verbal orders into written orders to the generals of the Allied Army. He also scanned incoming reports and summarised them for Ferdinand. In addition, he was responsible for the accounts with spies and for the courier service that carried messages. However, he was only admitted to secrets, though, when it became absolutely necessary, and was kept out of the business of planning operations. This was because he could not shed the attitude of a Hanoverian officer and nobleman, which Ferdinand, Westphalen and Bauer considered sloppiness and unmerited haughtiness. As a result, he was eclipsed by Westphalen and Bauer.

In 1781, Reden became Hanoverian commander-in-chief, and in 1784, a field marshal.

b. **Durand** (British service): No specific information could be found on Colonel Durand. A Colonel Durand surrendered in November 1745 to the Jacobites at Carlisle, but it is not known if both Colonels Durand were the same person. No biographical information could be found.

However, this Durand was sent to Germany in May 1758 as a commissioner to check on the strength of the Allied Army for which the British paid, and stayed at least until 1759, after the Battle of Minden. Ferdinand kept him in his headquarters, and Durand was apparently very impressed by Ferdinand.

c. Robert Boyd (* c.1710; + 13 May, 1794; British service): Boyd was employed by the British Army, from 1740 to 1756, at Minorca as a civilian storekeeper, and successor to his father. In 1756, he took part in the failed defence of Minorca and assisted as a witness in Admiral Byng's court martial for not having succoured the beleaguered garrison (Byng was found guilty and shot on the quarterdeck of his former flagship). From January 1758 onwards, he became successor to Colonel Amherst as British commissar. Effective as of March 1758, he was commissioned for his services during the Minorca siege as a lieutenant colonel in the army, that is, without an attachment to a regiment. Subsequently, perhaps at his own request, he became commissioner for the mustering the Hessian troops in British pay. Some sources claim that he later was made British commissary general in Germany under Lord Granby, but this could be wrong. In 1758, Duke Ferdinand also made Boyd one of his aides-de-camp. He was apparently a good organiser and tactician but had limited knowledge of practical warfare in the open field. However, he was used as an advisor for the defence of fortresses or employed in besieging them. In 1760, he was attached as a lieutenant colonel to the 1st Foot Guards Regiment and sent to Germany. He was also sent to England to report to the King and British government, e. g., in 1762 after the Battle of Wilhelmsthal.

In 1765, Boyd changed to the 39th Regiment of Foot, from 1766 onwards served as their colonel. He became a major-general in 1772 and a lieutenant general in 1777. From 1776 to 1777, he was acting governor of Gibraltar. During the defence of Gibraltar from 1779 to 1783, he was second in command under George Augustus Eliott, later Lord Heathfield. They would have become acquainted in Germany, when Elliott commanded the 15th Light Dragoon Regiment, which he had raised. At Boyd's suggestion, red-hot shot were employed for the destruction of the enemy's famous floating batteries. Apparently, he was knighted for his service. He was again acting governor of Gibraltar in 1790, and governor from 1790 to 1794. In 1793, he was promoted general.

d. **Martin Ernst von Schlieffen** (* 30 October, 1732; + 15 February 1825; Hessian service): Schlieffen belonged to a Pomeranian noble family, first mentioned in 1365, but as citizens of the town of Kolberg. He originally served in the Prussian Army, joining, in 1745, the von Bredow Garrison Infantry Regiment at Berlin. In 1749, he was transferred to the Guards Infantry Regiment, then at Potsdam. In 1755, he was discharged for health reasons, and was not taken back. From 1757, he entered Hessian service as a lieutenant colonel and subsequently a colonel. Ferdinand appointed him aide-de-camp, in 1758. In 1761/1762, he served several times as an independent commander of troops, between spells as aide-de-camp.

In 1772, Schlieffen was promoted Hessian lieutenant general and also acted as a Hessian minister of state. In 1789, after the death of King Frederick II, he went back to Prussian service and became governor of Wesel. He retired in 1792 and started to write a number of scientific and other works. In 1808, he became a member of the Prussian and Bavarian Academies of Science. In April 1813, he was made a baron of the Kingdom of Westphalia.

e. **Emmerich Otto August von Estorff** (* 28 October, 1722; + 19 October, 1796; Hanoverian service): Estorff belonged to a Hanoverian noble family, first mentioned in 1162. His mother was a Huguenot. In 1741, he was commissioned as an officer and, in 1753, became Rittmeister [cavalry captain] in the Hanoverian Life Guards. He was appointed, in 1757, brigade major (a wartime billet approximately an adjutant or chief-of-staff to a major general as a commander of a brigade – German armies having no brigadier rank). In 1759, he was promoted lieutenant colonel and became Ferdinand's 2nd Adjutant General besides Reden. He was promoted to colonel in 1761.

At the end of 1762 Estorff became Quartermaster General of the Hanoverian Army and colonel of the 3rd Cavalry Regiment. From 1766 onwards, he was colonel of the 6th Dragoon Regiment (in which Scharnhorst, the reformer of the Prussian Army, served as an ensign, before he changed over to the artillery). By 1777, he was a lieutenant general. After Count William of Schaumburg-Lippe had died and his military school was closed, in 1777, Estorff founded, in 1778, a cadet school (in which Scharnhorst taught) at Northeim, his regiment's garrison. In 1781, he was made inspector general of the entire Hanoverian cavalry.

f. **Charles Lennox, 3rd Duke of Richmond, 3rd Duke of Lennox** (22 February, 1735; 29 December; 1806; British service): Lennox inherited his titles in 1750. He became, in 1752, an ensign in the 2nd Foot Guards Regiment and, in 1753, a captain in the 20th Regiment of Foot. In 1755, he was made a fellow of the Royal Society. In 1756, he became lieutenant colonel of the 33rd Regiment of Foot and, in 1758, a lieutenant colonel and, subsequently, the colonel of the 72nd Regiment of Foot (ex 2nd/33rd, raised in 1757). Apparently in 1759, he was made Ferdinand's aide-de-camp. In 1761, he was promoted major-general.

In 1763, his 72nd Regiment of Foot was disbanded, but he was appointed Lord Lieutenant of Sussex. In 1765, he served as an ambassador extraordinary in Paris and as a privy counsellor, and in 1766 as secretary of state of the Southern Department (as the secretary for England and Wales and for foreign affairs with Catholic and Muslim countries was known until 1782). He was promoted, in 1770, to lieutenant general. In the House of Lords he supported the cause of American colonies, of Ireland and of parliamentary reforms. In 1777, he also became 3rd Duke of Aubigny in France. In 1782, he was promoted full general and served in 1782/1783 as the Master-General of the Ordnance. From 1784 to 1795, he became again Master-General of the Ordnance, reforming that authority. He was appointed, in 1795, colonel of the Royal Horse Guards and promoted field marshal.

g. **Charles Fitzroy** (* 25 June, 1737; 21 March, 1797; British service): In 1752, Fitzroy became an ensign in the 1st Foot Guards Regiment, in 1756 he was promoted to captain and in 1758 to lieutenant colonel. Apparently, in 1759, Ferdinand made him an aide-de-camp. By 1761, he was a colonel, and Ferdinand sent him to England with his report on the victory at Vellinghausen to King George III and the British government.

He was, from 1759 to 1780, a Member of Parliament, from 1760 to 1762, a groom of the bedchamber, and, from 1768 to 1780, Queen Charlotte's vice-chamberlain. In 1780, he was created 1st Baron Southampton.

h. **Friedrich Adolph Riedesel, Freiherr [Baron] zu Eisenbach** (* 3 June, 1738; + 6 January, 1800; originally Hessian, then Brunswick service): Riedesel belonged to a Hessian noble family first mentioned in 1226 that provided, from 1432 onwards, the hereditary marshal of the landgraves of Hessen and chairman of the assemblies of the Hessian entire nobility, even after the country was divided into Hessen-Kassel and Hessen-Darmstadt. Riedesel joined, apparently in 1755, the Hessian Army as an ensign and served with the Hessian troops in England, where he learned English and French.

He returned with the Hessians to Germany. In 1757, he became Ferdinand's aide-de-camp. After the Battle of Minden, he was promoted Rittmeister [cavalry captain]. He transfered to Brunswick service, in 1761, was made a lieutenant colonel and received the Brunswick hussar regiment (previously von Roth Hussar Regiment), which he forthwith commanded.

A younger brother, later becoming Hessian hereditary marshal, Johann Conrad, served in the Saxon Army and was, during the Seven Years War, an aide-de-camp to Prince Xaver, as Comte de Lusace commander-in-chief of the Saxon troops attached to the French armies.

After the war, Riedesel stayed in Brunswick service. He commanded as a major general the Brunswick troops in British pay during the American Revolution but was captured in 1777 at Saratoga with his troops and his wife and children. He was exchanged in 1778 or 1779 and served subsequently on Long Island and in Canada (it is reported that his family introduced the German custom of a Christmas tree to America, when Riedesel was commandant at Sorel, Canada). In 1783 or 1784, he and his family returned home. In 1787, he was promoted to lieutenant general, serving with Brunswick troops in the Netherlands. In 1793, he retired, but was appointed commandant of the city of Brunswick.

3. Other adjutants or aide-de-camps:

a. **von Alten** (Hanoverian service): He belonged to a Hanoverian noble family, first mentioned in 1182 that owned a number of manors around the city of Hanover, including Großburgwedel. He was a major, but only served for a short time an aide-de-camp of Ferdinand. No further information is available.

b. **August Christian Freiherr [Baron] von Bülow** (* 1728; + 24 September, 1760; killed in action at Stadtberge; Prussian service): Bülow was a member of a noble family originally from Mecklenburg, first mentioned in 1154, but later spreading over parts of Northern Germany, the Netherlands, Denmark and Livonia. He was the son of a Prussian minister and originally a lieutenant in Ferdinand's Prussian infantry regiment (unofficially numbered as No. 5). Ferdinand had asked King Frederick II for him to accompany him to the Allied Army as one of his two original aides-de-camp. He became, in 1760, as a major the commander of the Légion britannique, raised in British pay (also called Légion diabolique by the British, as not even such an experienced officer as Bülow could discipline this bunch, primarily consisting of deserters from the French Army).

c. **von Derenthal** (Prussian service): Derenthal was a member of an originally Westphalian noble family. He was an ensign in Ferdinand's Prussian infantry regiment, and also accompanied him to his new command as an aide-de-camp. He was later promoted lieutenant, and was, by 1759, a captain, but was apparently killed in action in 1761, some time before the Battle of Vellinghausen. No further information is available.

d. **Graf [Count] Georg Ludwig von Oeynhausen** (* 10 May, 1734; + 11 March, 1811; Hanoverian service): Oeynhausen belonged to a noble family first mentioned in the Bishopric of Paderborn, in 1237, that later expanded to Hanover and Mecklenburg. He was the son of Major General Count von Oeynhausen, the Hanoverian chief master hunter. His mother was a Huguenot. Count Wilhelm von Schaumburg-Lippe, a grandson of King George I by an illegitimate daughter, and the Allied artillery commander, was an uncle. He entered the Hanoverian Army, in 1748, as an ensign of the Guards Regiment on Foot. In 1757, after the lost Battle of Hastenbeck, he was transferred to the Hanoverian Leibgarde zu pferd as a captain lieutenant (that is, a staff captain – a lieutenant commanding a company belonging to a field officer; the Leibgarde had one squadron divided into three companies). From 1757 onwards, he served as an aide-de-camp to Ferdinand.

By 1793, he was a Hanoverian major general and fought the French in the Netherlands. By 1803, when the Hanoverian Army was disbanded, and he retired, he was a lieutenant general and colonel of the 7th Dragoon Regiment.

e. **von Malortie** (Hanoverian service): Belonging to an originally French family, probably Huguenots, he was a captain, in 1757, and took part, in 1761, in the Battle of Vellinghausen. However, it is not clear if he was, at that time, still an aide-de-camp or the commander of a battalion of the Légion britannique. No further information was available.

A Karl von Malortie (* 1734; + 1798) was later a Hanoverian lieutenant general and governor of two sons of King George III, both studying from 1786 onwards at Göttingen: Ernst August (* 1771; + 1851), later Duke of Cumberland (not the Zeven Cumberland), and from 1837 onwards, when Queen Victoria started ruling Britain and the personal union between Hanover and Britain was dissolved, King of Hanover, and Adolph Friedrich (*1774; + 1850), later Duke of Cambridge, and from 1816 until 1837 British viceroy of Hanover.

f. von Seyboldsdorff: He was only an aide-de-camp to Ferdinand for a short time, and no further information is available. The Seiboldsdorf family belonged to the Bavarian nobility, first mentioned already in 740, and were made counts of the Empire, in 1692.

g. von Wintzingerode or Wintzigerode: There is no further information on this particular member of a noble family from the Eichsfeld around Duderstadt, Heiligenstadt and Leinefeld-Worbis, first mentioned in 1209. However, he spoke not only French, but also English, as he conveyed Ferdinand's orders during the Battle of Minden to Lord Sackville in French, but expressly repeated them in English. In 1762, he apparently commanded the Hessian Jäges, but it is not clear if he did so while still one of Ferdinand's aides-de-camp.

He was not the Hanoverian officer Achaz Philipp von Wintzingerode-Bodenstein (* 1722; + 1758, killed in action), but perhaps Wilhelm Levin Ernst Freiherr [Baron] von Wintzingerode (* 1738; +1781) who was later a Prussian and Hessian colonel, or possibly Adolf Levin von Wintzingerode (* 1715; + 1778).

h. von Pentz: The noble Pentz family was first mentioned in Mecklenburg, in 1321, but also expanded to Denmark. Apparently, Ferdinand greatly appreciated him. During the Battle of Krefeld, in 1758, Pentz was Ferdinand's chief aide-de-camp, and, in 1761, at Vellinghausen a captain and commander of a battalion of the Légion britannique. There is no further information, though.

i. Graf [Count] Jakob Johann Taube von Kudding (6 May, 1727; + 19 March, 1799; Hanoverian service): Taube belonged to a noble family that may have originated Jutland, Denmark, and expanded into the Baltic countries, Sweden and Finland. He was born a Swede, and son of a Swedish Hofmarschall [literally, court marshal; lord steward]. He entered the Swedish Army, in 1738, as a non-commissioned officer. In 1742, he was commissioned as an ensign in the Upplands Infanteri Regemente. However, in 1744, he joined, as a cadet, the Hanoverian Army. In 1745, Taube was promoted lieutenant. He retired, in 1748, from the Swedish Army and completely entered Hanoverian service. In 1755, he became a captain lieutenant (that is, staff captain), and, in 1759, he was a captain and Ferdinand's aide-de-camp. In 1761, he was commandant at Liebenau and commanding officer of the 2nd Battalion of the Hanoverian Foot Guards. He was promoted, in 1762, to lieutenant colonel, and for some time was commandant at Alsfeld.

After the war, he returned to Swedish service, and was, in 1766, a regimental commander at Stralsund. He retired, in 1774, as a lieutenant general.

j. Edward Ligonier (* 1740; + 14 June, 1782; British service): Ligonier was the illegitimate son of Colonel Francis Augustus Ligonier, the brother of John Ligonier, 1st Earl Ligonier. The latter was a viscount and, from 1757 to 1759, the commander-in-chief of the British Army, as well as, from 1766 onwards, an earl in the Peerage of Great Britain. Edward Ligonier became, in 1759, a captain of the 1st Foot Guards Regiment and an aide-de-camp of Ferdinand.

He was appointed, in 1763, a royal aide-de-camp. From 1763 to 1765, he served as a secretary in the embassy at Madrid. In 1764, he was appointed a groom of the bedchamber to the Duke of Gloucester. In 1770, he inherited, from his uncle, the title of Viscount Ligonier of Clonmell and was created, in 1776, 1st Earl Ligonier, of Clonmell, both in the Peerage of Ireland. He was promoted to major general in 1775 and to lieutenant general in 1777.

In 1761/1762, there were also:

k. Carpenter: From his name, he might have been British. By 1761, he was one of Ferdinand's aides-de-camp as a captain. In 1762, he was seconded, at least for some time, to the Hessian hussars, and as a Rittmeister [cavalry captain] and regimental commander to Riedesel's Brunswick Hussar Regiment. There is no further information.

l. Valentin Anton Georg von Massow (* 1740; 20 September, 1786; Prussian service): Lieutenant von Massow belonged to a noble family in Pomerania, first mentioned in 1232, that furnished to Prussia, in the 18th century, a number of soldiers and civilian administrators. One had commanded King Frederick William's I Giant Grenadier Guards, and after this formation was disbanded, following King Frederick's II accession, to the throne (just one battalion remained, unofficially numbered as No. 6, while the remaining personnel were pensioned, promoted non-commissioned officers or used to reinforce the new Guards Regiment and other new regiments with crack soldiers) became responsible for organizing the procurement of uniforms for the entire Prussian Army. Massow's father was the president of the Prussian Kriegs- und Domainenkammer [War and Domain Chamber] at Minden, the regional administrative and government authority, and during the war was prominent for his intimate knowledge of Westphalian conditions in the British commissariat that furnished the Allied Army with victuals and fodder. Massow replaced, in July 1761, Captain von Derenthal who had been killed while serving as Ferdinand's aide-de-camp. He became brother-in-law to Riedesel, when Riedesel married his half-sister, in 1762.

After the war, Massow became a Prussian civilian Kriegs- und Domainenrat [war and domain counsellor] with the chamber at Halberstadt.

Perhaps, other aide-de-camps joined as well.

4. On the fringe of Ferdinand's staff was:

a. **John**, according to other sources **Charles Frederick, Beckwith** (* 1712; + 1787): He was a British officer from Yorkshire, serving with the troops sent to Germany, in 1758. Apparently, he initially commanded the 20th Regiment of Foot as a lieutenant colonel prior to and at Minden. In 1760, he became colonel and brigadier, commanding an elite brigade consisting of the then two existing British grenadier battalions and the two Highland battalions. In December 1762, he entered Prussian service, taking over the former Légion britannique, now the Légion prussienne in Prussian service. He was promoted to major general, in April 1763, and made Governor of Wesel, owning the fusilier regiment (unofficially numbered as No. 48) stationed at Wesel. In 1766, though, he resigned and returned to Britain.

In 1750, he had married Janet Wishart, daughter of the Reverend Dr. George Wishart of Pittarow, Dean of the Chapel Royal (Holyrood) at Edinburgh. Her mother was a Campbell and related to the earls of Argyll. Their five sons also served in the British Army, four becoming general officers. During the Seven Years War, Westphalen and Beckwith became friends, even if Beckwith is reported to have had quite a prickly character. Mrs. Beckwith came to Wesel, accompanied by her sister Jeanie (Jane, Jean or Jeanne). In 1765, Jeanie Wishart and Westphalen married.

5. Not part of Ferdinand's inner circle were the following:

a. **Jeffrey Amherst** was made colonel of the 15th Regiment of Foot, in 1756, and commissioner in mustering the Hessian troops in British pay serving in England. In 1757, the Hessians and he joined the Allied Army in Hanover under Cumberland and assisted in the lost Battle of Hastenbeck. After the convention of Kloster Zeven, he started to dismiss the Hessian troops from British pay, but then this convention was not ratified by King George II. However, while Ferdinand took over the Allied Army, in the winter of 1757/1758, Amherst was appointed in 1758 commander of the British expedition to Louisbourg. He then became commander-in-chief in North America, and colonel of the 60th Royal American Regiment of Foot. He took no further part in the war in Europe. In 1763, he visited biological warfare on American Indians taking part in the Pontiac risings by letting them capture blankets infected by smallpox.

Work for Ferdinand must have been very limited if it happened at all.

b. Ferdinand also inherited from Cumberland the Hanoverian Colonel von Borchmann as quartermaster general. However, he was too slow for Ferdinand, accustomed to the Prussian manner of executing business. So, he was sidelined, from 1759 onwards.

c. Cumberland's 2nd quartermaster general was the Hessian Major von Gohr, assisted by his brother, Lieutenant von Gohr. Ferdinand could not stand them and restricted them to subordinate tasks.

Look for more books from Winged Hussar Publishing, LLC and Nafziger Press – E-books, paperbacks and Limited-Edition hardcovers. The best in history, science fiction and fantasy at:
www. wingedhussarpublishing.com

or follow us on Facebook at:
Winged Hussar Publishing LLC

Or on Twitter at:
WingHusPubLLC

For information and upcoming publications